The Online Journalism Handbook

LONGMAN PRACTICAL JOURNALISM SERIES

Journalism Ethics and Regulation, 3rd edition – Chris Frost
ISBN 9781408244685

The Broadcast Journalism Handbook – Gary Hudson and Sarah Rowlands
ISBN 9781408245217
(new 2nd edition coming Autumn 2011)

The Broadcast Journalism Handbook – Gary Hudson and Sarah Rowlands
ISBN 9781405824347
(current edition)

The Online Journalism Handbook – Paul Bradshaw and Liisa Rohumaa
ISBN 9781405873406

The 21st Century Journalism Handbook – Tim Holmes, Sara Hadwin and Glyn Mottershead
ISBN 9781405846325
(coming Autumn 2011)

Design for Media – Di Hand and Steve Middleditch
ISBN 9781405873666

Law for Journalists – Frances Quinn
ISBN 9781408254141

The Online Journalism Handbook

Skills to survive and thrive in the digital age

Paul Bradshaw and

Liisa Rohumaa

Longman
is an imprint of

Harlow, England • London • New York • Boston • San Francisco • Toronto • Sydney • Singapore • Hong Kong
Tokyo • Seoul • Taipei • New Delhi • Cape Town • Madrid • Mexico City • Amsterdam • Munich • Paris • Milan

Pearson Education Limited
Edinburgh Gate
Harlow
Essex CM20 2JE
England

and Associated Companies throughout the world

Visit us on the World Wide Web at:
www.pearsoned.co.uk

First published 2011

ISBN: 978-1-4058-7340-6

British Library Cataloguing-in-Publication Data
A catalogue record for this book is available from the British Library

Library of Congress Cataloging-in-Publication Data
Bradshaw, Paul
The online journalism handbook : skills to survive and thrive in the digital age / Paul Bradshaw and Liisa Rohumaa. — 1st ed.
p. cm.
Includes bibliographical references and index.
ISBN 978-1-4058-7340-6 (pbk. : alk. paper) 1. Online journalism.
I. Bradshaw, Paul. II. Title.
PN4784.O62.R64 2011
070.4—dc22

2011003393

10 9 8 7 6 5 4 3 2
15 14 13 12

Typeset in 9/12, Giovanni-Book by 73
Printed by Ashford Colour Press Ltd., Gosport

Brief contents

BRIEF CONTENTS

Full contents

Acknowledgements

Author acknowledgements

Paul Bradshaw

Thanks to all of the following who either improved the book by posting comments on the Online Journalism Blog, through private correspondence, or in conversation:

Andy Anderson, Kevin Anderson, Charles Arthur, Pete Ashton, James Ball, Jeremy Bante, Caroline Beavon, Zach Beauvais, Martin Belam, Daniel Bennett, Sarah Booker, Nick Booth, Jon Bounds, Andy Brightwell, Heather Brooke, Julian Burgess, Brenda Burrell, Dan Davies, Stijn Debrouwere, Murray Dick, JC Dill, Mark Donoghue, Andy Drinkwater, Alex Gamela, Joanna Geary, Alison Gow, Michael Grimes, Mary Hamilton, David Hayward, Iain Hepburn, Tony Hirst, Graham Holliday, Neil Houston, Amber Iler, Martyn Inglis, Steve Jackson, Nicolas Kayser-Bril, Stef Lewandowski, Nico Luchsinger, Sergio Marchesini, David McCandless, Dr Kelly Page, Christian Payne, Meg Pickard, Richard Pope, Marc Reeves, Jonathan Richards, Adrian Short, Karen Strunks, Chris Taggart, James Thornett, Simon Waldman, Matt Wardman, Adam Westbrook, Tom Whitwell, Gavin Wray.

Thanks also to my family for keeping me sane.

Liisa Rohumaa

Many thanks for guidance and help to: Pete Clifton, John Domokos, Vanessa Edwards, Karen Fowler-Watt, Alastair Good, Sian Grzeszczyk, Alex Gubbay, Iain Hepburn, Tom Hill, Victor Keegan, Robert Minto and Laura Oliver, as well as colleagues past and present at Bournemouth University's Media School and the *Financial Times*.

Special thanks and dedication to the late Peter Martin for his encouragement during the early days of FT.com.

Publisher acknowledgements

The publishers would like to thank the many reviewers who have commented upon, and helped improve, the original idea, and the draft chapters, for this book.

We also gratefully acknowledge the contribution and efforts of the two authors, to Liisa especially for conceiving the original idea and taking the project through to a successful conclusion, and to Paul for so ably complementing Liisa's talents and bringing additional energy, ideas and expertise. Both have been a pleasure to work with.

We are grateful to the following for permission to reproduce copyright material:

Photos

(Key: b-bottom; c-centre; l-left; r-right; t-top)

Alamy Images: CJG-Technology 16, David J Green 93, NetPhotos 12, PhotoEdit 9; **Flickr:** 112c, Michael Hernandez 112b; **Guardian News and Media Ltd.:** 43; **Iain Hepburn:** 94; **iStockphoto:**

Alex Slobodkin 89, Damir Cudic 112t, Temistock Lucarelli 13; **John Domokos:** 105; **Laura Oliver:** 40; **Press Association Images:** Paul Sakuma/AP 19c; **Rex Features:** Matt Baron/BEI 7; **Telegraph Media Group:** Andrew Crowley/2006 32; **TopFoto:** ullsteinbild 19l, 19r.

Screenshots

Plate 2: Newsmap – a treemap visualization of the news (2004) by Marcos Weskamp. http://newsmap.jp; Plate 3: Mountains Out of Molehills by David McCandless, www.informationisbeautiful.net/visualizations/mountains-out-of-molehills/; Plate 6: Anatomy of a Tweet by Raffi Krikorian, http://mehack.com/map-of-a-twitter-status-object; Plate 7: The Guardian Open Platform, www.guardian.co.uk/open-platform; Plate 8: The Guardian Interactive Guides, www.guardian.co.uk/interactive; Plate 13: Twitter Network of Arab and Middle East protests, www.guardian.co.uk/world/interactive/2011/feb/11/guardian-twitter-arab-protests-interactive?CMP=twt_gu; Screenshot on page 43 from www.guardian.co.uk/global-development.

The Financial Times

Plate 12: FT.com UK Deficit Buster, Financial Times, http://cachef.ft.com/cms/s/0/abe91fdc-4e08-11dfb43700144feab49a.html#axzz1IuwZn0iJ

Text

Article on page 110 from www.telegraph.co.uk/journalists/alastair-good/, © Telegraph Media Group Limited, written by Alastair Good; Article on page 151 from www.guardian.co.uk, written by Meg Pickard.

In some instances we have been unable to trace the owners of copyright material, and we would appreciate any information that would enable us to do so.

About the authors

Paul Bradshaw

Paul publishes the Online Journalism Blog and is the founder of the investigative journalism crowdsourcing site Help Me Investigate (shortlisted for 2010 Multimedia Publisher of the Year). He is described by UK Press Gazette as one of the country's 'most influential journalism bloggers' and by the Telegraph's Shane Richmond as 'The UK's Jeff Jarvis'.

Paul has a background in magazine and website management, and taught for nine years at Birmingham City University, where he established the MA in Online Journalism. He continues to lead that MA and teach at City University in London, where he is a Visiting Professor. He has contributed to a number of books about journalism and the internet and speaks about the subjects in the media regularly both in the UK and internationally.

In 2008 Paul was ranked the UK's 4th 'most visible person on the internet' by NowPublic, and in 2009 ranked 36th in the 'Birmingham Power 50'. In 2010 he was listed on both Journalism.co.uk's list of leading innovators in media, and the US Poynter Institute's list of the 35 most influential people in social media.

His 'Model for the 21st Century Newsroom' and 'BASIC Principles of Online Journalism' series have formed the basis for newsroom operations and journalism education around the world, where they have been translated into a number of languages.

In addition to teaching and writing, Paul acts as a consultant and trainer to a number of organisations on social media and data journalism. You can find him on Twitter @paulbradshaw.

Liisa Rohumaa

Liisa lectures in journalism and online communication at Bournemouth University's Media School. While news editor of FT.com she was appointed as the university's first online journalist in residence by the Centre for Excellence in Media Practice to develop the online journalism components of the BA and MA in Multimedia Journalism programmes.

Liisa started her career in journalism as a reporter for the Surrey Comet where one of her jobs was to report on new arrivals at Chessington Zoo. She has worked for BBC Worldwide, the Daily Telegraph and Financial Times. She is particularly interested in digital connectivity and is a researcher on the New Dynamics in Ageing project, a multidisciplinary research initiative with the ultimate aim of improving quality of life of older people. Liisa blogs at baltblog.wordpress.com and tracks the good, bad and the ugly of user generated comment via Twitter @snarkmouth.

Edgar Forbes

Chapter 11: Law

Edgar is an in-house counsel and specialist in media law and intellectual property.

He trained as both a lawyer and journalist and was formerly global head of rights management for international news agency Reuters.

He regularly provides training and lectures on media law and IP issues and is a regular commentator on the media through his blog mediabeak.com

Chapter 1

Introduction

We're all online journalists now. Whether we work for a newspaper, a broadcaster or an online outlet, our stories, pictures, audio and video appear online and what started out in print becomes archived on the web – from ink to hyperlink.

Some fear that 'traditional' skills of news gathering and news writing will disappear, and that technology will become more important than stories. This is not what this book believes. Traditional skills remain central to the journalist's craft. The ability to spot a story, to gather and convey information effectively, and the talent to communicate a story accurately are, in an information-overloaded world, essential. The internet has given us more tools with which to do these things. But it has also given us tools to do things that we never thought possible before: the ability to engage directly with readers and collaborate with them; the ability to allow users to interact with different parts of a story in different ways; and the ability to understand our former audiences in ways far removed from crude circulation figures or viewing peaks.

Using technology is one thing. Getting the technology to do the right thing is quite another. And getting the technology to do the *write* thing is yet another. Doing the *write* thing, the journalism, requires new skills and new ways of thinking about how to get the story across and engage readers – not necessarily in that order. The following chapters aim to give context, guidance and practical training for beginners, mid-career journalists and those considering specialising in a particular area such as video or podcasting. Sections on blogging, interactivity, data journalism and user-generated content reflect the new world we live in. Readers, viewers and listeners – now also *users* – want to contribute to forums, discussions, blogs and polls, adding their own commentary, analysis, updates and context. Citizen journalists are cutting out mainstream media, reporting news events both global and hyperlocal, allowing their words and multimedia to be emailed, texted, downloaded and published anywhere in the world. Governments, celebrities and advertisers are not far behind.

Online journalism is evolving and reporters have to be adaptable. The increasing need to understand the production process should not be underestimated. Good navigation, links and search engine optimisation – tagging stories and tailoring headlines so they are easily found on traffic drivers such as Google and Facebook – are critical elements of the job. There are no delivery vans online – and users increasingly expect the news to come to them, whether via email, mobile, social networks, personalised news services or a casual search.

Stories can be conveyed using a selection of text, video, audio, picture galleries, blogs, maps, timelines and links to resources. Where once a journalist knew that the story facing them would have to be shaped into a 500-word report or a 3-minute package, now before they even leave the office they must decide whether to take along a digital camcorder, camera or audio recorder; whether to put out a quick update on Twitter or Facebook; and if the story will need streaming live on their mobile phone or mapping later on Google Maps.

Journalists used to treading a geographical 'beat' are having to learn to tread a virtual one too: checking blogs and social networking sites for mentions of their local area or specialism; enlisting the support of an online community to get to the bottom of an issue. Meanwhile, computer assisted reporting helps journalists trawl through statistics and obscure reports to find connections and stories they might otherwise have missed.

The most significant change is the transformation of the relationship between journalist and reader. The internet gives readers access to media around the world, alternative perspectives from local, national, international and independent organisations and individuals. And readers can challenge journalists via their blog, Twitter account or comments section. Equally, journalists now have much greater access to their audience. They can reach out to those affected by an issue, or those with expert knowledge. They can conduct polls at the click of a button. Editors can set up forums to allow readers to talk to each other, offering advice or support, or arrange a live chat so that users can talk directly to those in the news. Journalists with a story too big or inaccessible to pursue on their own can call on their readership to collaborate via 'wikis' and a process called 'crowdsourcing'.

This book believes these changes offer ways to re-engage with readers who have become suspicious of journalists' over-reliance on official sources and PR companies. Technologies that now surround us mean that journalism can become about listening to readers – and working with them – as much as talking to them.

The biggest challenge facing journalists in this new media age is knowing which tools to use, when. It is not about technical skills (although access to these is always a factor), but about conceptual ones: thinking creatively about storytelling and news gathering – and, increasingly, distribution too.

This book aims to give guidance about the new media landscape and, based on that, conceptual skills to make the right choices in navigating through it.

This book should make you question things, make you try new things, but, above all, make you better at what you do. And if you're fortunate, it will help you do the same for your readers, too.

Paul Bradshaw
Liisa Rohumaa

Chapter 2

History

This chapter will cover:

- Pioneers
- Early adopters
- Dotcom boom
- . . . and bust
- Closer look: Why were newspapers slow to respond to the net?
- Case history: *The Huffington Post* – credible competitor?
- Timeline of web journalism
- Blogs, wikis, podcasts and participatory media
- New frontiers

Introduction

When journalists were first given personal access to the internet the response was positive. Email allowed them to be good at something they liked to do – talk to each other. The idea of having a conversation with the reader was some way off and the 'Big Conversation' theory of citizen journalism advocate *Dan Gillmor* outlined in his book *We, the Media* was just a whisper. Any kind of 'have your say' reader feedback was consigned to the letters page.

In the early 1990s most journalists got their first introduction to the internet via email, intranets, newsletters and basic information sites. Few could have predicted how this new medium, characterised by global reach and interactivity, would provide exciting challenges and opportunities while at the same time threaten the print industry in which many of them worked. Big media was still confident and newspapers had survived the competitive onslaughts of radio and television. Journalists and proprietors were still in charge of content and distribution. The business model for print media had stayed the same for over a century. The choice for the consumer was clear: you bought a paper or switched on the TV or radio. Yet those at the centre of news or the millions affected by it had little voice, just the slim chance of being quoted by a reporter or having an opinion broadcast as a soundbite.

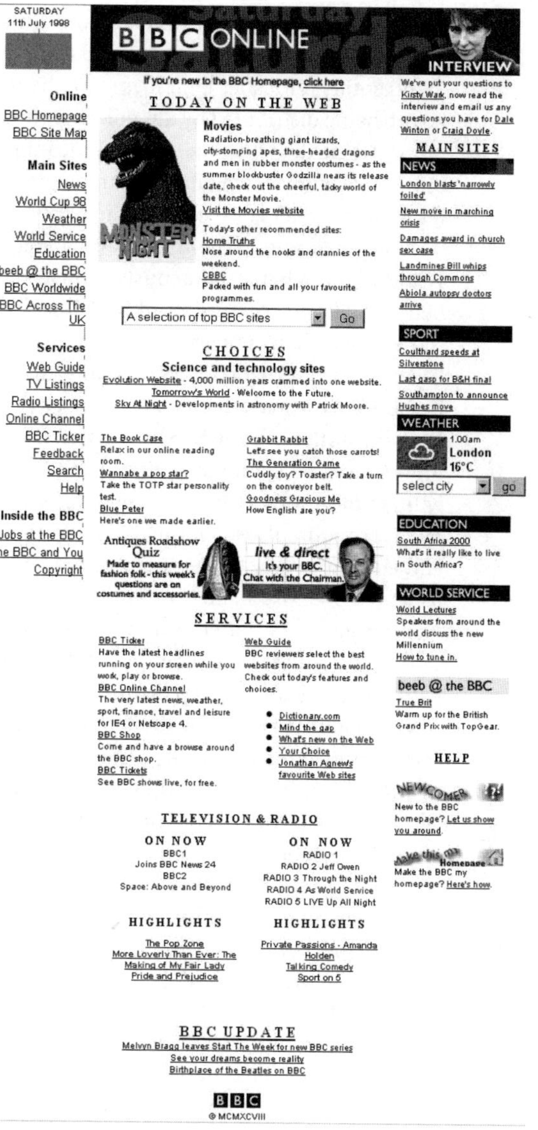

An early BBC homepage
Source: bbc.co.uk

The interactive nature of the internet allowed ordinary people to share and check information. They could circumvent the information powerbrokers, newspaper proprietors, network executives, media moguls and journalists. By sharing information they could challenge received wisdom and publish their own version of events. The media revolution of the last decade means anyone can broadcast 24/7 to the world; share and exchange information in real time; challenge vested interests and even defy censorship.

Today we use text, pictures, video, podcasts, blogs, interactive graphics, user-generated content and tools such as mobile telephony, social media networks and services such as Twitter. So, how did we get here and if anyone can do it what does this mean for journalists and journalism?

Pioneers

While the technology of mass communication advanced after the Second World War the tools of the trade remained the same right up to the 1980s: a notebook, a pen, a typewriter, two sheets of paper, a 'black' (photocopy paper), and a metal spike.

A typed report went to the printers where experts in movable type (of the kind pioneered by 15th-century publisher Johannes Gutenberg) would ensure it rolled out on huge printing presses before being distributed by air, rail, ship, lorry and newspaper boy. Corrections were done on the 'stone' where demarcation of duties meant journalists had to ask printers to literally move lumps of hot metal typesetting under extreme pressure of deadlines and financial penalties. Of course, if the story wasn't good enough the editor had his own archive system – the spike.

Now, the tools of the trade have changed: a story can be published and distributed on the World Wide Web instantaneously from a lap-top computer or a hand-held device such as a BlackBerry or iPhone. And the word 'spike' seems as antiquated as the metal em rulers once used by sub-editors to lay out pages.

For many journalists, their first introduction to digital technology was the personal computer in the 1970s. Microsoft emerged as a key player but while some had PCs at home few had access to them in the office where typewriters were still the norm. From the mid-1980s newspapers moved towards computerisation. In the UK, regional newspaper proprietor Eddie Shah battled with print unions to bring in new technology and launched his national newspaper *Today* in 1986. For journalists working on *Today* this was the first chance to input copy directly, to write and edit on screen, bypassing printing colleagues. Rupert Murdoch's News International, publishers of *The Times* and *The Sun*, were the next to go head to head with print unions fighting to keep jobs. The bitter Wapping dispute following News International's decision to build a state-of-the-art printing plant in London's Docklands ended in 1987 with lay-offs and, for some within the industry, a deep distrust of new technology and its implications.

Some journalists, many of them savvy technology specialists, were aware that this was just the start. Tim Berners-Lee, at the European Centre for Nuclear Research (CERN), was developing a computer language and address system that would lead to the launch in 1991 of what we now call the World Wide Web. The internet, the 'network of networks' which allowed computers to speak to each other, had already been developed using technologies that had their origin in the space race of the late fifties and early sixties. Simply put, the internet with its network services, such as email, now had its own hypertext language to link electronic documents.

The World Wide Web was first seen as an academic tool with only a handful of hosts serving websites, but by 1993 it had taken off with the introduction of Mosaic, the first web browser that could display text as well as graphics.

By the mid-nineties journalists were using the web for work, media outlets were experimenting with the medium and some individuals were starting to set up their own websites. The US took the lead and the White House was one of the first information portals. It was also one of the web addresses that gave journalists their first taste of the vagaries of the net. A simple search often led them not to the government site but to one of the new upstart sites from the area that was to make the most money from the internet – the porn industry.

How does the internet work? See: Technology, Chapter 3.

Early adopters

The first incarnation of online journalism came in the form of bulletin boards, electronic newsletters and paid-for information services. Early pioneers worked for outlets such as OnLine Today and The Source.

However, mainstream media was still slow to embrace the web and appeared to have a 'you go first policy.' A notable exception in the UK was *The Daily Telegraph*, which launched what it called the *Electronic Telegraph* in 1994. A year earlier a team at the University of Florida's journalism school laid claim to the launch of the first journalism site (at the same time the USA allowed commercial traffic on the internet), but it was left to other industries to demonstrate the capabilities and potential of the internet. In 1995 search engine Yahoo! opened for business as did the bookseller Amazon and the ads site Craigslist. This year also signalled the start of online shopping and auction site eBay.

Some of that entrepreneurial zeal rubbed off on a self-styled libertarian called Matt Drudge who founded an email newsletter which he would later transform into one of the most influential and notorious news aggregation sites. Detractors criticised him for his mix of news and gossip. However, Drudge was more concerned by the practicalities of web journalism. He told Sky News in 2007 the secret of his website was 'To keep it going.' Today, drudgereport.com, which broke one of web journalism's first scoops – the news of Bill Clinton's affair with Monica Lewinsky – still attracts millions of visitors.

Source: Rex Pictures/Matt Baron

Matt Drudge

Dotcom boom

By the late 1990s most journalists were adept at getting their information online even if they were not working on a website. Newspapers, magazines, TV and radio organisations had websites run by small teams and presented them as a showcase for their brand. The majority of articles were 'cut and paste' content from the parent organisation, creating an impression that online journalism was just 'shovelware'.

BBC Online, launched in 1997, was a natural destination for many but there were other webzines and sites (many with a technology or business bent) such as The Register, The Street, Slashdot, Salon and Slate making innovations in news delivery and allowing readers a say in forums.

Salon, in particular, staffed by former journalists of the *San Francisco Examiner*, demonstrated that print journalists could reinvent themselves. During a strike in 1994 a few of them had taught themselves HTML and launched an online newspaper marketed as a 'smart tabloid'. Its conversational tone and forums pointed to a new relationship between the journalist and reader, a sense of community.

The success of these start-ups undoubtedly helped to galvanise newspapers' online strategies and persuade them to invest more in terms of technology and staff. Several nationals in the UK including *The Guardian* and the *Financial Times* invested millions into their online 'product'.

However, there were other key factors behind this confidence:

- Sites could make money through adverts and subscriptions.
- Search engines such as Google contributed to a surge in traffic and new, untapped markets.
- Papers started to see classified adverts migrate to the web.
- Open source technology allowed people to create content such as blogs cheaply.
- Market confidence in e-commerce spurred stock prices.
- Venture capitalists backed net products hoping for the next Amazon.

Dotcom bust

Unfortunately this speculative bubble was to burst. By 2001 many enterprises had spent too much, produced no profits and gone bust. Revenue from the net was minuscule in comparison with that delivered by newspapers.

No coherent business model had emerged that would secure profits for online news sites. Many journalists lost their jobs during a period of retrenchment with little investment in audio, video and interactive features. In some quarters blogging was derided as a fad.

Even though enterprises such as Amazon and Lastminute.com demonstrated modest profits, there was little optimism among journalistic enterprises that they could justify any more investment. But dotcom journalists weren't down and out. The twin engines of technology and big news stories would drive the next phase of the multimedia evolution.

Closer look Why were newspapers slow to respond to the net?

The newspaper industry was slow to respond to the challenges presented to it by the internet. In 2005 (the same year he bought MySpace) News Corp chief Rupert Murdoch admitted the industry had been complacent and warned that established rivers of revenue such as classified ads would dry up.

There had been warnings before. Professor Philip Meyer in his book *The Vanishing Newspaper* forecast that most newspapers in the USA would die out by the mid-point of this century. News was cheap, a freely available commodity, and if papers were to survive they must trade on their influence and powers of analysis.

The closure of newspapers, decline in circulations and failure to come up with a winning business formula for print and online unsettled a once confident industry.

So, why was it slow to embrace new media? First, it is worth remembering that the decline in newspaper sales and advertising revenue had started long before the widespread use of the internet in the nineties.

Newspapers in the post-war period saw readers migrate to magazines, TV and radio. Reading habits and loyalties changed – and journalism changed as cutbacks altered priorities. Investigative journalism, involving teams such as the *Sunday Times* Insight team which exposed the Thalidomide scandal in the late sixties, was costly. Column inches devoted to features and celebrity journalism were much cheaper. Regional newspapers have cut back in response to competition from freesheets and, of course, the web.

Why has the newspaper industry struggled to take advantage of the internet?

- Newspapers were surprised by the pace of new technology and therefore slow to respond.
- Newspapers were profit-making monoliths. Why change working practices, retrain journalists or invest if there was no proven business model?
- Newspapers had lasted for hundreds of years and survived TV and radio – why would the internet be a threat?
- Newspapers were averse to change. A print redesign might take years to plan and roll out. *The Times* spent several years planning the launch of its Compact edition which came off new presses in 2004.

- Journalists and management were suspicious of new technology and new working practices. Bitter disputes over the introduction of new technology in the eighties underpinned fears that the internet would also mean job losses.
- Stop! Newspapers were not complacent but hard-headed. There was very little indication, initially, how they would make any money out of the internet so why threaten the revenues of the print product to invest in an unproven medium? Who could argue with this, particularly when the dotcom bubble burst in 2000?

The road to convergence

One of the most damaging barriers to progress was the seeming ambivalence of newspapers to their dotcom operations, creating an artificial 'us' and 'them' culture between print journalists and their dotcom colleagues. In the nineties it was not unusual for web journalists to be given separate contracts, moved to another floor or even another building (the *New York Times* only moved journalists into the same building in 2007. It is now seen as a model of convergence). The resulting breakdown in communication, as well as duplication of content and roles impaired the quality of web journalism.

The integrated approach of the last few years in which journalists work together was fashioned out of financial expediency, improvements in technology and the success of sites in generating traffic, new audiences and advertising. Newspapers scurried to tell the story of the September 11 terrorist attacks but by the next day front page news stories already looked out of date. Everyone had turned to the TV and radio as their first news source but millions had also bombarded the internet for information (causing news sites to crash). Not only that, but they were posting their own comments and experiences and seeking out blog sites. The Iraq war, the Tsunami and the London terror attacks showed that it wasn't just journalists who could tell the story.

Newspapers were slow to recognise the importance of search engines such as Google. Even though it has said it has no ambition to be a content provider its power over online news distribution and rankings is undeniable. Google was viewed as a threat even though it denied any such ambition. At the International Press Institute's conference in Edinburgh in 2005 the Google presentation was one of the most eagerly anticipated and highly attended sessions. Many print journalists bristled as Krishna Bharat, Principal Scientist of Google and creator of Google News, talked about online journalism, gave a history of the printed daily and referred to 'our industry'.

In the aftermath of dotcom failures post 2000 most newspaper sites saw cutbacks but journalists started to work in teams and web and paper operations started to cross-promote and offer 'bundled' ad deals. Papers put up their cover prices or changed format – *The Times* became a Compact and the *Guardian* relaunched in a smaller size called Berliner. Some made savings on print costs by dumping data that was freely available on the internet. Others looked at the free newspaper market pioneered by Swedish company Metro or to regions such as Asia where newspaper sales showed growth.

Rupert Murdoch's speech in 2005 to the American Society of Newspaper editors warning of complacency is frequently cited as the tipping point for newspapers and attitudes to change in the digital era. He portrayed himself as a 'digital immigrant' and added: 'The challenge for us . . . is to create an internet presence that is compelling enough for users to make us their home page. Just as people traditionally started their day with coffee and the newspaper, in the future, our hope should be that for those who start their day online, it will be with coffee and our website.'

His speech spurred a change in the working practices of his newspapers and more investment into thesun.co.uk (once currantbun.co.uk) and timesonline. Other newspaper groups responded and online journalists welcomed the renewed impetus and momentum to the 'new newsroom'. While guardian.co.uk (formerly Guardian Unlimited) is viewed as one of the most successful and innovative sites for online journalism, others have forged ahead to present distinct, competitive offerings. In 2006 *The Telegraph* and the *Financial Times* rolled out integrated newsrooms with journalists producing content for both platforms. (See: Multimedia and convergence journalism, page 31)

Today, the buzzwords are convergence (the combination of various forms of media), geolocation (being able to target information based on the user's mobile phone location) and the semantic web (where the meaning of information is defined so that the web can understand the requests of people and machines – often seen as the most likely basis for 'Web 3.0'). The challenge for journalists will be their agility to respond by providing Web 3.0 journalism. Pressure remains to provide content worth paying for that is rich in analysis or information that readers can't get anywhere else.

CASE HISTORY *The Huffington Post* – credible competitor?

The response from mainstream media to the launch of *The Huffington Post* in 2005 gives us many clues about the attitudes in the newspaper industry that made it slow to respond to the challenges of the internet.

The blog site founded by journalist Arianna Huffington, former AOL Time Warner executive Kenneth Lerer and viral marketing expert Jonah Peretti is hardly radical in its content or presentation. Its mix of news, political commentary, policy analysis, entertainment and academic debate has drawn upon contributions from politicians, journalists and celebrities including Barack Obama, Michael Moore and Donatella Versace as well as established bloggers such as Jay Rosen. Yet, it was initially viewed with scepticism. Few forecast that within two years it would recruit more journalists and become a 24-hour news site capable of breaking and responding to news. Now owned by AOL, it bills itself as 'The Internet Newspaper' and is rated as the world's most popular blog site (most linked to) by Technorati. (See: *The Huffington Post*, Plate 19)

Detractors gave no hint that they feared it might rival established news sites or be quoted in the same breath as the *Washington Post*. No one predicted that it might steal a march by giving readers an opportunity to post back comments.

Arianna Huffington, a relative newcomer to the blogosphere, was known for her Washington connections and stellar contacts. She campaigned to be governor of California in 2003 and is the former wife of businessman and Republican politician Michael Huffington. *The Huffington Post* initially came under fire for disparaging comments left by the public. At a practical level, the heady mix of celebrity and politics did not fit the editorial ethos of many of the leading news sites.

However, Alan Rusbridger, editor of *The Guardian*, was one of the first to acknowledge the Post's influence. Talking to a Harvard audience about *The Guardian's* Comment is Free site in 2006 he said: 'It's as if *The Huffington Post* existed in the same space as the *New York Times*. Difficult to imagine, perhaps, and quite often a bumpy ride. But all part of the continual experimentation demanded of media organisations by the Web 2.0 era.'

But what do you think? Go to: www.huffingtonpost.com

Timeline of web journalism

* **1991:** Tim Berners-Lee releases World Wide Web browser and server software
* **1994:** *Daily Telegraph* launches Electronic Telegraph
* **1994:** Launch of Drudge Report. Founder Matt Drudge breaks first big online scoop in 1998 with Monica Lewinsky story
* **1995:** Craig Newmark sets up Craigslist, an online noticeboard where people post ads
* **1997:** Launch of BBC Online
* **1999:** Pyra Labs creates Blogger, free software that allows anyone to set up their own blog
* **1999:** Launch of Guardian Unlimited. Relaunched as guardian.co.uk in 2008
* **2001:** Readers flood websites for news following terrorist attacks of September 11
* **2002:** US Senate Republican Leader Trent Lott stands down after bloggers pick up remarks that were ignored by mainstream press
* **2004:** Flickr becomes source for images as site allows users to upload and share photos
* **2004:** CBS anchorman Dan Rather resigns after bloggers raise questions about accuracy of CBS report on George W. Bush's National Guard service
* **2004:** Asian tsunami on Boxing Day demonstrates reach of web from inaccessible areas as images and video are published to web from mobile phones
* **2005:** Podcasts take off as iTunes adds them to its jukebox
* **2005:** Rupert Murdoch tells newspaper industry that it has been slow to respond to digital developments. Buys social networking site MySpace
* **2005:** July 7 attacks on London Underground see emergence of digital citizen as mobile phone images flash around the world. Sites use user-generated content to tell story
* **2005:** News organisations scour web in aftermath of Hurricane Katrina for eyewitness accounts and images posted on blogs
* **2007:** Mainstream media reports Virginia Tech massacre using information from Facebook and other social networking sites
* **2007:** Myanmar protests are tracked via blogs and social networking sites because journalists were blocked from entry
* **2008:** News of Chinese earthquake spreads via Twitter
* **2008:** Journalists look to Twitter as a tool after terrorist attacks in Mumbai are reported in real time by the microblogging service
* **2010:** Citizen journalism site iReport is used to track and connect relatives after the Haiti earthquake

Blogs, wikis, podcasts and participatory media

The phenomenal growth in broadband during the last decade has meant millions more potential readers have access to high-speed internet. Services allow them not only to receive information but to partake in a medium that allows them to set up websites for free, upload and share digital photos, respond to journalists via comments fields, create and add to wikis, and send mobile phone text, images, sound and video that can be seen around the world in a matter of minutes.

Major news stories such as the terrorist attacks on New York in September 2001, the Iraq war in 2003, the Asian tsunami in 2004 and the London Underground bombings in 2005 demonstrated the appetite for information on the web and the agility of the medium to respond in real-time.

Journalists have had to learn to respond to a web evolution that has seen the launch of Wikipedia, MySpace, Flickr, Facebook, YouTube and Twitter. They have also had to develop a new language and intrinsic understanding of how the web works, whether it be SEO (search engine optimisation), 'trolls' (mischief makers spreading disinformation), fixing text with HTML, or analysing site traffic and knowing the difference between hits and unique users.

New frontiers

Convergent technology has forced journalists to work in a more integrated way, in newly designed converged newsrooms for a multimedia environment where the idea of being a 'print' or 'online' journalist is looking increasingly old-fashioned. Journalists have had to learn new skills but more significantly they have had to learn and experiment with a medium that throws up almost daily challenges, not least the emergence of citizen journalism.

Anyone can now create their own blog or website and influence the news agenda. Journalists blog but also track news and comment from the blogosphere using sites such as Technorati and Twitter trends. Where once they kept up with the news by reading what other journalists had to say, they now have to also keep up with news, analysis, opinion and agendas created by their audience. User-generated content such as images, audio, video and blogs has developed alongside the letters page. (See: How to Blog, Chapter 6)

National and regional news sites have seen growth and in some cases modest profits. The reach of the web has been alluring for advertisers who now scrutinise ABC Electronic figures for trends in traffic growth. The Mail Online, one of the last newspaper sites to launch in the UK, has positioned itself as a major competitor to Guardian.co.uk and Telegraph.co.uk. More recently, however, there has been a backlash against the pursuit of traffic for its own sake by some publishers (notably those whose sites do not get the highest traffic), who have described casual visitors to news websites as 'window-shoppers' with little value to their publications or to advertisers. Some sites charge for their content via subscriptions. *The Times* is experimenting with a paywall policy that means readers can pay for content on a daily, weekly or subscription basis which gives them access to the newspaper and the website.

Regional UK newsgroups have seen growth online but not enough profit to underpin both print and online operations. Many local newspapers have shut down, a pattern repeated in even more dramatic fashion in the US.

The growth of hyperlocal news websites (often a blog) in the US where amateurs and professionals work together on community news has inspired start-ups in the UK. Some have tried to fill the void left by papers; many have micro readerships of just a couple of thousand.

They are unlikely to replace local papers, argues Roy Greenslade, media commentator for *The Guardian*. But he does see this as an opportunity for trained journalists to collaborate with local amateurs. 'If they [publishers] really want to find a way of doing more than cutting costs, they might think about backing initiatives that offer a genuinely new gateway to a different digital journalistic future.'

Summary

Online journalism is evolving and creating new ways of engaging the reader on a global and real-time basis. Whether you are a young journalist just starting out or someone who grew up with print and broadcast, the key skills of journalism – getting the story and telling it in an accurate and compelling fashion – are still fundamental. But *how* you tell and distribute the story is being driven by technology and influenced by new forms of journalism such as blogging and citizen journalism. Digital skills are a prerequisite of the modern journalist, as is an understanding of multimedia platforms such as mobile telephony and mobile phone applications. Convergence presents new challenges to media outlets as they seek to organise their journalists and output across several platforms.

The internet provides journalists with an exciting opportunity to re-engage with readers who also want to tell the story. The citizen journalism revolution may only just have started, its main proponents using the blogosphere and other platforms rather than distinct websites. However, the web still provides another opportunity to do what journalists have been striving to do for hundreds of years – engage with their audience. Journalists may find themselves working alongside their audience much more in the future. Or even for them.

Source: iStockphoto/Temistock Lucarelli

Activities

Archive research

Chart the development of a major news site such as nytimes.com by using the web to go back in time.

1. Go to the Waybackmachine site at www.archive.org which stores 150 billion pages.
2. Using the search engine field, type in the web address of your site.
3. By clicking on the years displayed you will build up a picture of how many pages, multimedia features and designs the site has had.
4. What multimedia features did it use to report big news stories such as the 9/11 attacks in New York?
5. Answer the following questions: in which year did it launch interactive features, forums, blogs, podcasts, video, user-generated content?
6. Now use the search engine again to track the history and development of the Waybackmachine site!

Further reading

Allan, S. (2006) *Online News: Journalism and the Internet,* UK and USA: Open University.

Allan, S. and Thorsen, E. (2009) *Citizen Journalism: Global Perspectives,* USA: Peter Lang.

Editors (2008) *The Huffington Post Complete Guide to Blogging,* USA: Simon and Schuster.

Gillmor, D. (2006) *We The Media, Grassroots Journalism by the People, For The People,* USA: O'Reilly Media.

Greenslade, R. (2009) *Who Will Fund Hyperlocal Start-ups?* Guardian.co.uk, April 14, 2009, www.guardian.co.uk/media/greenslade/2009/apr/14/digital-media-local-newspapers

Jarvis, J. (2009) *What Would Google Do?,* USA: Collins.

Meyer, P. (2009) *The Vanishing Newspaper: Saving Journalism in the Information Age,* USA: University of Missouri Press.

Trippi, J. (2006) *The Revolution Will Not Be Televised: Democracy, the Internet, and the Overthrow of Everything,* USA: HarperPaperbacks.

Chapter 3

Technology

This chapter will cover:

- Why do journalists need to understand technology?
- Closer look: 'How I use technology'
- What is the internet?
- Language and design
- Exercise: HTML – the basics
- Convergence
- Search
- Closer look: Web analytics
- Social media marketing (SMM) and social media optimisation (SMO)
- Content management systems (CMS)
- Closer look: Using the technology – what's out there for journalists?
- What kit do I need?

Introduction

The last decade has seen a revolution in the way we distribute and consume information and the next will see even more innovation. The internet has given journalists the means to publish at the touch of a button so that stories can (also at the touch of a button) be read globally and in real-time. But before we click to 'publish' there are many stages in the journalistic process we need to consider, not least the way we think about what the reader wants and how they want to receive it, search for it, subscribe to it, react to it and share it.

Journalists need to understand how technology is driving the delivery of content across platforms and devices, whether it is via a text message or a hyperlink from a laptop or a smartphone or an e-reader such as the iPad. They need to understand the 'how' because this will help them determine the 'what' in terms of making sure stories are searchable and presented in an effective format using words, pictures, audio, video and interactive features.

Journalists need to figure out how convergent technologies shape convergence journalism. They also need to understand that their industry is changing in response to the challenge of technology and new media competitors. When Bill Keller, executive editor of *The New York Times*, said at the end of 2009: 'We want to make sure we have the best possible working relationship between technology, product, and the newsroom. We understand that *The New York Times* is and has to be a technology company as well as a journalism company,' his team was preparing to launch the newspaper as an application on Apple's iPad.

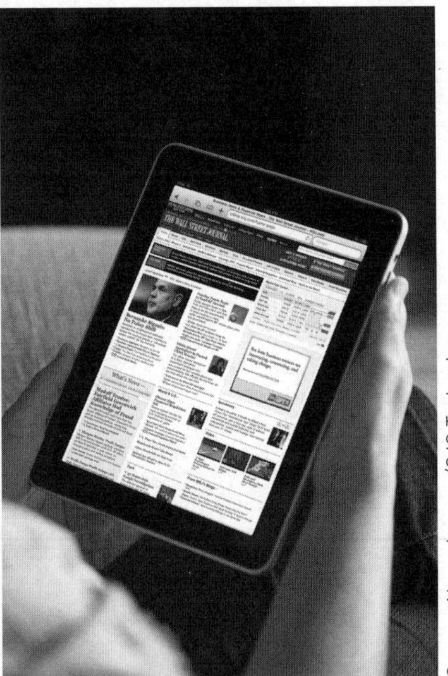

Source: Alamy Images/CJG Technology

Apple iPad

Internet communication has become more accessible and the growth in technology is exciting and challenging. The pace of change can also be frustrating and a little scary – journalists have to learn new skills to keep up. As well as the jargon, acronyms and buzzwords such as convergence there are the practical issues of what kit to use and tracking the latest developments in how readers are using the technology, whether it be messaging via Twitter or downloading mobile phone applications.

This chapter deals with what you need to know from RSS to SEO. It explains how the internet works and how journalists are using technology to enhance their journalism, engage with readers and pioneer new forms of storytelling. As Michael White of *The Guardian* put it when commenting on how technology has transformed the nature of political reporting in the last 40 years: 'Do I miss the old ways? Of course. But the new interactive, crowdsourced and accountable ways can be fun too, even the online abuse. And I no longer have the old reporter's anxiety dream of not being able to find a phone box. You can always file your story with a laptop and a Wi-Fi connection. Now I dream of power points.'

Why do journalists need to understand technology?

A web journalist does not need to have the skills of an information architect to create a website or publish to it. Where once it was necessary to be an expert in HTML (Hyper Text Markup Language) to create a hyperlink or an expert in design and site management software programs such as Dreamweaver, today's publishing or content management systems (CMS) have tools and features that make this an easier process, helping you to do this speedily and efficiently. You do not need to be a super-geek or computer programmer to publish to the web, although some journalists will undoubtedly want to have more of a command of the technology than others. Some will choose to specialise in a particular area such as audio or video while others will find their careers take them down another route to being a data researcher or journalist programmer experimenting with interactive technologies. An informed overview of how technology works will, however, help the journalist or editor make the right choices for story delivery and help them troubleshoot when things go wrong.

There are other reasons why journalists need to have an overview of how technology works for them.

- Technology can help you do your job more efficiently: getting information takes minutes rather than days; you can file multimedia using text, pictures, video and audio; you can use the web to email, tweet, map, analyse data, translate; you can conduct a video interview using a service such as Skype.
- Convergence journalism is not only about the overlapping of technologies but also how we organise our multimedia news rooms. Remember: you may have a good story but that doesn't mean you have to tell it five different ways for five different platforms just because you have the technology to do so.
- Interactive features mean instant feedback and conversation with the reader.
- The onus is on journalists to drive site traffic by making sure their articles are optimised for search engines, and to allow readers to recommend and share articles using sites such as Facebook, Twitter, Digg and Delicious.
- Web analytics tells us more than how many hits a website receives; it can also deduce how many times someone has clicked on to an article, how they got there, where they are regionally and globally, and where they went when they left a site.
- The quality of tools and devices to help you do your job is constantly improving – you will always need an upgrade.
- The rise of 'mojo' journalism – journalists are using their mobile phones to write, edit, publish and distribute.
- Journalists need to understand 'the language' so that they can communicate ideas with colleagues such as web developers – do you know your cookies from your breadcrumbs?
- Troubleshooting – when something goes wrong is it just a loose cable, user error (you hit the wrong button) or something that needs specialist attention?
- The cheap, fast and effective delivery of information means more competition from – and opportunities for collaboration with – citizen journalists and new media companies such as Google.

Closer look 'How I use technology'

'The big change for me has been a move to Twitter (twitter.com/vickeegan) as a major source of news and views, replacing the increasingly slow Google news alerts. The key is who to follow – I choose a small number of experts in their field who filter their news for all of us in a way they never used to. I don't seek followers for their own sake but go for loyal ones who will retweet thereby creating leverage.

'I get a lot of stories from social networks (in the real world not online) because most journos are in the office twittering and blogging and don't get out so much. I still use the phone, especially Skype or Truphone for long distance, but email exchanges or chat give an exact record of what was said (useful if there is comeback).

'Now I have left *The Guardian* and on my own I have set up a blog for creative uses of new technology (www.victorkeegan.com). I have dipped my toe into iPhone apps (City Poems) and regularly cross refer to photos or paintings of mine in Flickr.com to generate a community. Everything is now going mobile creating exciting new opportunities. We mustn't get left behind.'

Victor Keegan, former technology columnist for guardian.co.uk

What is the internet?

The internet is often referred to as the 'network of networks', the infrastructure which connects computers around the world. As soon as you sign up with an internet service provider (ISP) your computer is hooked up to the internet and probably the first application you will use will be email. The 'internet' should not be confused with the World Wide Web, the technology developed by Tim Berners-Lee which interlinks hypertext documents so that we can exchange text, pictures, data, audio and video.

To access a website you use a software application called a browser and then type in your address or uniform resource locator (URL) such as www.bbc.co.uk, which will take you to the BBC website and should take only seconds with a broadband connection. If you see http:// in the web address this means Hyper Text Transfer Protocol, which allows your web browser to communicate with the server of the website (the computer on which the site is stored). The domain name is the registered web address of a site. Many companies on the internet now specialise in hosting and registering domain names, although the price for this can vary.

I'm logged on, so why do I need to know about browsers?

A browser is the software application which displays your web page. To help you, some pages have breadcrumbs, links which usually appear at the top and are a trail for the user to go back through previous levels in the site structure (e.g. Chelsea > Premiership > Football > Sport > BBC News).

Many sites use cookies to store information about users – partly for the user's convenience (e.g. password, location, favourites), but also for commercial reasons (e.g. where a user came from, search terms, etc.). Most browsers will allow you to reject or accept cookies – the text files placed on your computer by many websites to track registration details and site traffic, for example. The option to do so may affect your choice of browser. But for those building and designing websites the main issue is how a browser will affect the finished product – the choice of browser used by the reader can determine its capability, particularly its appearance.

In the early days of internet journalism, Netscape and Internet Explorer fought it out to be the most popular browser. Now there are more options such as: Microsoft Internet Explorer, Apple Safari, Mozilla Firefox, Google Chrome, Flock and Opera. The battle for dominance in this market has been termed 'browser wars' as each seeks to prove it is faster and has more efficient anti-virus software.

Mozilla Firefox

Google Chrome

Internet Explorer

Language and design

Hyper Text Markup Language is the computer language for formatting on the web. HTML creates pages and the hyperlinks which allow you to navigate from one area of the page to the other, to another page or another website entirely. Hyperlinks are key to the information highway that is the web – they can get you to where you want to go, help you navigate your way round the web and drive traffic (readers) to your site.

HTML uses tags to format text and pictures. However, publishing systems have become so sophisticated that journalists do not need to be able to write HTML to publish online. Most systems work in WYSIWYG (what you see is what you get) so that you can edit without seeing code. Free systems such as WordPress allow you to set up a site without any knowledge of HTML.

A more sophisticated enterprise which demands video, animation and sound does need expertise in HTML or at least proficiency in any number of web development tools such as Dreamweaver, Flash and Javascript. What needs to be allied with these skills is a knowledge of design and usability. Is the site easy to read and easy to navigate? Are the interactive features user friendly? A team of experts specialising in these areas is employed for the bigger websites which use content management systems. And when it comes to HTML they will also be expected to be up to speed with its extension, XHTML.

So, do you need to know XHTML? The simple answer is no. But when it comes to HTML, a little knowledge is useful to correct small formatting mistakes which can often have a big impact on how an article is displayed.

Exercise

HTML – the basics

Hyper Text Markup Language is the computer language for publishing on the web. It is possible for an internet journalist to publish online without any knowledge of it. For the more adventurous, call up any site and click on View in the tool bar and then Source – this shows the HTML and can look a little scary.

What am I looking at?

The formatting language displays pages and information that are recognised by the browser. The browser reads the information contained within tag brackets <> which can format text into web pages, headings, lay-outs and hyperlinks.

For example:

```
<html>
      <head>
      <title> web page </title>
      </head>
      <body>
      <p>
Web journalists don't have to be experts in HTML but a little knowledge is a good thing.
      </p>
      <body>
</html>
```

This is a web page but the only thing you will see on your browser will be:

Web journalists don't have to be experts in HTML but a little knowledge is a good thing.

Simple HTML will create a page and a template within which the content sits. It can also control formatting including font size, colours and alignment. However, modern web design recommends using cascading style sheets (CSS) for these elements, so that design is separated from content. CSS allows you to specify different styles for different situations – for example, if the page is being viewed on a mobile phone, or printed. It's unlikely you will need any understanding of CSS to produce journalism, but if you are adjusting the design of a site – particularly on a platform such as WordPress – then you will.

The most common troubleshooting for web journalists is the dead link – a hyperlink that does not work when you click on it. It could be that you need to check the web address again, or you have incorrectly cut and pasted the URL (one common mistake is missing out 'http://'). Or it could be a formatting error. A hyperlink in the main body of the page looks like this:

```
<a href=http://www.webjournalism.com>Web Journalism</a>
```

The reader of the website only sees Web Journalism which is often highlighted in another colour; they can click on it and go direct to the website.

Convergence

Convergence is a term that has been applied to describe technologies, content and strategy. Convergence journalism, which sees journalists coming together to produce multimedia, is underpinned by the technologies that allow us to produce, merge and distribute content across a number of different platforms. For example, a newspaper will have journalists who produce stories for the paper and its website and organise its workflow with a convergent publishing system.

Computers and digitisation allow us to produce text, pictures, audio and video for the internet accessed by computers and mobile phones. The technology allows us to combine, overlap or produce distinct content. Radio broadcasts can be delivered 'live' over the net and archived as podcasts. Pictures and video can be captured on a phone. The same phone will allow you to text, email and download music. TV programmes and films can be downloaded on to a computer or accessed via services such as the BBC's iPlayer. Newspapers and novels can be read on e-readers such as the Kindle and iPad. A 'one screen fits all scenario' has often been forecast in which everyone can access television programmes and internet content from the same piece of hardware – although the reality appears to be heading in the opposite direction, with the same content becoming accessible across a proliferation of screens, from digital cinema screens to smartphones.

How will this affect me?

Convergence for journalists means using operating systems to publish and distribute stories across several platforms. It means integrated newsrooms (think about the BBC producing content for radio, TV and online) producing multimedia presentations, and an integrated approach with journalists commissioning and producing content in appropriate formats. Convergence does not mean that a journalist needs to be expert at every aspect of technology – there will always be a need for specialists – but it does mean new skills and a new approach that involves getting the best out of technology to offer what the reader/user/viewer/listener wants in the format of their choice.

Search

The internet is so vast it is essential that we find what we are looking for quickly and efficiently. It is vital that we understand how it works to make sure our journalism is findable – in other words, to make sure that it has good search engine optimisation (SEO). Search engines such as Google, Ask and Yahoo! allow us to find a story or a website without the need for a URL; we can just search for it using keywords or phrases. Most of these engines index the information using 'spider' technology to 'crawl' the web looking for pages. A search engine such as Google uses an algorithm to search its own database of pages that use the keywords, or which were linked to with those keywords (you can make sure a search is limited to pages that contain a particular word by placing a + sign immediately before it, with no space).

Search engine optimisation

Internet journalists make it their business to use keywords in their headlines, URL and page title so that their articles can be found more easily. This is one of the most basic ways of ensuring good SEO (see Writing for the web, Chapter 4).

Websites can pay for prominent (but clearly labelled) positions in a search results page, and advanced content management systems factor in SEO so that content can be more easily found.

You can improve SEO of content to drive more traffic to articles and attract more unique users by:

- using keywords in articles, intros, headlines and subheadings – names, places rather than generic terms;
- tagging content with keywords that define content – most publishing systems allow you to do this;
- using links in your articles where relevant;
- updating the page frequently where possible (user comments will achieve a similar result);
- and, most importantly, writing compelling, unique content that other people will link to. Links to your content are the primary factor influencing how well you rank on a page of search results.

Closer look Web analytics

Along one wall of the open plan offices of *The Daily* and *Sunday Telegraph* there is an enormous bank of screens. They display 24-hour news channels, webpages and – on one screen – the most read pages for *The Telegraph* website for that day, week and month – for every section.

These are known as web analytics – or metrics – and they are to online publishing what circulations are to print, and ratings to broadcast. They dictate how much a publisher can charge for advertising or sponsorship on a site – and how inflated or deflated a journalist's ego might be.

The Telegraph is just one of an increasing number of publishers who circulate information on the month's most popular articles and sections – indeed, some US websites have experimented with basing part of a journalist's pay on how many visits their articles receive.

In this context it is vital that a journalist understands the language around web analytics. Here are some of the key terms to familiarise yourself with:

Page views: Quite simply how many times a page has been viewed.

Unique visitors: This refers to how many individuals have accessed your site. This is important because one visitor may look at several pages, or even look at one page more than once – so a high number of page views may not mean you have large numbers of visitors.

Page views per visit (or visitor): The two statistics above allow you to work out how many pages each visitor looks at on average. If you have low page views per visitor it means you have a lot of people visiting but not sticking around to look at more than one page; if you have high page views per visitor then you are likely to have a more loyal group of users that returns to read, or spends time browsing around the site. This is the sort of visitor advertisers like.

Time on site: This tells you how long users stick around for – and again, the longer the better, generally speaking, as it means that they are either spending time reading articles in full, or clicking through to other articles. If visitors are not spending very long on your site, you might want to think why that is: are you giving them other articles to click on once they're finished? Could you produce content that is more immersive, such as audio slideshows or online community? Content that keeps people on your site is often called 'sticky' and many publishers work hard to identify 'sticky content'.

Bounce rate: The percentage of visitors who left your site without looking at more than a single page. This may be because that page was not what they were looking for, or because it was *all* that they wanted to read. Once again, the challenge is: how can we make them want to read more?

Traffic source: Where the visitor came from. A large percentage of visitors will, invariably, come from search engines – Google in particular. Another significant source of visitors will be social networks such as Facebook and Twitter. If a major site links to you you will notice it in these figures, as you will see a sudden surge of visitors coming from one particular webpage: the page that links to you. Looking at your sources is a good way to find other websites in your field, and also to identify where you might concentrate your distribution efforts. Not getting enough traffic from Google? It may mean you need better search engine optimisation.

Search terms: For those visitors coming via search engines, this will tell you what they searched for. Again, this can be extremely useful in shaping your content strategy. A good exercise is to conduct a search yourself on those terms and see how high you come up – although it should be noted that your site will be ranked differently on a particular search depending on who is searching (for example, a UK site will rank higher on a set of search results if someone is searching in the UK).

You can use any of a number of free web analytics tools on your own website or blog. WordPress has its own analytics built in, which will tell you how many people have visited each day, what pages they visited, and what search terms they used to find your site. Google Analytics is the best known free analytics tool, and in addition to all the above it will tell you what countries your visitors come from, what sort of browser they are using (e.g. Internet Explorer, Firefox), how long they spend on your site, and what page they leave on.

Social media marketing (SMM) and social media optimisation (SMO)

Related to SEO is the practice of social media marketing (SMM) or social media optimisation (SMO). The objective here is twofold: first to increase traffic through sharing of links on social media, and secondly to increase search engine ranking as a side-effect of that. Simply, SMO tactics include:

- using social networks such as Twitter and Facebook to post links;
- allowing users to distribute stories with links to social bookmarking sites such as Digg and Delicious and community sites such as Stumbleupon;
- posting comments with links.

It is important to make a distinction between links within articles and links on social media: typically links on blog comments, forums and social networks are not counted by search engines when they rank your website. This is done by including a <nofollow> tag on all links which tells search engines not to follow them. This avoids the system being abused by spammers and advertisers.

Content management systems (CMS)

A content management system (CMS) manages the content of a website and allows collaboration with other members of a team. Journalists can file to a single production system. They can also write, edit, upload and publish concurrently. To write and edit using the CMS you will log on and give your password. What you will see are the folders and structure of your CMS which determines your work flow. You will be given access to certain parts of the system depending on your role as a content producer or editor. Within the system there will be templates which you will use to write your story and tools which allow you to perform simple functions such as making a hyperlink or uploading a picture or video without the need to use HTML.

There are many types of CMS which use convergent technologies and are customised or updated according to the type of media company. For example, a media enterprise that has a newspaper and a website can have a system which allows them to edit stories for both platforms. A single story could be edited for the paper in three different templates for three separate editions of the story. It could also be called up in its web template ready to have images, hyperlinks, and embedded audio and video added before it is published to the web. The story could also be edited and published from a number of different locations – from offices, the journalist's home or via a laptop out in the field.

Systems are becoming more sophisticated as media companies invest millions in technology which goes beyond content storage and retrieval. Content management systems now have to rise to the challenge of providing for different platforms, syndication, web feeds, social tools, and collaborative content with readers.

Open source and free software

For journalists who want access to free software to build a website with built-in CMS there is open source and free software. Open source software makes its source code available to users, meaning that others can add to it, adapt and improve it.

For many developers and journalists the open source movement is a philosophical approach to the internet which allows collaboration by sharing, developing and using software for the benefit of all. For the majority it is just a free, practical approach to publishing on the internet. Its main influence on journalism has been the ease of access to blogging software. Anyone can use Joomla or WordPress, for example, to set up a blog with functionality and design without the need to pay for a host or domain name (see How to blog, Chapter 6).

Closer look Using the technology – what's out there for journalists?

Every day there is the launch of a new website, blog, device, tool or upgrade that can help journalists. Sometimes it is easy to forget things that we take for granted, such as email, text and access via the internet to broadcasts. Also it can be challenging to learn new skills. But by using and experimenting with technology journalists not only find out what works for them (sometimes it is just a matter of preference) but what is working for their audience.

Mobile journalism

Nowhere is this more apparent than in the area of mobile telephony. An increasing number of people are accessing information from the web via their phones, forcing journalists and designers to think about content for what is a developing medium for distribution. Many news organisations, such as the BBC, Reuters and CNN, are specifically tailoring their output for the mobile market.

Mobile phone journalism, as a medium in itself, is also developing as 'mojo' journalists discover they can cover stories effectively and speedily using their handy, pocket-sized device. For example, reporters can video interviews on the fly and get them online in minutes, giving breaking news stories a 'live' quality. Teams of reporters covering events find they can communicate effectively with one another using phones and respond rapidly if the story changes. One of the main drivers of mobile journalism is the increased quality of video and video editing facilities. Journalists are also finding that interviewees, familiar with what a mobile phone can do, are less intimidated than if they were speaking to someone carrying the bigger kit associated with film crews.

Investigate the following:

- Use applications that you can download to your phone. Some are free and some you have to pay for. There are many apps that are useful for journalists: subscriptions to news sites, access to radio stations (Wunder Radio), a storage facility for files (Dropbox), recording and editing (Poddio), and simple apps that allow you to do the basics such as write or record your notes.
- Keep up with breaking news by signing up for news alerts via email or web feed to your computer or phone or both.
- Use RSS (Really Simple Syndication) so you don't have to check your most viewed websites all the time for updated content. Many sites have an orange RSS logo at the top of the page. This is a web feed direct to your desktop and allows you to subscribe to a site for the latest content in your chosen area.
- To subscribe to RSS feeds, look into setting up an RSS reader. There are both web-based RSS readers (such as Google Reader) and desktop-based ones (such as FeedDemon). Both can be very powerful, with synchronisation and the ability to access them anywhere – including on the go, which can be very useful if you want to catch up on things when you're on the move. Just find the one you're most comfortable with – you can always export your subscriptions to another RSS reader later.
- Join social networks such as Twitter and Facebook to exchange and search for information.
- Bookmark your websites at Digg or Delicious.
- Use VoIP (Voice over Internet Protocol) which allows calls and videocalls via your computer. Services such as Skype are free to use and downloadable, and also offer chat and text options.
- Upload and store pictures to sites such as Picasa and Flickr.
- Create a wiki (a collaborative CMS such as Wikipedia) for a group project using twiki.org.
- While out on a story you can view maps, your location and get directions – Google Maps has a free download.
- Use translation services.
- Test the latest voice recognition technology, which transcribes speech into text – Apple's Scribe application is one of the latest.

What kit do I need?

A single device serving the spec requirements of a journalist as a computer, phone, camera, video, audio and notepad tool hasn't yet been invented despite the claims of various manufacturers. Yet the day can't be far off when a device fulfils the key components of accessibility, stability and sound and picture quality. There are many sophisticated audio and video recording devices but as a start a web journalist needs:

- the failsafe option of a notepad and pen.

- a mobile phone with fast internet browser, camera, video and audio recorder, ideally 3-G enabled with Wi-Fi connectivity. There are many mid-range phones on the market which have these capabilities but for every journalist who recommends a top-of-the-range BlackBerry citing its email capabilities there is another who prefers the touch screen technology of Apple's iPhone, or the flexibility and affordability of phones using Google's Android operating system.
- a lap-top computer – again, it is a matter of budget and preference: netbooks are light, cheap and flexible; bigger laptops and MacBooks will give you more power and software, but are heavier and cost more – but make sure your broadband access at home is the fastest you can get. Note, too, that upload speeds are often a fraction of the advertised download speeds.
- chargers, power cables, batteries. When travelling, always carry two chargers for your mobile, one in the suitcase and one for your pocket, a set of batteries for your computer and take your power cable. Your destination may have Wi-Fi but travelling light can sometimes mean a phone that needs to be charged and a computer's batteries packing up at the worst possible moment.

Tips

- It is worth investing in some headphones. Remember, if you are attending an event with other journalists, you will want to listen but not necessarily want to broadcast your work to the world before hitting the publish button. Ideally, get a headset with a microphone that is compatible for VoIP and Skype calls.
- Get a separate keyboard and mouse for your laptop for long periods of work in front of the screen. Most laptops are not very ergonomic, so to prevent RSI (repetitive strain injury, which often starts with pain in the wrists and fingers) invest in a docking station which allows you to set up your computer with a separate keyboard and mouse. If your computer is Bluetooth (open wireless) enabled, you can install your Bluetooth enabled keyboard and mouse, as well as other devices such as mobile phones, digital cameras and printers.
- Remember to back up your files! If your computer goes wrong or it is stolen at least you will be able to access your files if you have back-up by saving your data on a CD or memory stick. There are many online services that allow you to save your data so you don't have to save information on a disk or CD. You can then download your files when you have computer access again.

Think about:

- a digital recorder which plugs into your computer and saves recordings in a straightforward, compatible format such as MP3;
- a Flip, Kodak or other small video camera – low-budget, widely used. Make sure it shoots non-HD for faster uploading;
- smarter smartphones – for example, journalists are testing the capabilities of Google's Android system which has apps aimed at journalists (such as Qik which allows you to record and stream video from your phone);
- an ebook reader – it is early days but journalists are testing the Kindle and iPad and thinking about how multimedia journalism can be designed for ebooks.

A distinction should be made between open source and free software – some blogging software is free but the source code is not available to adapt, while the owners of that software and code can decide to pull the service or start charging, as the previously free social network service Ning did in 2010. To access and download free open source software go to sourceforge.net, which claims it has the largest collection of open source tools and applications on the net.

Summary

Journalists in the future will have to engage with advanced technologies including a more 'intelligent web'. As publishing systems, devices and tools improve and change, this means learning new skills while keeping an eye on how the consumer is using equipment and influencing manufacturers.

Where once the typewriter and computer were the main tools used by journalists, the mobile phone is emerging as an accelerant to publishing breaking news and accompanying words, pictures and video out on the web in a matter of minutes.

Journalists work in the new digital economy and should be aware of how governments are using legislation to clamp down on illegal downloads and file-sharing. Many journalists have concerns about powers that can be used to block internet sites that they claim give a platform for free speech.

The web continues to present us with even more challenges, a new era called Web 3.0. The inventor of the World Wide Web, Tim Berners-Lee, sees a 'semantic' web of the future where it is envisaged that we go beyond a collection of hyperlinked documents to a collection of hyperlinked data and facts. Colin Meek, an investigative journalist who specialises in getting the most out of search engines, explained the concept in an article at www.journalism.co.uk: 'The terminology used to describe the semantic web is often hard to penetrate, but the best way to understand it is to view the technology as an attempt to link up various clouds of information: flight times, weather forecasts, social network bookmarks and news stories are all delivered in different formats and readable only by different applications.'

Activities

1. YouTube is the popular choice to view video but why not try one of the other options? Sign up for Vimeo.com and compare key features such as quality and sharing options with YouTube.

2. Now search for Bill Keller's presentation on his seven digital priorities for *The New York Times*, which has its own research and development team. You will see that this video was put on the Vimeo website by niemanlab.org. Take a look at the Nieman Journalism Lab to find out more about this digital journalism project based at Harvard University.

Further reading

Berners-Lee, T. (1999) *Weaving the Web: The Past, Present and Future of the World Wide Web*, UK: Orion.

Kolodzy, J. (2006) *Convergence Journalism*, USA: Rowman and Littlefield.

Meek, C. (2008) *Web 3.0: what it means for journalists*, journalism.co.uk (October 23, 2008), www.journalism.co.uk/5/articles/532631.php

Nielsen, J. (2004) *Designing Web Usability: The Practice of Simplicity*, USA: New Riders Publishing.

Nielsen, J. (2007) *Homepage Usability: 50 Websites Deconstructed*, USA: New Rider Press.

Quinn, S. Filak F. V. (2005) *Convergent Journalism*, UK: Focal Press.

White, M. (2010) *Open door*, guardian.co.uk (April 19, 2010), www.guardian.co.uk/commentisfree/2010/apr/19/michael-white-open-door-election-reporting

Whittaker, J. (2000) *Web Production for Writers and Journalists*, 2nd edn, UK: Routledge.

Chapter 4

Writing for the web

This chapter will cover:

- What is online journalism?
- Multimedia and convergence journalism
- Search
- Research and organisation
- Writing for the web
- Writing for SEO
- Scannability
- How to use hyperlinks
- Tagging
- Editing
- FAQ
- Closer look: Online journalism tips
- Creating packages
- Closer look: guardian.co.uk/global-development

Introduction

'I use a 16-year-old computer. She can launch a Russian satellite with the thing she has.'

Cal McCaffrey, the investigative reporter in the film *State of Play*, complains to his editor about special treatment for his online colleague.

Online journalists use the internet to publish and distribute their journalism. But that is just one small part of a much bigger story. The distinctiveness of the online medium in its ability to provide networked information via hyperlinks to a global audience in real-time, and to let that audience interact with each other, has given journalists the opportunity to shape new, distinctive forms of journalism based on sharing information and the participation of readers.

Internet journalists are just as keen as their print, radio and television colleagues to get the story. While the internet is a good source of stories and a place to gather information, web journalists still need to get out of the office to talk to people.

Technology allows them to file stories using a combination of text, pictures, video, audio, animation and interactive features – and to distribute it via websites, blogs, texts and emails, and social networks.

They can use maps, gather information via crowdsourcing, make links between various sets of data, use external sources such as graphics and data to create 'mashups,' and they can call upon readers to provide user-generated content (UGC). But they still need to have the skills and know-how to effectively write, present and deliver stories for websites, e-readers and mobile phones. In addition, they need to be aware that journalistic content is also being produced by bloggers and citizen journalists.

Separate chapters in this book go into detail about technology, blogging, interactivity, UGC and legal issues and how to produce podcasts, slideshows and video. This chapter outlines the skills and principles of online journalism and is a primer for the next chapter which takes an in-depth look at investigative techniques associated with computer-assisted reporting and data journalism.

What is online journalism?

What are the defining characteristics of online journalism?

- Journalists use the internet as a platform for their stories.
- Hyperlinks – the click-through connections that flow information across networks.
- Non-linear storytelling. Readers determine how, when, what and where they consume content. They decide their entry point to a story when they access it via a link or a search engine. Online journalists break out (or chunk) parts of the story to reflect this and provide readers with different entry points depending on the angle that might interest them.
- Multimedia in the form of text, pictures, audio, video can be used.
- Journalists can report a story in real-time and distribute that story concurrently to several sites on several platforms. The story might start with a tweet on a breaking news story and might be read via a news site, a blog, a Twitter feed on a laptop or as a news alert on a phone.

- Interactivity – readers can engage with journalists, leave comments, talk to each other on forums, create or reinforce community.
- Accessibility – information can be accessed globally and around the clock.
- Transparency – journalists can use hyperlinks to give readers access to documents, press releases and to give attribution to quotes, facts and figures.

Online journalists have to be agile and adaptable as they react to stories. They are also challenged by the fact that they are not always constrained by traditional deadlines and a required length of story.

They have to determine the value of a story, how best to tell it, at what point the story is good enough to publish and at what point they have finished it in terms of added value such as extra links and background stories. As new media commentator Jeff Jarvis puts it: 'Online, the story, the reporting, the knowledge are never done and never perfect. That doesn't mean that we revel in imperfection . . . that we have no standards. It just means that we do journalism differently, because we can. We have our standards, too, and they include collaboration, transparency, letting readers into the process, and trying to say what we don't know when we publish – as caveats – rather than afterward – as corrections.'

For citizen journalism advocate Dan Gillmor it is no longer about what online journalism is and who is doing it. 'We are all creating media. Any one of us can, and many of us will, commit an act of journalism. We may contribute to the journalism ecosystem once, rarely, frequently or constantly. How we deal with these contributions – deciding to try one, what we do with what we've created, and how the rest of us use what's been created is going to be complex and evolving. But it's the future.'

Multimedia and convergence journalism

A multimedia journalist is someone who has the skills to work in print, television, radio and online. Many student journalists train in these areas before deciding which area to specialise in. But even if your ambition is to work for a radio station or a glossy magazine it is unlikely you will concentrate on only audio or print. The radio station will have a website, a Facebook page, a Twitter page (as will the individual programmes and the journalists) and the glossy magazine will have a website where journalists can blog and provide video and podcasts.

The advent of convergent newsrooms providing journalism across several platforms, for instance newspapers that have websites, means that a specialisation in one area is less important than media literacy in as many fields as possible such as news writing, blogging, podcasting, video, data investigation, slideshows, mapping, information design and interactive features.

Where previously a journalist would know what medium they were going to use whenever they encountered a story, now they must first identify which tools and techniques might be most appropriate. Is this story best told with text or audio? Are there strong images that need bringing out with photography or video? Will users want to interrogate the background through raw data, maps and links? This decision will often need to be taken quickly, and the journalist needs to either draw on their own multimedia skills to tell the story, or to call on others in their team with specialist knowledge of areas such as flash interactivity, microblogging, live web chats, mapping and mashups (a web page that uses several sources to create a story).

To make this work journalists have to skill up, communicate effectively and have strong editorial leadership that has clear, common news values. 'Newsrooms tackling convergence vary greatly in how they go about using the strengths of each medium to best get news and information out to an increasingly scattered and diverse public. Using all media available – print, broadcast, and online – convergence journalists believe they can inform more people, at more

Exercise

Go to YouTube to watch *The Daily Telegraph* newsroom in action.

Source: Telegraph Media Group/Andrew Crowley

The convergent newsroom

times, and in more places, about the world. They also believe that not every story works best in every medium. They say the key to making convergence work is to understand how to tell stories in newspapers, on television and online and to allow the readers, viewers, and users to reap the benefits' (Kolodzy, 2006).

While online journalists often complain about newspaper colleagues not understanding the internet it is also important that *they* also make an effort to learn about the print process.

Search

A knowledge of how search engines work is now central to what journalists do – both to be able to research as quickly and effectively as possible, and to write 'search engine optimised' content so that readers can access their work easily.

Search engines such as Google, Yahoo! and Bing crawl the web recording the pages that they find alongside keywords and phrases in headlines and text, alongside images, in page titles and URLs, and in links that lead to the pages in question. When you conduct a search the search engine matches the words that you are searching for against its database, and ranks the results based on a calculation of hundreds of variables – not just whether the words appear on the page (or in pages that link to it) and where, but how often and when the page has been updated, its 'authority' (how many other pages link to it) and the 'authority' of the pages that link to it.

One result of Google's algorithms (the calculations it makes to rank search results) is that older web pages are privileged over newer ones. This is because they tend to have accumulated more links pointing to them. Likewise, frequently updated sites such as news websites and blog posts tend to fare better than those that are left dormant for years.

Typically, search engines provide a number of filters (dates, regions, maps, blogs, media type) to help journalists find information. Google even provides a 'search within search results' function. And its advanced search facility allows users to specify date ranges and file formats.

It is tempting to just use Google but it won't be able to find everything. Journalists digging for information can also use subject directories such as Wikipedia and 'meta search' engines such as monstercrawler.com and dogpile.com which give results from a number of different search engines. Technorati is also a good place to search blogs as well as topics and trends that are popular in the blogosphere, and you will find other 'vertical' search engines that focus on a particular medium (for instance, video) or subject (for example, science).

Search engine tips

Google provides a number of filters but simple commands can help the search process. Most of these are accessible from the Advanced Search page, but knowing the procedures below can save you time:

- By using + (plus) you force Google to include words it might ignore. For example, a search for sixties graphics designer Grace Sullivan could be problematic as Sullivan is a common name and Grace is unlikely to be recognised as a keyword. A search for grace+sullivan gives you a better set of results.
- By placing + immediately before a word (e.g. +Volkswagen), you restrict results to pages containing the word. Without this you may get results that are *linked to* that word, but do not contain it themselves.
- If you are looking for an exact phrase use quote marks – "UK trade deficit". Again, this is particularly useful for names.
- To exclude words, use − (minus) for example, using −Volkswagen in a search for 'Golf' can be useful if you are searching for the sport, not the car.
- ~ for synonyms, as in NHS ~investigation which will also search for NHS probe.
- OR to search for two terms, for example taliban OR taleban.
- Use * for a wildcard match – for example 'tal*ban' will search for taliban, taleban and any other misspelling such as talaban or taloban.
- Site: to restrict results to one site. For example: Iran site:cnn.com.
- Date: restrict search to that timeframe.
- Allintitle: to restrict results to all the keywords used.
- Allintext: to restrict results to all the keywords used in body text.
- Filetype: to restrict results to a specific file type. For example, filetype:pdf will only return PDF files in your results, which can be useful if you're looking for reports.
- for content that has been removed from a site type in your search and click on the cached (saved versions of pages) link.

If you have difficulty finding information it may be buried in what is termed the 'invisible web'. This is where information, documents and data reside that search engines cannot access and index. There are a number of reasons for this but search engines cannot find information on pages that are in the wrong file format, and some sites have been specifically programmed to deter engines from crawling over them. Journalists can still access 'hidden' information by using websites which give access to pages in databases. Among the most popular are:

completeplanet.com – database directory

dmoz.org – open directory project

resourceshelf.com – guide to free resources

infomine.ucr.edu – academic

intute.ac.uk – academic directory

ipl.org – used by librarians

pipl.com – people finder

bubl.ac.uk – catalogues web resources chosen by UK academic librarians

Chapter 5 on data journalism details more resources and advanced techniques for searching databases.

Research and organisation

Journalists get stories by talking to people, by making connections, by covering breaking news, analysing data and trends, from press releases and by research and planning.

The online journalist is no different: it is important to get out of the office and not fall into the habit of recycling information that has already appeared on the internet. Indeed, if it has already appeared online then the most efficient way to report it is simply to link to it, and move on (unless something needs chasing up or verifying).

Preparation and organisation is essential when so much information is available online. How does the online journalist keep on top of what is happening and find relevant content?

- Use RSS news feeds to get automatic updates on topics of interest.
- Sign up for text and email news alerts.
- Use online calendars such as Meetup.com and Upcoming.com to identify useful events.
- Follow sites and contacts via Twitter.
- Use and join social networks to find people and pictures (Facebook, LinkedIn, Flickr).
- Join discussion groups.
- Use 192.com to find people and businesess, their address, telephone number, and electoral roll details.
- Track the popularity of content at social bookmarking sites such as Digg, Delicious and StumbleUpon where users can bookmark and vote on articles.
- Store and share bookmarked articles at one of these sites.

Writing for the web

The principles of good journalism – a story which engages the reader and answers the questions of who, what, where, when, why and how? – apply also to online journalism.

The medium, however, demands that the presentation of content differs from print. A story with an ambiguous headline is unlikely to engage the reader because without keywords for search engine optimisation (SEO) it will get buried further down the search engine results page (SERP).

If the story is one long piece of text taken from the print product without related links that give more value added content, this is 'shovelware', a form of lazy journalism that makes no attempt to make the most of the online medium. Stories need to be written for SEO and made accessible so that readers can find and navigate text easily as they scan the page. This has implications for how we write headlines, intros and subheads.

The journalist needs to keep in mind:

- the reader – how they get to the story. They choose their point of entry whether it is from elsewhere within the site or through links on other sites, blogs, social networks, search engines, news feeds and text alerts. The number one source of traffic to any given article is normally search engines, followed by social networks. Users might be less interested in your news story and go straight to related stories in a package in search of analysis, facts, figures and hyperlinked resources. Storytelling, therefore, is non-linear because readers make the decision about what they read and in what order.
- the medium – using appropriate content. Does the story need a timeline for context? A poll? Will it be enhanced by links to blogs and UGC?
- the platform – this could be a computer, laptop, e-reader or mobile phone. Media organisations are thinking about how to target and present content specifically for these platforms.

The inverted pyramid

Journalists are trained to write stories that get to the point in the first paragraph. The inverted pyramid style of writing where the nub of the information in the first sentence is backed up in subsequent paragraphs with quotes and background information works well online. A colourful intro or dropped intro where the writer builds up to a revelation does not work on the internet. Think about how articles appear in search results. Readers see a small excerpt – either of the intro or the passage surrounding the words being searched for – so if it is not clear what the piece is about they will not click on to it.

And the who, what, where, when and how questions can also be developed and broken out into separate stories. For example:

who = a profile, a picture story, a video, a podcast

what = link to documents, official reports, write an FAQ (frequently asked questions), pictures, ask readers to send in views and pictures about what happened, link to special blogs, start a blog about a specific issue/event

where = maps, graphics, data on regions and countries

when = dates, background, context, a calendar, a timeline of significant dates and events

how = analysis, Flash interactive or animation, live Q&A for readers to engage with expert/issue

Exercise

Select the top news story of the day. Search for it online. Does your search take you to the main news story? Or did you find it via a blog or multimedia element? How has the story been developed online? What else does it need – an audio slideshow, links to useful resources, a poll, a forum, links to Twitter comments?

Now look at a competitor site's treatment of the story. How have they made it relevant to their target audience? Finally, which site do you think did the better job? Why?

Writing for SEO

Online journalists need to be aware of search engine optimisation when they write headlines, intros, subheadings and image captions. Think about how your article will be found by readers using a search engine. They will type in specific words – keywords – and phrases. Search engines 'spider' sites, index content and look for keywords. Words such as 'the', 'and', and 'it' are not keywords, nor are 'people', 'person' 'man'. Keywords and phrases with names, places and figures are more effective at improving ranking of content.

Think about the reader – they only see the headline and a passage of text when they get search results or when they see a story on their phone.

For example: a headline which says, 'Wetherby schoolboy drowned' has keywords and gives information. 'Child confirmed dead' will be lower down in search results and is unlikely to catch the eye.

An intro which says, 'John Smith was thrown in river by school bullies, say Yorkshire police' tells the reader the news and will make them read on. It contains keywords. An intro that starts 'It's the news no mother wants to hear. As the police knocked at the door she burst into tears' is too vague.

Web usability expert Jakob Nielsen cites the BBC's news site as a good example of SEO with clear, concise headlines that use keywords. He says journalists need to make every word work hard for its living, as in the headline 'Italy buries first quake victims'. Because readers tend to scan pages in an F pattern he recommends: 'Start subheads, paragraphs, and bullet points with information-carrying words that users will notice when scanning down the left side of your content in the final stem of their F-behaviour. They'll read the third word on a line much less often than the first two words.'

Tagging and categorising content is also important in SEO. Most content management systems (CMS) allow you to do this when composing an article. Categories tend to be broad 'sections' that you cover regularly, such as 'boxing' or 'health'; tags tend to be specific people, locations or organisations mentioned in the article such as 'diabetes' or 'Wayne Rooney'. You should make sure your writing is well tagged and categorised to help search engines.

Other factors you should be aware of when looking at search engine optimisation include the URL (address of the webpage) and the page title (that appears on the strip across the top of the web browser, and is used to title the page if you bookmark or save it). These will be dictated by how the CMS works, but a good CMS should ensure that the article headline is used as the page title, and keywords used in the URL (WordPress, for example, allows you to edit the URL to improve search engine optimisation or make it more memorable). A search engine friendly URL should look something like localpaper.com/wayne-rooney-manchester-united-injury. If it looks like localpaper.com/123450909 then see if that can be changed.

Finally, the most important element of search engine optimisation is how many people link to your webpage. The best way to make that happen is to write fantastic, compelling, unique content that people want to share and link to. No amount of SEO techniques can avoid the need for great journalism.

Scannability

Over hundreds of years print newspapers and magazines have developed a number of techniques to help 'browsers' – the headline, the sidebar, the photo, the caption, the subhead, and the inverted pyramid. Broadcast news also has its techniques: the intro, the establishing shot, the actualité.

Online news borrows from both, but because it is a medium where users are *active* readers scannability is key to effective online journalism. There are several techniques that enhance the scannability of any webpage.

Clear, unambiguous headlines: a reader scanning down a list of search results is not always going to be willing to decode cryptic or punny headlines. They just want to know what the article is about. Also, an online audience is an international audience. They may not understand a culturally specific pun or clever wordplay, so keep your online headlines clear, functional and unambiguous. More to the point, if you use a keyword or phrase in your headline – such as the name of the subject of the story – it will improve your search engine rankings for that word or phrase. For example, *The New York Times* print headline 'For the Young, Politics Is Social' was reheadlined '*Finding Political News Online, the Young Pass It On*' because people are more likely to search for 'finding political news online'.

Intro-as-summary: having your first paragraph sum up what the story is about is useful for many reasons: it is likely to be displayed alongside a link to the story in search results; readers using screen readers will know quickly if the story is relevant to them; and readers using RSS readers will be able to see at a glance whether the story is worth reading. Also, search engines attach more importance to the first paragraphs of a webpage, so including keywords there will improve your search engine ranking.

Subheadings: breaking an article every few paragraphs with subheadings that indicate the content to come gives the reader numerous entry points into the text. Again, make them as clear as possible.

Bullet or number lists: such lists tend to catch your eye as soon as you look at the page. These work brilliantly online – any chance you get, use them.

Indented quotes: users often look for direct quotes. Help them by indenting any quote that runs over one line (blogs do this very well).

Hyperlinks: the conventional blue, underlined text screams 'click me' and, in blog convention, shows you are supporting your argument.

Emboldened or highlighted words: this is a good way of highlighting key phrases or words in your piece and again gives the user entry points into the text. Use it sparingly or it loses its impact (note: some websites render links as highlights, in which case avoid. And never underline text for emphasis – it will look like a link and frustrate the user).

How to use hyperlinks

Hyperlinks allow us to navigate the web. Without links there would be no web. Links let the reader click from one article to another, to navigate around a site or click on to an external page or site. They are often coloured or underlined.

Content management systems and blogging services make it easy to create hyperlinks without any knowledge of the code that makes them work. It is usually as simple as highlighting the relevant phrase, title, name or word you want to be a link, clicking on the link tool button (looks line a chain) and copying and pasting in the web address (URL) of the page you want to link to.

Journalists use links to other content such as articles, video, background information, archives, documents and resources. Links are used to:

- help readers navigate and drive traffic on a site;
- provide transparency by giving the reader access to where the information came from;

- serve as attribution and authority when referring to researched content such as quotes from an external source;
- save the user time and effort in finding out more.

Links allow the journalist to cross-refer to relevant information and related articles to the original story. They can demonstrate depth of research and help support an argument, particularly useful for the commentator or blogger. They can also save you having to repeat what someone else has already explained or reported.

Links are a service to the reader, and readers increasingly expect them: failing to link to your sources means you risk looking either ignorant (not knowing the source) or arrogant (seeing the user as someone who does not need to know any more about the subject). Linking to external sites will mean they leave your site, but they will come back if it is a useful link.

Tagging

A tag is the metadata which describes, labels or categorises the content. As explained earlier, content management systems including blogging services such as WordPress and Blogger allow you to tag and categorise your content when you write it. But many other media platforms allow tagging too – Flickr, SoundCloud, Vimeo and YouTube are just a few.

Sites often show a 'tag cloud' – a list of tags that give an indication of the content of the site and its popularity. By clicking on one of the tags you will go to a list of all the stories related to that tag term.

Bookmarking services such as Delicious allow you to bookmark online sources and categorise them via tags. You can easily access them but you can also make them available to users, via a link. You can even get an RSS feed of a particular tag term – a feed for 'Obama' will allow you to get a feed of all bookmarked webpages about the US president.

Journalists can also use geotagging which gives geographical information about content and helps users find content by using postcodes and geographical search tools.

Hashtags – most commonly used on Twitter, and created by using # before a word – help readers find tweets under that category. You will often see them high up on trending topics (topics that are being discussed most on Twitter). Putting a # sign before a word also makes it into a link on Twitter that users can click on to see all other tweets using that hashtag.

Any tag that is associated with your content will help search engines and other tools find and categorise it. It will also make it easier for you to re-find it if you need to use something again in the future.

Editing

Online journalists take responsibility for checking their articles just as they take responsibility for publishing stories and checking that they appear online in the correct format. Those working in smaller teams or on their own, especially bloggers, do not have the luxury of a team of sub-editors to revise and improve their work. In larger organisations with content management systems that have a workflow which determines editing roles, stories can be edited and revised by a number of journalists and formatted for the required medium.

The nature of online journalism is that a story will be updated many times as the journalist improves the story with more information, hyperlinks and links to related information. Journalists need to:

- preview the story before publishing;
- check spelling, grammar, punctuation;
- write headlines and intros for SEO;
- check that hyperlinks work and stories format properly;
- be clear about attribution and source material – state who or what it is and hyperlink to it;
- be careful about cut and paste – using a phrase or a sentence from someone else's article even inadvertently might still bring an accusation of plagiarism.

Journalists also need to be aware of libel or linking to potentially libellous material. Use as much original material as possible and steer clear of copyrighted material unless you have permission to use it.

See Law and online communication, Chapter 11, which looks at challenges facing online journalists and issues such as defamation, jurisdiction, copyright, data protection and regulation.

FAQ

How long should a story be?

Some websites set the length they want stories to be. Look at news stories on bbc.co.uk/news which are generally 100–300 words long. There is no set rule on this but remember readers don't like to scroll down blocks of heavy text. Long-form journalism still works on the web but features need to be broken up with headings, bold text, pictures and features such as audio clips.

Do I really need to use keywords?

Only if you want people to find, read and link to your stories.

How many hyperlinks should I use?

Every story should have hyperlinks but keep them to relevant and specific information – 'deep links' that go to a specific page deep within a website, rather than a homepage. Don't scatter random hyperlinks to information on sites such as Wikipedia that readers could easily get themselves. They are reading your story in the expectation of original journalism and links that demonstrate you have done all the hard work and research for them.

Why use external hyperlinks and send readers to other sites?

Without hyperlinks the web wouldn't work. Readers appreciate intelligent hyperlinks and will come back to reliable sources. Linking is simply good journalism.

Do I need to write 'click here' before every hyperlink?

No, but there may be occasions when you want to alert the reader to helpful links further down the text.

Closer look Online journalism tips

'You still need the traditional skills of spotting a story, sifting information and getting the facts right. The internet has given journalism an adrenaline shot by giving us the tools to monitor and filter that information. We have to try out these new tools as much as possible without feeling we have to use all of them all of the time. My advice to upcoming journalists is to:

Laura Oliver

- Nurture your contacts online and offline. Use Twitter – it's good for contacts but has a serendipitous element when it comes to sparking ideas, tracking trends and finding nuggets of information.
- Be sociable. Talk to people. Use social networks to find stories but join in and be part of them as well. Don't just storm in and plunder information without checking information and responding to fellow users.
- Develop an etiquette that means you cross-refer and hyperlink to sources and resources.
- Take part in the 'conversation.' Join forums and respond to reader comments and tip-offs.
- Use the technology. It can be liberating and make you more efficient and creative. Try out new tools on the web and think of them as an aid to help your journalism.
- Talk to commercial colleagues. You do not have to blur the line between editorial and advertorial but you need to be aware of the competitive nature of the new media landscape. You can't afford to be ignorant of how the website works and pays for itself.
- Be aware and track changes in the way new media is influencing journalism – the journalist's role, the way stories are conveyed, the language used – whether that is through citizen journalism, hyperlocal news sites or social networks where more and more people are getting and sharing their information.'

Laura Oliver,
guardian.co.uk

What if I make a mistake, e.g., misspell someone's name?

Correct immediately and put a note on the story stating the nature of the correction and the date you made it.

What if someone writes negative comments about a story?

You can always politely respond to or challenge comments – or choose to ignore them. But remember that an untended garden tends to grow wild, and if you don't listen to other people they are unlikely to listen to you.

Are spelling, grammar and punctuation still important?

Yes. Mistakes make stories hard to read and the reader will doubt the professionalism and accuracy of your journalism.

What is chunking?

Readers prefer shorter articles. Longer pieces can be split into parts and complex stories work better if you chunk it out into background pieces and multimedia elements such as interactive graphics, video and audio.

Is Wikipedia a reliable source of information?

The online encyclopedia is useful but cross-check facts, go to source material and get on the phone.

Can I use text language?

No. Txt ok 4 fones but do u wanna rd 300 wrds like this?

Creating packages

Articles tend to be shorter online than in print because readers don't like scrolling through long pieces of text – not least because screen resolution is lower than print resolution, and so your eyes have to work harder to read.

This doesn't mean the death of long-form journalism in the form of a feature, or that online journalism is inferior to print. A feature can be split into several parts (chunking) and be available in full-text form for those who like to print out articles. Investigative stories can be chunked out into a package of elements that give analysis and context.

First comes the story. The key to telling it well is in choosing the appropriate elements to tell it. The online journalist can use:

- hypertext to link to information
- video
- audio
- still images
- audio slideshows
- animation
- interactivity
- community elements such as polls, forums, social networks
- blogs
- data
- maps
- timelines
- FAQs and Q&As
- User-generated content

You do not need all of these elements to tell the story. A good online journalist thinks:

- This story would have impact if we used video of the event or the people involved.
- An interactive graphic would help people visualise this (Haiti earthquake).
- A blog commentary would keep people up to date with what is happening.
- Involving the community might bring out some great leads and angles we wouldn't have thought of.
- This is a picture story (Chelsea Flower Show).
- This exclusive interview needs to be a podcast people can download.
- This story has history so we need a timeline (key dates and events).
- Lots of questions from readers need to be answered by a FAQ (Frequently Asked Questions) section.
- We have fantastic access to and relationships with sources or experts – a live Q&A would be an event readers could take part in.

And when there is a breaking news story they also need to think:

- Get first few paragraphs of the story online alerting the reader more is to follow.
- Make sure readers are alerted by email, text alerts and a line on Twitter and other social networks.
- Assign roles to team members – lead writer, editor, pictures.
- Call to action to readers to submit text, pictures, audio, video. Lead by example – share prolifically yourself.
- Track blogs, Twitter and other social networks. Use advanced search techniques to find people close to the action, or with specialist expertise.
- Rely on your own reporters to verify facts and identities.
- Take deep breaths and keep a clear head before . . .
- taking stock of what you have so far.

When building the package of stories it is not just a question of choosing what elements might suit the story. Think also about the resources you have at your disposal – it is easy to become sidetracked when you should be concentrating on getting the story right. Journalists are competitive by nature and want to be the first to publish the story or a new angle. But don't rush your work – readers are much more interested in accuracy and uniqueness than who got the story out first.

Closer look guardian.co.uk/global-development

The Guardian's special report on global development issues is a good example of convergence journalism in which journalists working in print and online produced a package of stories in formats that best suited the newspaper and the website.

The newspaper produced a front-page news story and a four-page special report focusing on how world leaders were tackling development goals on poverty and ill-health. Journalists profiled ten African children over a five-year period and the paper printed their stories, pictures, plus fact files and data about each child and country, and the debt and mortality rates for children. The stories and data appeared on the website and readers were alerted to online extras in a sidebar in the newspaper.

The website provided:

- an audio interview with a family from Malawi;
- archive information about the children when they were born;
- a picture gallery of the children;
- data and interactive features to track how development money is spent;
- a forum for readers to share their knowledge of the issues;
- an opportunity for readers to record individual messages to world leaders using the microblogging service Audioboo;
- an email newsletter for readers to keep up to date on summit news.

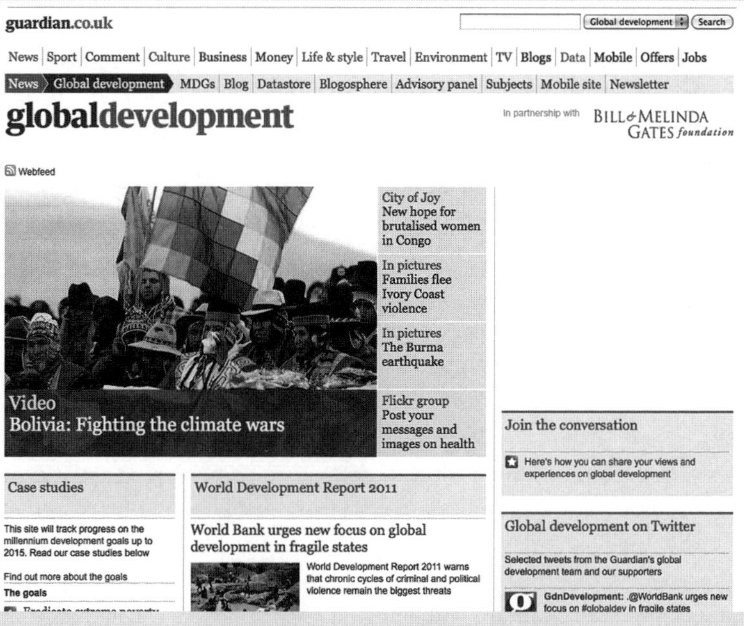

Guardian.co.uk's package on global development

Source: Guardian News and Media Ltd

Exercise

Read the package online and have a look at the picture gallery at guardian.co.uk/africaschildren. This is a long-term investigation which stems from *The Guardian*'s Make Poverty History campaign. What other story ideas would work? And in what format – think about maps, blogs, video, useful links.

Summary

The internet is often criticised for giving us information overload. But for journalists there is never a case of too much information. Online journalism is a developing form of communication that at its best should help people to find out what is happening in the world. It should be accurate, go to the truth and, via the hyperlink, go to the source of that information so that people can decide for themselves. Many users will want to analyse the information themselves on a blog or through a social network. They may come up with an angle the journalist hasn't even thought of. They may want to share it with the journalist or use a hyperlink to tell everyone through the internet.

Online journalism is still about getting the story, but it is also about interacting with the reader and sharing information. To do this, journalists need to engage with the technology that enables them to interact effectively – and they also need to know how their audience is engaging with technology. Alex Gubbay, Social Media Editor at BBC News, says: 'Journalists need to appreciate that working with UGC [user-generated content] and directly with your audience can sometimes be labour-intensive and take time to do properly. That's because it's important to authenticate and verify any content you are looking to use – especially if working with photos or video. It's also crucial to speak to those involved to corroborate what they have said or to get their permission to either use their material and potentially use them live on your own services.'

Story-telling is non-linear because the reader dictates how, when and where they engage with a story. Journalists need to write with search engine optimisation in mind – because being clear and easy to find is part of communicating effectively – and understand the strengths of multimedia elements to be able to present stories in an effective and compelling way. Traditional skills of good writing, research, accuracy and building contacts are still vital.

Computer-assisted reporting has revitalised journalism, helping reporters to gather information, filter it and present it in a way that is accessible and makes sense – for example, building data into interactive maps.

Database journalism, covered in the next chapter, helped to break the UK MPs' expenses scandal and presents another challenge and opportunity for journalists digging for stories. However, we should remember that while computers process information, humans can too. In the middle of all this are journalists who make it their business to find out what it all means.

Activities

1. Research and report

Track your local MP for stories. What are they saying? What are they up to? Bookmark and archive background and profile information using Delicious.com. Search for their website, blog, Wikipedia entry, Facebook, Twitter, YouTube, Flickr and other social networking sites and sign up for RSS feeds. Subscribe to their email and newsletter services. Search on Technorati for blog entries about them and get RSS feeds of political blogs that might mention them.

2. Create a package

Report a local event. Upload your story to your blog. Now search for it on Google using keywords. Could you improve the headline for SEO? Create two other background stories. These could be a profile, timeline, picture gallery, FAQ, podcast, video – select what you think is appropriate. Put hyperlinks on these stories to each other and back to your original story. Create hyperlinks to your package of stories on the original news story. Use Facebook and Twitter to link to and promote your package.

3. Contribute to a hyperlocal site

Find out if your local newspaper group has a hyperlocal community news site that you can contribute to. If not, set up your own by getting together with a group of friends. Choose a local area (beat) that doesn't get much coverage – it could be a village, town or small community. It could be a community with a common interest such as football or a campaign such as saving the local school. Set up your site as a news blog using WordPress and give it an RSS feed.

Further reading

Allan, S. (2006) *Online News: Journalism and the Internet,* Open University.

Friend, C. and Singer, J. B. (2007) *Online Journalism Ethics: Traditions and Transitions,* USA: M.E. Sharpe.

Gillmor, D. *Who's a journalist? Does that matter?,* www.salon.com/technology/dan_gillmor/2010/08/26/who_is_a_journalist/index.html

guardian.co.uk/global-development

Jarvis, J. *Product v. process journalism: The myth of perfection v. beta culture,* www.buzzmachine.com/2009/06/07/processjournalism/

Jenkins, H. (2006) *Convergence Culture: Where Old and New Media Collide,* USA: New York University Press.

Kolodzy, J. (2006) *Convergence Journalism,* USA: Rowman and Littlefield.

Nielsen, J. *Writing for the web,* www.useit.com/papers/webwriting/

Useful websites

guardian.co.uk/media

holdthefrontpage.co.uk

journalism.co.uk

journalists.org

nctj.com

news4media.com

ojr.org

onlinejournalismblog.com

paidcontent.org

pewinternet.org

poynter.org

pressgazette.co.uk

slashdot.org

TechDeepWeb.com

useit.com

wikileaks.org

wired.com

Chapter 5

Data journalism

This chapter will cover:

- Data journalism in action
- Finding data
- Gathering data yourself
- Interrogating the data
- Closer look: Cleaning up data
- Closer look: Quickly generating averages and percentages using spreadsheets
- Closer look: Tips from a pro: David McCandless
- Visualising data
- Mashing data
- Closer look: How to publish a spreadsheet online
- Closer look: Using Yahoo! Pipes to create a sports news widget
- Closer look: Taking it further – resources on programming
- Closer look: Anatomy of a feed

Introduction

> '[*Telegraph* journalist Holly] Watt had set up a spreadsheet which listed MPs' names, the addresses of properties on which they had claimed, whether each was rented or mortgaged, and notes of other points about their claims. By the middle of the second week . . . she had a potential breakthrough. As she typed in the address of the second home of Ian Cawsey, an obscure Labour MP, a box popped up on her screen with the rest of the address. This 'auto-complete' function meant she had already typed in the address for another MP.
>
> '"Bingo!" Watt shouted across the office.
>
> 'Scrolling back up the spreadsheet, Watt found that Cawsey's London address was shared with [another MP] . . . In other words, the taxpayer was being billed twice for the same property.'
>
> *No Expenses Spared*,
> Robert Winnett & Gordon Rayner, 2009, p. 220

The biggest political story of the 21st century was, at its heart, about data. A disk containing the expenses claims of hundreds of MPs landed on a desk in Buckingham Palace Road – and *Telegraph* journalists had less than a week to decide if, somewhere inside the millions of documents it contained, there was a story worth paying for. The decision that there was saw the newspaper dominate the news agenda for the following six weeks, thanks to a combination of traditional news-gathering skills with a newer skillset: the ability to find the story behind the data.

Journalists have always had to deal with certain types of information. From eyewitness accounts and official documents, to research papers, reports and press releases – part of a journalist's talent has been their ability to cut through the fat to the meat of the story.

The potential of databases for news gathering was identified as early as the 1960s, when US reporter Philip Meyer used them to investigate race riots. In 1973 Meyer published a seminal work in the field, *Precision Journalism*. The practices established in that book, and practised by others, became known as computer-assisted reporting, and the field gained an institution of its own in 1989 with the founding of the National Institute for Computer-Assisted Reporting (NICAR).

However, as the profession moved into the 21st century the focus broadened – from databases (private, inaccessible, few) to data (public, accessible, many). Joe Hellerstein, a computer scientist at the University of California in Berkeley, calls it 'the industrial revolution of data'. Others call the phenomenon 'big data' (Cukier, 2010).

'Data' has always been a vague term. To some, it refers to statistics and facts; to others, it is something specific: structured information in a particular format. For the purposes of this book, it is perhaps best defined as 'information that can be analysed with computers'. This can range from numbers to reams of text (what are the most common terms used?), images and video (which colours and patterns recur most?), and even behavioural data (when are people most active? Where do they cluster online?). If information has been digitised, then there are patterns to be found there.

But, however you define data, it is clear that there is an increasing amount of it around. Spreadsheets and databases have become a part of everyday life in business, government, and even entertainment and sport – and increasingly widespread publication of these online is proving to be a goldmine for those who know how to use them, whether analysing football results or investigating the awarding of government contracts.

At the same time, a number of leading figures on the World Wide Web, including its inventor Tim Berners-Lee, have been leading a movement to make it easy for computers – and people – to make links between various sets of data.

In particular, this has produced increasing pressure on governments to release data about their activities to the public, and to do so in a way that made it as easy as possible to interrogate (so, for example, you might be able to quickly spot that Politician X and the son of Politician X worked for the same company).

Coinciding with – if not preceding – this 'open data' movement has been the introduction of a series of Freedom of Information laws around the world that have given citizens the right to access data generated by public bodies, from crime information to details on how public money is spent; from inspection reports to information held about yourself.

As governments have released data, bloggers, scientists and web developers have been among the first to start doing interesting things with it – distributing it, analysing it, and 'mashing' it up with other sources to display it on a map, for example, or in comparison with other data sets. As these pioneers streaked ahead, journalists and news organisations were being left behind, but by early 2009 a vanguard of publishers had developed with coherent strategies around data-driven journalism.

Data journalism may be a new term, but the idea of ploughing through information to find the story is as old as journalism itself – the difference is that the internet and computing power are giving us new tools to help at every stage of the journalistic process.

Whether it's finding data in the first place, or interrogating it in order to find a story; whether you are visualising data in meaningful ways to tell a story, combining it with other information to create new insights, or simply releasing it in a way that makes it as easy as possible for users to do their own digging, data journalism is a key feature of the future of journalism on all platforms, but particularly online.

This chapter explores all these stages of data journalism, looking at some of its most high-profile examples, and providing practical advice on how to start developing your own data journalism skills.

It is the most challenging chapter in this book, but the lessons it contains are perhaps the most important for journalism's future, because data journalism is one of the key ways in which journalists and citizens can expose ignorance and challenge prejudice, make complex facts accessible, and hold power to account. And that, after all, is what journalism should be about.

Data journalism in action

> 'More than 12,000 flight plans were now stored in my computer. I was trying to narrow things down – find the pattern that lurked beneath all this data and the identity of the CIA's planes that might be involved in rendition. When I started my investigation, I had almost no information but now I was almost swamped. I turned to a software programme called Analyst's Notebook, a tool used normally by the police or intelligence organisations to solve complex financial crimes or even murders. Its job was to find connections within exactly such a mass of data.'
>
> *Ghost Plane: The Inside Story of the CIA's Secret Rendition Programme,* Stephen Grey, 2006, p. 107

Data journalism takes many forms. Sometimes the data itself tells the story so clearly that the journalist's job is merely to present it in such a way that its meaning is as clear as possible, or so that users can add to it. Sometimes the data is the starting point for an investigation that takes the journalist to meet others who can shed light on the questions it raises. And sometimes the data does not exist anywhere, and the journalist must gather it by meeting sources and visiting libraries, until they have enough to put together the data they need.

One of the pioneers of modern data journalism is Adrian Holovaty. Holovaty launched ChicagoCrime.org in 2005 – a 'mashup' which placed public crime data on a map of the city and instantly provided citizens with an important source of information on local crime. The idea was widely imitated by other newspapers, and ChicagoCrime eventually received funding to relaunch as EveryBlock (everyblock.com), which extended the concept to show planning applications, alcohol licences, restaurant inspections and street closures – among other pieces of data. It has also expanded to cover more than a dozen US cities – and with the technology behind the site released as 'open source', this means that anyone else can use it for other cities, anywhere in the world. Meanwhile, other news operations – such as MSN Local in the UK (local.uk.msn.com) – have adopted similar data-driven approaches.

Holovaty sees journalism as involving three core tasks – gathering, distilling and presenting information. Doing journalism through computer programming – just one form of data journalism – is, he says, just a different way of doing those tasks:

> 'Each weekday, my computer program goes to the Chicago Police Department's website and gathers all crimes reported in Chicago. Similarly, the U.S. Congress votes database I helped put together at washingtonpost.com works the same way: several times a day, an automated program checks several government websites for roll-call votes. If it finds any, it gathers the data and saves it into a database.
>
> '[And] just as an editor can apply editorial judgment to decide which facts in a news story are most important . . . on chicagocrime.org I decided it would be useful if site users could browse by crime type, ZIP code and city ward. On the votes database site, we decided it would be useful to browse a list of all the votes that happen late at night and a list of members of Congress who've missed the most votes. Once we made that decision of which information to display, it was just a matter of writing the programming code that automated it.
>
> 'Presentation is also automated. This is particularly complex, because in creating websites, it's necessary to account for all possible permutations of data. For example, on chicagocrime.org I had to account for missing data: how should the site display crimes whose data has changed? What should happen in the case where a crime's longitude/latitude coordinates aren't available? What should happen when a crime's time is listed as "Not available"?'
>
> 'The programmer as journalist: a Q&A with Adrian Holovaty', *Online Journalism Review,* Robert Niles, 2006

Although Holovaty's project involved programming, it is also possible to create similar, more basic mashups with just a few clicks, thanks to free web services like Yahoo! Pipes (see below).

Sometimes data journalism involves accessing or creating databases of information. In *Ghost Plane*, the story of Stephen Grey's investigation into a CIA practice of flying terror suspects to countries where they would be tortured, the *Sunday Times* investigative journalist talks about his global journey to visit sources as he gathered the evidence he needed to put together a picture of 'extraordinary rendition'. Data provided a key element of his investigation – specifically, databases of flight plans (which allowed him to verify the accounts of terror suspects who had been transported) and of people (which allowed others at the *New York Times* to establish the creation of fake identities that masked the existence of an airline run by the CIA).

At the BBC, Dominic Casciani drew on immigration data to produce a website looking at the subject (Casciani, 2005). Like much data journalism, the site allowed users to interrogate the issue in their own way, while also providing an editorial overview. In a similar vein *The Telegraph* added to its MPs' expenses database to create a powerful tool that readers could use to find out about all candidates in the run-up to the 2010 election (Bradshaw, 2010), while Channel 4 created 'Who knows who' to show 'the connections between politicians, celebrities and business leaders, and where power really lies in the UK.' Similar ideas have been developed by Silobreaker's Network (silobreaker.com/FlashNetwork.aspx?q=) and They Rule in the USA (www.theyrule.net).

Again, while these projects involved building in-house databases, there are free tools – such as DabbleDB and even Google Docs – that allow anyone to do the same.

This is becoming increasingly important as news organisations and journalists look to users of their website to help dig deeper into a story. When the official MPs' expenses documents were released by parliament, for example, *The Guardian* published them all online and invited readers to help spot possible stories and to build a more effective database, which both readers and journalists could then scrutinise. The same paper had earlier published MPs' travel expenses which Tony Hirst, publisher of the blog OUseful, visualised on a map in a way that made it easy to tell at a glance which MPs were claiming more for travel than other MPs who lived nearby (Arthur, 2009a).

Maps are particularly useful devices for the data journalist, especially when they are dealing with information that includes latitude and longitude, a postcode or placename. During one US election, for example, a number of map-related 'mashups' appeared showing Twitter tweets, YouTube videos or other election-related material displayed on a Google map. During the Beijing Olympics BBC Sport used similar technology to display tweets, blog posts and photos on a map of the Olympic village (Hamman, 2008).

Data is particularly useful in sport, where statistics and location are often both important and real-time information is in high demand. BBC Sport experimented with one 'widget' that combed a selected group of feeds for the latest news during the last days of the football transfer window. This chapter will explain how you can create a similar mashup using Yahoo! Pipes.

Before that, the chapter will seek to provide an overview of four basic stages that a data journalism project may go through: finding data; interrogating it; visualising it; and mashing it (Figure 5.1). The field of data journalism is so diverse that any one project might take in only one of the stages – finding information to share easily with users, for example. But the more stages you experience, the wider you read on the methods involved, and the more you experiment, the better your journalism will be.

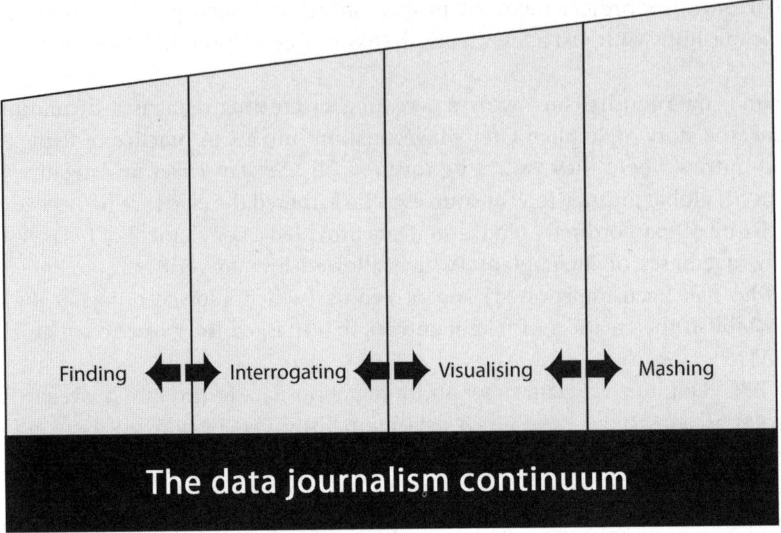

Figure 5.1 The data journalism continuum

Finding data

The first stage in data journalism is sourcing the data itself. Often you will be seeking out data based on a particular question or hypothesis (for a good guide to forming a journalistic hypothesis, see Mark Hunter's free ebook *Story-Based Inquiry* (2010)). On other occasions, it may be that the release or discovery of data itself kicks off your investigation.

There is a range of sources available to the data journalist, both online and offline, public and hidden. Typical sources include:

- national and local government;
- bodies that monitor organisations (such as regulators or consumer bodies);
- scientific and academic institutions;
- health organisations;
- charities and pressure groups;
- business;
- and the media itself.

One of the best places to find UK government data online, for example, is Data.gov.uk, an initiative influenced by its US predecessor Data.gov. Data.gov.uk – launched in January 2010 with the backing of the inventor of the World Wide Web, Sir Tim Berners-Lee – effectively acts as a search engine and index for thousands of sets of data held by a range of government departments, from statistics on the re-offending of juveniles to the Agricultural Price Index. The site also hosts forums for users to discuss their use of the data, examples of applications using data, further information on how to use the data, and technical resources. For archive material NDAD (the National Archives' National Digital Archive of Datasets) is worth a visit at www.ndad.nationalarchives.gov.uk.

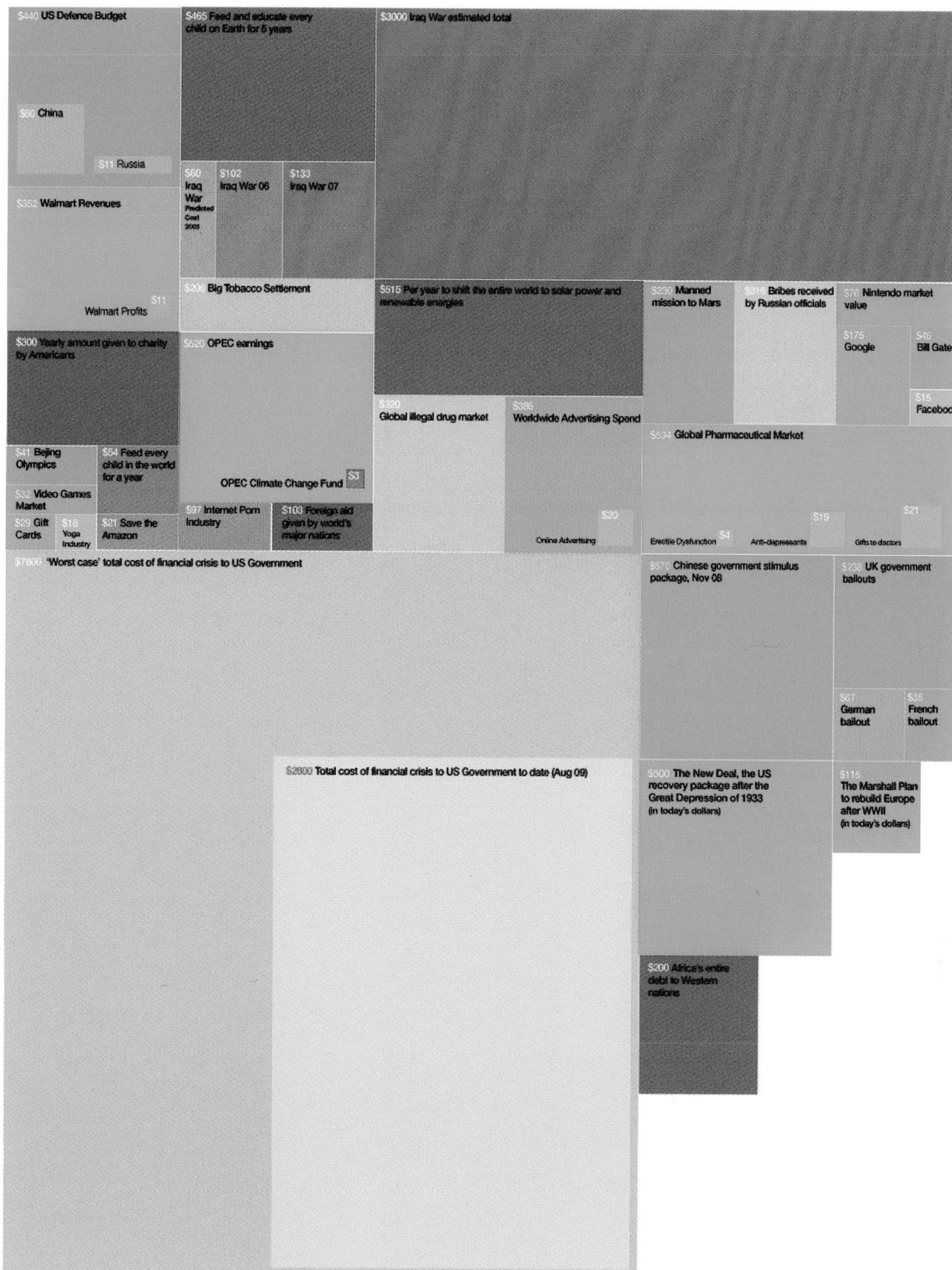

PLATE 1 The Billion Dollar Gram: A treemap of spending that allows you to quickly put government spending into context

David McCandless, www.informationisbeautiful.net/visualizations/the-billion-dollar-gram/

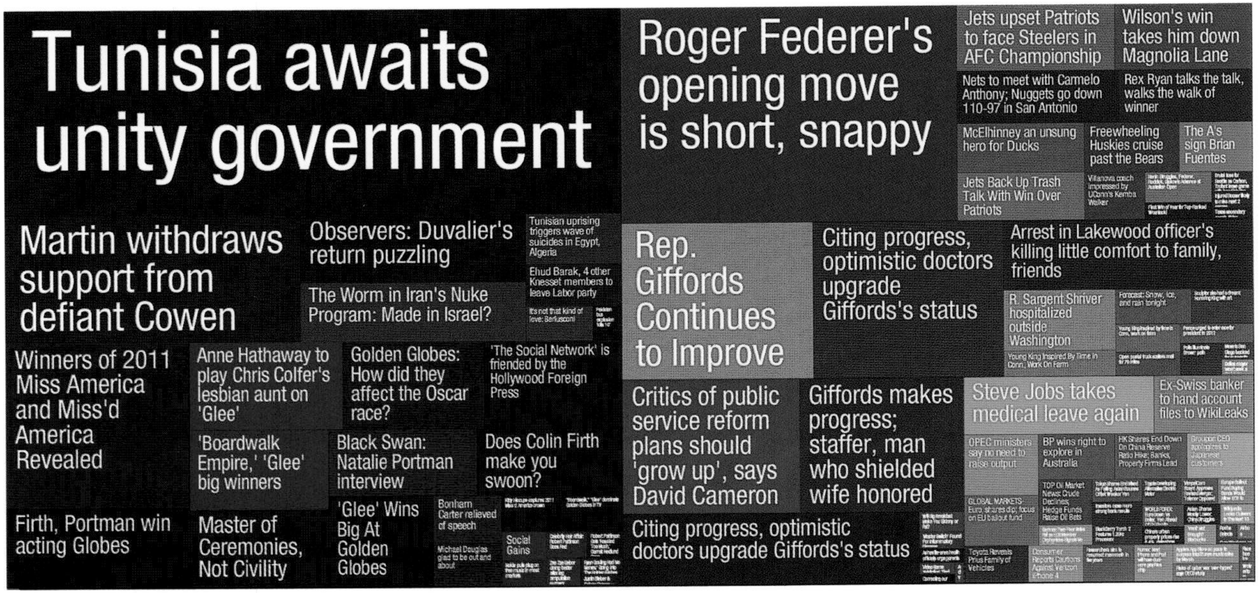

PLATE 2 The News Map: A treemap of news coverage on Google News
Marcos Weskamp, http://newsmap.jp/

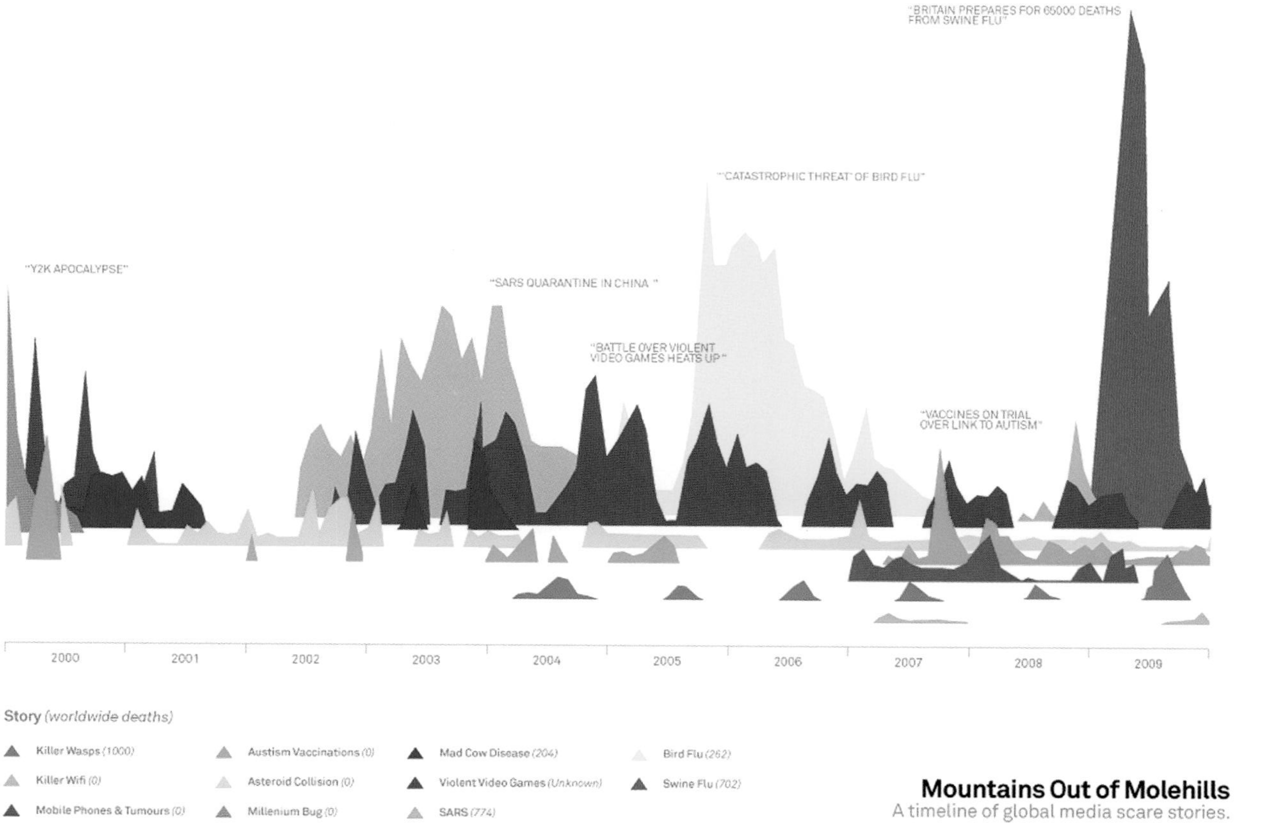

PLATE 3 Mountains Out of Molehills: A timeline of media scare stories

David McCandless, www.informationisbeautiful.net/visualizations/mountains-out-of-molehills/

PLATE 4 Stop, Question and Frisk in New York Neighbourhoods

New York Times, www.nytimes.com/interactive/2010/07/11/nyregion/20100711-stop-and-frisk.html?ref=nyregion

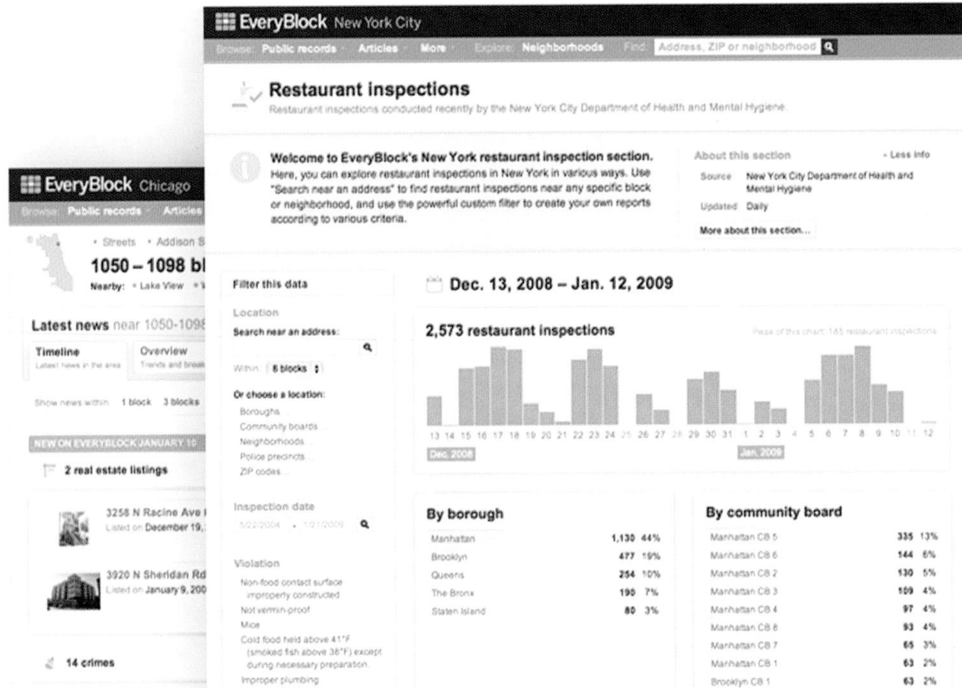

PLATE 5 EveryBlock: A newsfeed for your block

EveryBlock, http://media.everyblock.com/images/newhome_screenshot.png

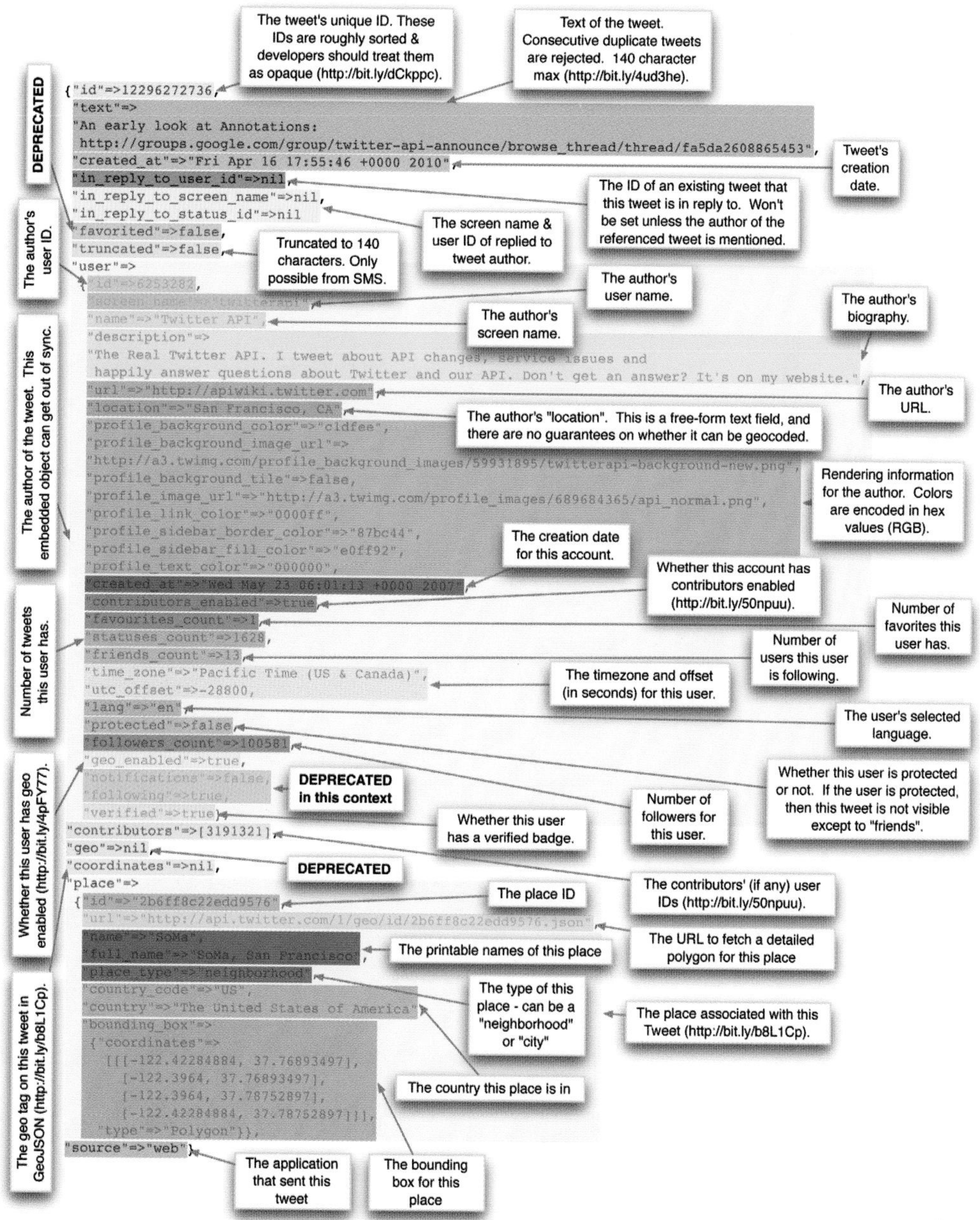

PLATE 6 Anatomy of a tweet

Raffi Krikorian, http://mehack.com/map-of-a-twitter-status-object

OPEN PLATFORM

Build applications with theguardian

Case studies

Recipe Search

The recipe search engine from WhatCouldICook .com is now also running on guardian.co.uk. Learn about how it works and what kinds of commercial possibilities the case study demonstrates.

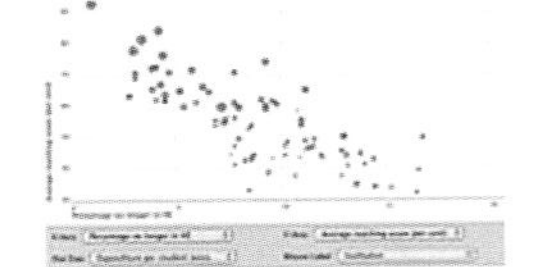

PLATE 7 The Guardian Open Platform
Guardian News and Media Ltd, www.guardian.co.uk/open-platform

guardian.co.uk

News | Sport | Comment | Culture | Business | Money | Life & style | Travel | Environment

Multimedia > Interactive guides > Video | Audio & podcasts | In pictures | Audio slidesh

interactive guides

Webfeed

By section

- Books
- Business
- Culture
- Education
- Environment
- Life and style
- Media
- Money
- Politics
- Science
- Society
- Technology

Recent

Iraq war stories, 2003-10
24 Aug 2010

Social Enterprise 2010
24 Aug 2010

Chile: trapped miners found alive
23 Aug 2010

Enjoy England interactive map: Share your trip ideas

Northern Ireland's upsurge in violent attacks
22 Aug 2010

Gap year travel guide: what's hot in 2010
21 Aug 2010

PLATE 8 Guardian Interactive Guides
Guardian News and Media Ltd, www.guardian.co.uk/interactive

PLATE 9 Being A Black Man: Washington Post interactive
Washington Post, www.washingtonpost.com/wp-srv/metro/interactives/blackmen/blackmen.html

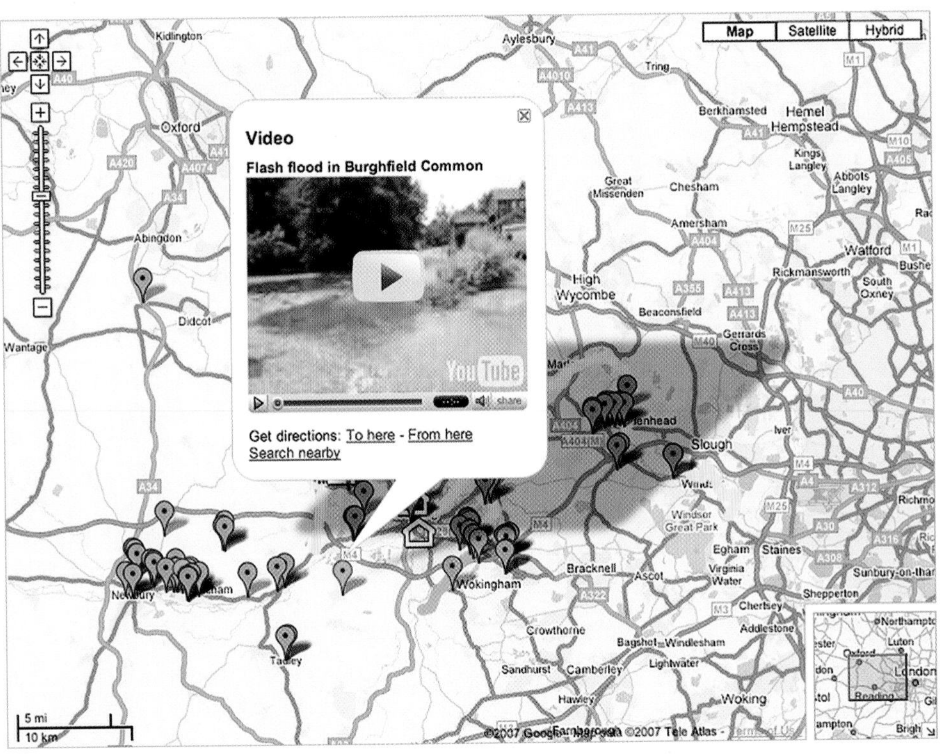

PLATE 10 BBC Berkshire flood map
Robin Hamman, Cybersoc, http://cybersoc.blogs.com/photos/uncategorized/2007/07/24/berkshirefloodmashup.jpg

At a regional and local level, Oneplace (oneplace.audit-commission.gov.uk) was a good source of information (the assessments upon which the data was based ended in June 2010), while individual local authorities are also releasing information that can be used as part of data journalism projects. The quality and quantity of this information varies enormously by council, but there is continuing pressure for improvement in this area.

There are also volunteer projects, such as OpenlyLocal and Mash The State, that make local government data available in as accessible a format as possible, while the organisation MySociety operates a group of websites providing easy access to information ranging from individual politicians' voting record (TheyWorkForYou) to local problems (FixMyStreet) and information about a particular area's transport links and beauty (Mapumental). MySociety also runs a petitions website for Downing Street, and websites that allow people to pledge to do something if other people sign up too (PledgeBank), to find groups near you (GroupsNearYou), contact your MP (WriteToThem) or be contacted by them (HearFromYourMP).

In the private sector, organisations regularly release data online, from tables and research reports published on company websites to the annual reports that are filed with bodies such as Companies House. Also worth looking at is the web project Open Corporates (opencorporates.com), which seeks to make company information more easily accessible.

The Charity Commission is an excellent source of information on registered charities, which must file accounts and annual reports with the organisation. The commission also conducts occasional research into the sector.

NHS foundation trusts likewise must file reports to their regulator, Monitor. You will find similar regulators in other areas such as the Financial Services Authority, Ofcom, Ofwat, Ofqual, the General Medical Council, the General Social Care Council and the Pensions Regulator, to name just a few.

For academic and scientific research there are hundreds of specialist journals. Most have online search facilities which will provide access to summaries. To get access to the full paper you will probably need to use the library of a university, which involves a subscription. For access to a journal on midwifery, for example, your best bet is to make a quick call to the nearest university that teaches courses in that field. Although university libraries increasingly limit access to students, you can request a special pass. For access to the data on which research is based it is likely you will need to contact the author. Also of potential use in this area is the UK Data Archive (data-archive.ac.uk).

Media organisations such as *The Guardian* and *The New York Times* publish 'datablogs' that regularly release sets of data produced or acquired by investigations, ranging from scientific information about global warming to lists of Oscar winners. These can be a rich source of material for the data journalist, and a great starting point for the beginner as they are often 'cleaner' than data from elsewhere. Also worth investigating are websites such as WikiLeaks and ScraperWiki, which provide a repository for sets of data.

The Guardian and *The New York Times* websites are also among an increasing number of web platforms generally which are making their own data available via APIs (application programming interfaces). Social networking sites (such as Flickr and Twitter) also provide APIs.

Accessing this data generally requires a level of technical ability, but can be particularly useful in measuring activity across social networks (for example, sharing and publishing). Even if you don't have that technical ability, understanding the possibilities can be extremely useful when working with web developers on a data journalism project (see the part of this chapter on mashups for more information on APIs).

Using search engines to find data

If you are using a search engine to find the data you are looking for, you should familiarise yourself with the advanced search facility, where you can often specify the format of the file you are looking for. Searching specifically for spreadsheets (files ending in .xls), for example, is likely to get you to data more quickly. Similarly, official reports can often be found more effectively by searching for PDF format, while PowerPoint presentations (.ppt) will sometimes contain useful tables of data. You can also include 'XML' or 'RDF' in your search terms if you think your data may be in those or other formats.

Advanced search also allows you to specify the type of website you are searching for – those ending in .gov.uk (government), .org and .org.uk (charities), .ac.uk (educational establishments), .nhs, .police.uk and .mod (Ministry of Defence) are just some that will be particularly relevant (you can also specify an individual site – for instance, that of a local council). A basic familiarity with these search techniques – for example, limiting your search to spreadsheets on .gov.uk websites – can improve your results.

To use advanced search, look for an 'advanced search' link. Or you can use particular syntax – for example, adding `site:gov.uk` to a Google search will limit results to sites ending in .gov.uk; likewise `site:bolton.gov.uk` would limit it to the Bolton Council website. Adding `filetype:pdf` will limit results to PDFs, and so on. For an extensive guide to Google search, see: www.googleguide.com/advanced_operators.html.

You should, however, remember that Google only searches a small part of the internet and there may be other search engines that give better results for different searches. Wolfram Alpha, for example, is a 'computational knowledge engine' that searches a range of data sources from around the world, allowing you to type intelligent queries such as 'UK GDP 2000–2009' and see where the data is pulled from by clicking on 'Source information' below the results. There are also various specialist 'vertical' search engines such as Microsoft Academic Search (http://academic.research.microsoft.com/).

Live data

Another type of data to think about is live data that is not stored anywhere yet but, rather, will be produced at a particular time. A good example of this would be how newspapers are increasingly using Twitter commentary to provide context to a particular debate. Part of *The Guardian*'s coverage of Tony Blair's appearance at the Chilcot Inquiry into the Iraq War, for example, used the data of thousands of Twitter updates ('tweets') to provide a 'sentiment analysis' timeline of how people reacted to particular parts of his evidence as it went on (*The Guardian*, 2010a, 2010b). Similar timelines have been produced for political debates and speeches to measure public reaction.

Preparation is key to live data projects – where will you get the data from, and how will you filter it? How can you visualise it most clearly? And how do you prevent it being 'gamed' (users intentionally skewing the results for fun or commercial or political reasons)?

Legal considerations

Whatever data you are acquiring, you will need to consider whether you have permission to republish that data (analysing the data privately in the first place is a separate issue and unlikely to raise legal issues).

Data may be covered by copyright, or may raise issues of data protection or privacy. Even apparently anonymous information can sometimes be traced back to individual users (Barbaro & Zeller, 2006), and while government information is paid for by public money, for example, it is, strictly speaking, often covered by Crown Copyright, while organisations like Ordnance Survey and Royal Mail have been notoriously protective of geographical information and postcodes (see Heather Brooke's book *The Silent State*, 2010, for more on the tactics used by organisations to prevent access to 'public' data).

In addition, if you are using free online tools to visualise or share your data (see below), you may want to check the terms and conditions of those services in case they conflict with the terms under which you obtained the data or intend to use it.

Books and Freedom of Information (FOI)

Of course, there is also a rich range of data available in books that data journalists should familiarise themselves with – from books of facts and statistics to almanacs, from the Civil Service Year Book (also online) to volumes like Who's Who (online at ukwhoswho.com – your library may have a subscription).

Particularly useful is the data held by public bodies which can be accessed through a well-worded Freedom of Information (FOI) request. Heather Brooke's book *Your Right To Know* (2007) is a key reference work in this area, and the online tool WhatDoTheyKnow is particularly useful in allowing you to submit FOI requests easily, as well as allowing you to find similar FOI requests and the responses to them. In addition, you should look to see if an organisation publishes a disclosure log of the FOI requests it has received (tip: use Google's Advanced Search to look for 'disclosure log' within a particular website or domain such as .gov.uk).

When requesting data through an FOI request, it is always useful to specify the format that you wish the information to be supplied in – typically a spreadsheet in electronic format. A PDF or Word document, for example, will mean extra work at the next stage: interrogation.

Gathering data yourself

Of course, the data you need for a particular story may not exist at all in either books or online – or the data you do find is out of date, flawed, scattered across several sources, or needs checking. In that case you'll need to gather data yourself.

There are two basic approaches you can take in gathering data: compiling it from other sources such as newspaper or other reports (secondary research), or collecting it yourself through methods such as observation or surveys (primary research).

Whichever method you use, you should understand potential weaknesses in the methodology and seek to address these. The selection, size and generalisability of the sample; the selection and phrasing of questions; the environment; the use of a control group; your own presence; and myriad other factors must be taken into account to ensure that your methods stand up to scrutiny.

Needless to say there are countless books covering research methodology and you should read these if you are to do any research of your own. Even if you don't, they will give you an understanding that will prove very useful in looking at the methods used to gather other data that you might use. For an accessible read on the subject see Ben Goldacre's *Bad Science* book (2008) and blog (www.badscience.net), or one of the increasing number of 'sceptics' blogs such as Quackometer (www.quackometer.net).

Interrogating the data

'One of the most important (and least technical) skills in understanding data is asking good questions. An appropriate question shares an interest you have in the data, tries to convey it to others, and is curiosity-oriented rather than maths-oriented. Visualising data is just like any

> other type of communication: success is defined by your audience's ability to pick up on, and be excited about, your insight.'
>
> Fry, 2008, p. 4

Once you have the data, you need to see if there is a story buried within it. The great advantage of computer processing is that it makes it easier to sort, filter, compare and search information in different ways to get to the heart of what – if anything – it reveals.

The first stage in this process, then, is making sure the data is in the right format to be interrogated. Quite often this will be a spreadsheet or CSV (comma-separated values) file. If your information is in a PDF you may not be able to do a great deal with it other than copy or re-type the values into a new spreadsheet (making sure to check you have not made any errors). In some cases you can use optical character recognition (OCR) and 'export to spreadsheet' to extract the data, but it's better if you don't have to face that problem.

A Microsoft Word or PowerPoint document is likely to require similar work. Note: if you're pasting into Excel it has a useful tool for cleaning up data that is in rows but not in a recognised columnar format: paste into a column and select Data > Text to Columns.

If the information is already online you can sometimes 'scrape' it – that is, automatically copy the relevant information into a separate document. How easy this is to do depends on how structured the information is. A table in a Wikipedia entry, for example, can be 'scraped' into a Google spreadsheet relatively easily (Tony Hirst gives instructions on how to do this at: http://blog.ouseful.info/2008/10/14/data-scraping-wikipedia-with-google-spreadsheets/), and an online CSV file and certain other structured data can be scraped with Yahoo! Pipes

Closer look Cleaning up data

Whether you have been given data, had to scrape it, or copied it manually, you will probably need to clean it up. All sorts of things can 'dirty' your data, from misspellings and variations in spelling, to odd punctuation, mixtures of numbers and letters, unnecessary columns or rows, and more. Computers, for example, will see 'New Town', 'Newtown' and 'newtown' as three separate towns when they may be one.

This can cause problems later on when analysing your data – for example, calculations not working or results not being accurate.

Some tips for cleaning your data include:

- Use a spellchecker to check for misspellings. You will probably have to add some words to the computer's dictionary.
- Use 'find and replace' (normally in the Edit menu) to remove double spaces and other common punctuation errors.
- Remove duplicate entries – if you are using Excel there are a few ways to do this under the Data tab – search for duplicates in Help.
- Watch out for extra spaces at the beginning and end of text; they are often easy to miss and may prevent matching in some programs.

The free tool, Google Refine, is also worth exploring.

For more tips on Excel specifically, see this guide: http://office.microsoft.com/en-us/excel/HA102218401033.aspx

(see http://www.daybarr.com/blog/yahoo-pipes-tutorial-an-example-using-the-fetch-page-module-to-make-a-web-scraper and below for more on using Yahoo! Pipes). You can also use the Firefox extension OutWit Hub which presents you with a step-by-step guide to extracting data from a webpage of your choice. A lot of scraping, however, will involve programming – the online tool ScraperWiki provides one environment to help you do this. For more information on scraping and scraping tools, see the links at: www.delicious.com/paulb/scraping.

Sometimes data is incomplete: for example, it may be lacking a person's first name or date of birth, which makes it hard to connect with other sources. For this reason and all those above, it is a good idea to develop your own databases, and publish where legally possible.

Spotting the story

Once your data is cleaned you can start to look for anything newsworthy in it. There are some obvious places to start: if you are dealing with numbers, for example, you can work out what the 'mean' is (the average age of chief inspectors, for example). Similarly, you might look for the 'mode' – the term or value which appears most often (e.g. the most common reason given for arresting terrorist suspects) or the 'median' – the middle value in the range covered. Typically, medians are best used for financial statistics such as wages, means are best used for physical characteristics, and modes are best used to illustrate the 'best seller' or 'most used'.

All of these come under the vague term 'average', and are subject to abuse (see *How to Lie With Statistics*, Huff, 1954, for more on this and other statistical tricks). Amber Iler, commenting on a draft of this chapter on the Online Journalism Blog, puts it this way:

> 'Means can be abused by averaging over time: for example, an average increase of 20 cement trucks/day on a road may not seem like a lot until you look at the median increase and see that they all use the road between 7–9 AM. You get a very different picture when you think about sharing the road with 20 trucks spread out over the course of a day than you do imagining the congestion of 20 trucks on your road during rush hour.'

Kaiser Fung, a statistician whose blog Junk Charts is essential reading in the field, notes the dangers in lazily reaching for the average when you want to make an editorial point:

> 'Averaging stamps out diversity, reducing anything to its simplest terms. In so doing, we run the risk of oversimplifying, of forgetting the variations around the average. Hitching one's attention to these variations rather than the average is a sure sign of maturity in statistical thinking. One can, in fact, *define* statistics as the study of the nature of variability. How much do things change? How large are these variations? What causes them?'
>
> Fung, 2010, p. 4

So, while averages can be interesting discoveries, they should most often be used as a starting point for more illuminating investigation.

If you are looking at data over time, you can look to see what has increased over that period, or decreased – or disappeared entirely. You will need to make sure you are expressing percentages correctly. If the amount spent by an organisation on recruitment, for example, rises from £200,000 to £250,000 this represents a 25 per cent increase; the reverse, however (£250k to £200k), would be a decrease of 20 per cent.

Calculations like these can be made easily with spreadsheet software such as Excel and the spreadsheet in Google Docs (see *Closer look: Quickly generating averages and percentages using spreadsheets* on page 58). Many journalists in the field of computer-assisted reporting (CAR) will also use database software such as Access and languages such as SQL which provide very powerful ways to interrogate thousands or millions of lines of data. This is an area worth exploring if you become serious about this aspect of data journalism.

You will also need to gather further data to provide context to your figures. If, for example, more council staff are receiving bonuses, is that simply because more staff have been employed? How much is spent on wages, and how do your figures compare? If you are comparing one city with another, understand how their populations differ – not just in aggregate, but in relevant details such as age, ethnicity, life expectancy, etc. You will need to know where to access basic statistics like these – the National Statistics website (www.statistics.gov.uk) is often a good place to start.

As a journalist you should double-check your findings wherever possible with statisticians in the field you're covering. The Royal Statistical Society maintains a list of media contacts you can contact across sectors from finance and the environment to DNA, forensic evidence and health.

Sometimes a change in the way data is gathered or categorised can produce a dramatic change in the data itself. In one example, designer Adrian Short obtained information (via an FOI request) on parking tickets from Transport for London that showed the numbers of tickets issued against a particular offence plummeted from around 8,000 to 8 in the space of one month (Arthur, 2009b). Had people suddenly stopped committing that parking offence, or was there another explanation? A quick phone call to Transport for London revealed that traffic wardens

Closer look Quickly generating averages and percentages using spreadsheets

Spreadsheet packages can save you a lot of time as a journalist. Excel and the free spreadsheet software in Google Docs can quickly generate an average or percentage from sheets of numbers using formulae. Here are a few useful formulae that you can adapt for your own data (some spreadsheet packages may use different formulae):

```
=average(a2:a300)
```

This will generate a mean from all the numbers between cells A2 and A300 (A is the first column; the number 2 refers to the row – change these to fit where your own data is in the spreadsheet).

```
=median(a2:a300)
```

This will give you the median value of all the numbers between cells A2 and A300.

```
=max(a2:a300)
```

This will give you the maximum number within that range.

```
=countif(a2:a300,140)
```

This will count how many times the figure '140' is mentioned in the numbers between cells A2 and A300.

```
=(b2-a2)/a2
```

This will calculate a percentage increase between two figures, as long as B2 is the new figure and A2 is the old figure.

To find formulae for other calculations just do a quick search on what you want to do and the word 'spreadsheet formula'.

Closer look Tips from a pro: David McCandless

David McCandless is a writer and designer, and author of the book and website *Information is Beautiful* (2010). His work has appeared in *The Guardian*, *The Independent* and *Wired* magazine. These are his five tips for visualising data:

1. Double-source data wherever possible – even the UN and WorldBank can make mistakes.
2. Take information out – there is a long tradition among statistical journalists of showing *everything*. All data points. The whole range. Every column and row. But stories are about clear threads with extraneous information fuzzed out. And journalism is about telling stories. You can only truly do that when you mask out the irrelevant or the minor data. The same applies to design, which is about reducing something to its functional essence.
3. Avoid standard abstract units – tons of carbon, billions of dollars – these kinds of units are overused and impossible to imagine or relate to. Try to rework or process units down to 'everyday' measures. Try to give meaningful context for huge figures whenever possible.
4. Self-sufficiency – all graphs, charts and infographics should be self-sufficient. That is, you shouldn't require any other information to understand them. They're like interfaces. Each should have a clear title, legend, source, labels, etc. And credit yourself. I've seen too many great visuals with no credit or name at the bottom.
5. Show your workings – transparency seems like a new front for journalists. Google Docs makes it incredibly easy to share your data and thought processes with readers – who can then participate.

were issued with new handsets around the same time. *Guardian* journalist Charles Arthur hypothesised:

> 'Could it be that s46 [another offence which had a steep rise at the same time] is the default on the screen to issue a new ticket, and that wardens don't bother to change it? Whatever it is, there's a serious problem for TfL if those aren't all s46 offences which have been ticketed since August 2006. Because if the ticket isn't written out to the correct offence, then the fine isn't payable. Theoretically, TfL might have to pay back millions in traffic fines for people who have been ticketed for s46 offences when they were actually committing s25 or s30 offences.'

That particular story came about at least in part because the information was easy to visualise.

Visualising data

> 'At their best, graphics are instruments for reasoning about quantitative information. Often the most effective way to describe, explore, and summarise a set of numbers – even a very large set – is to look at pictures of those numbers.'
>
> Edward Tufte, *The Visual Display of Quantitative Information, 2001*, p. 9

Visualisation is the process of giving a visual form to information which is often otherwise dry or impenetrable. Traditional examples of visualisation include turning a table into a bar chart, or a series of percentage values into a pie chart – but the increasing power of both computer analysis and graphic design software has seen the craft of visualisation develop with increasing sophistication, adding animation and personalisation, among other things. More recently, the spread of social media and the widespread distribution of 'Big Infographics' (Yau, 2010) have also added to their popularity.

In larger organisations the data journalist may work with a graphic artist to produce an infographic that visualises their story, but in smaller teams, in the initial stages of a story, or when speed is of the essence they are likely to need to use visualisation tools to give form to their data.

Broadly speaking, there are two typical reasons for visualising data: to find a story or to tell one. Quite often, it is both.

In the parking tickets story above it was the process of visualisation that tipped off Adrian Short and *Guardian* journalist Charles Arthur to the story – and led to further enquiries.

In most cases, however, the story will not be as immediately visible. Sometimes the data will need to be visualised in different ways before a story becomes clear. An understanding of the strengths of different types of visualisation can be particularly useful here.

Types of visualisation

Visualisation can take on a range of forms. The most familiar are those we know from maths and statistics: *pie charts*, for example, allow you to show how one thing is divided – for example, how a budget is spent, or how a population is distributed. Pie charts are thought to be particularly useful when the proportions represented are large (for example, above 25 per cent), but less useful when lower percentages are involved, due to issues with perception and the ability to compare different elements. Slices in pie charts should be ordered clockwise, from largest to smallest, and there should not be any more than five slices.

More useful for lower percentages are *bar charts* or *histograms*. Although these look the same there are subtle differences between them: the bars in bar charts represent categories (such as different cities), whereas bars in histograms represent different values on a continuum (for instance, ages, weights or amounts). The advantage of both types of chart over pie charts is that users can more easily see the difference between one quantity and another. Histograms also allow you to show change over time. You should avoid using 3D or shadow effects in bar charts as these do not add to the information or clarity.

Pictograms are like bar charts but use an icon to represent quantity – so a population of 50,000 might be represented by five 'person' icons. It is not advisable to use pictograms if quantities are close together as the user will find it harder to discern the differences.

Also useful for showing change over time are *line graphs*. Lines are 'suited for showing trend, acceleration or deceleration, and volatility, including sudden peaks or troughs' (Wong, 2010, p. 51). In addition, a series of lines overlaid upon each other can also quickly show if any variables change at different points or at simultaneous points, suggesting either relationships or shared causes (but by no means proving it – these should be taken as starting points for further investigation. You should also avoid plotting more than four lines in one chart for purposes of clarity.). Line graphs should not be used to show unrelated events, such as the test scores of a group of people.

Scattergrams are similar to line graphs, showing the distribution of individual elements against two axes, but can be particularly useful in showing up 'outliers'. Outliers are pieces of data which differ noticeably from the rest. These may be of particular interest journalistically when they show, for example, an MP claiming substantially more (or less) expenses than their peers.

A number of charts can be visualised together in what are sometimes called ***small multiples***, enabling the journalist or users to display a number of pie charts, line graphs or other charts alongside each other – allowing comparison, for example, between different populations.

Two increasingly popular forms of visualisation online are treemaps and bubble charts. Unlike other charts which allow you to visualise two aspects of the data (i.e. their place on each axis) ***bubble charts*** allow you to visualise three aspects of the data, the third being represented by the size of the bubble itself. A particularly good example of bubble charts in action can be seen in Hans Rosling's TED talk on debunking third-world myths (www.youtube.com/watch?v=RUwS1uAdUcI) – a presentation which also demonstrates the potential of other forms of visualisation, and animation, in presenting complex information in an easy-to-understand way. You can recreate Rosling's talk and play with visualising similar data using Gapminder (www.gapminder.org).

Treemaps visualise hierarchical data in a way that might best be described as rectangular pie charts-within-pie charts. This is particularly useful for representing different parts of a whole and their relationship to each other, for instance, different budgets within a government.

Perhaps the best-known example of a treemap is Newsmap (http://newsmap.jp/), created in 2004 by Marcos Weskamp (Plate 2). This visualises the amount of coverage given to stories by news organisations based on a feed from Google News. Weskamp explains it as follows:

> 'Google News automatically groups news stories with similar content and places them based on algorithmic results into clusters. In Newsmap, the size of each cell is determined by the amount of related articles that exist inside each news cluster that the Google News Aggregator presents. In that way users can quickly identify which news stories have been given the most coverage, viewing the map by region, topic or time. Through that process it still accentuates the importance of a given article.'
>
> Weskamp, 2005

More broadly, *maps* allow you to visualise information geographically. This can be done with points (such as the locations of crimes in an area) or lines (the routes taken) or with colouring – for example, illustrating how often crimes are committed in a particular area by giving it a colour on a spectrum from yellow to red. Maps coloured this way are called *chloropleth* maps. Care should be taken in choosing how to split data between different colour categories in a chloropleth map so as not to mislead readers.

These are examples of the most common forms of visualisation, but there are dozens more to explore.

Considerations in visualisation

When visualising data it is important to ensure that any comparisons are meaningful, or like-for-like. In one visualisation of how many sales a musician needs to make to earn the minimum wage, for example, a comparison is made between sites selling albums, sites selling individual tracks, and those providing music streams. Clearly this is misleading – and was criticised for being so (Yang, 2010).

Visualisation should also be used only when it adds something to a story. Staci Baird (2010) compares its role with that of headlines and photos in attracting readers, while warning that 'overly complex graphics will quickly convince readers to ignore your article.'

Baird advises being concise in your information design to convey one idea really well, and a good infographic, she suggests, shouldn't need a legend to be understandable. She recommends avoiding over-used chart types such as pie charts or bar charts if possible – or mixing different types together for variety – while including visuals, illustrations and photos to make visualisations more attractive. On a more practical level, you should design for the final intended viewing size (don't require users to click away from an article to see a graphic), and always include copyright, data sources, credits and other information on the graphic itself.

The Times' Julian Burgess says the key thing with visualisation is simply 'Lots of practice.'

> 'Use stuff like Excel, so you get a feel for how graphs and visualisations work, what quantities of data you can deal with. If you're dealing with even slightly large amounts of data, then looking at using a database will be well worth it. They are much quicker and hard to screw up your data compared to spreadsheets. Access is okay for lightweight stuff, beyond that MySQL is free and good, but quite geeky to start with.
>
> 'Use visualisations for research/exploring data, it can help you see a story in the data, where to target your research/legwork. Often it might be nothing significant, but you might need to write about it, explain it, and sometimes it will be the gem of the story.
>
> 'Displaying for the web is often quite tricky compared with the stuff above. Good data doesn't necessarily lead to something cool which can be displayed. Logarithmic scales are often required for displaying data in a meaningful way, but they can't really be used for public facing stuff as they are generally considered too complex outside academia.'

The Wall Street Journal Guide to Information Graphics (2010) offers a wealth of tips on elements to consider and mistakes to avoid in both visualisation and data research. Here is just a selection:

- 'Choose the best data series to illustrate your point, e.g. market share vs total revenue.
- 'Filter and simplify the data to deliver the essence of the data to your intended audience.
- 'Make numerical adjustments to the raw data to enhance your point, e.g. absolute values vs percentage change.
- 'Choose the appropriate chart settings, e.g. scale, y-axis increments and baseline.
- 'If the raw data is insufficient to tell the story, do not add decorative elements. Instead, research additional sources and adjust data to stay on point.
- 'Data is only as good as its source. Getting data from reputable and impartial sources is critical. For example, data should be benchmarked against a third party to avoid bias and add credibility.
- 'In the research stage, a bigger data set allows more in-depth analysis. In the edit phase, it is important to assess whether all your extra information buries the main point of the story or enhances [it].'

Visualising large amounts of text

If you are working with text rather than numbers there are ways to visualise that as well. *Word clouds*, for instance, show which words are used most often in a particular document (such as a speech, bill or manifesto) or data stream (such as an RSS feed of what people are saying on Twitter or blogs). This can be particularly useful in drawing out the themes of a politician's speech, for example, or the reaction from people online to a particular event. They can also be used to draw comparisons – word clouds have been used in the past to compare the inaugural speeches of Barack Obama with those of Bush and Clinton; and to compare the 2010 UK election manifestos of the Labour and Conservative parties. The *tag cloud* is similar to the word cloud, but typically allows you to click on an individual tag (word or phrase) to see where it has been used.

There are other forms for word visualisation too, particularly concerning showing relationships between words – when they occur together, or how often. The terminology varies: visualisation tool ManyEyes, for example, calls these *word trees* and *phrase nets* but other tools will have different names.

Visualisation tools

So, if you want to visualise some data or text, how do you do it? Thankfully there are now dozens of free and cheap pieces of software that you can use to quickly turn your tables into charts, graphs and clouds.

The best-known tool for creating word clouds is Wordle (www.wordle.net). Simply paste a block of text into the site, or the address of an RSS feed, and the site will generate a word cloud whose fonts and colours you can change to your preferences. Similar tools include Tagxedo (tagxedo.com/app.html), which allows you to put your word cloud into a particular shape.

ManyEyes also allows you to create word clouds and tag clouds, as well as word trees and phrase nets that allow you to see common phrases. But it is perhaps most useful in allowing you to easily create scattergrams, bar charts, bubble charts and other forms. The site also contains a raft of existing data that you can play with to get a feel for the site. Similar tools that allow access to other data include Factual, Swivel, Socrata and Verifiable.com. Google Fusion Tables is particularly useful if you want to collaborate on tables of data, as well as offering visualisation options. A more powerful service is offered by Dabble DB, which allows you to create, share and collaborate on online databases, as well as visualise them.

More general visualisation tools include Widgenie, iCharts, ChartTool and ChartGo. FusionCharts is a piece of visualisation software with a Google Gadget service that publishers may find useful.

If you want more control over your visualisation – or want it to update dynamically when the source information is updated, Google Chart Tools is worth exploring. This requires some technical knowledge, but there is a lot of guidance and help on the site to get you started quickly.

Tableau Public is a piece of free software you can download (tableausoftware.com/public) with some powerful visualisation options. You will also find visualisation options on spreadsheet applications such as Excel or the free Google Docs spreadsheet service. These are worth exploring as a way to quickly generate charts from your data on the fly.

For visualising maps, Google Maps is an obvious place to start. Beginners can add data manually or use a tool like Map A List to publish their spreadsheet to Google Maps or Google Earth. Also worth exploring is the open source option Open Street Map. Spreadsheets can also be converted to KML format, which opens up various possibilities related to mapping data that you should explore further if you want to develop skills in this area. More broadly, there is a whole school of geovisualisation and geographic information systems (GIS) that you might want to read up on.

Publishing your visualisation

There will come a point when you've visualised your data and need to publish it somehow. The simplest way to do this is to take an image (screengrab) of the chart or graph. This can be done with a web-based screencapture tool like Kwout, a free desktop application like Skitch or Jing, or by simply using the 'Print Screen' button on a PC keyboard (cmd+shift+3 on a Mac) and pasting the screengrab into a graphics package such as Photoshop.

The advantage of using a screengrab is that the image can be easily distributed on social networks, image-sharing websites (such as Flickr), and blogs – driving traffic to the page on your site where it is explained.

If you are more technically minded, you can instead choose to embed your chart or graph. Many visualisation tools will give you a piece of code which you can copy and paste into the

HTML of an article or blog post in the place you wish to display it (this will not work on most third-party blog hosting services, such as WordPress.com). One particular advantage of this approach is that the visualisation can update itself if the source data is updated.

Alternatively, an understanding of Javascript can allow you to build 'progressively enhanced' charts which allow users to access the original data or see what happens when it is changed.

Showing your raw data

It is generally a good idea to give users access to your raw data alongside its visualisation. This not only allows them to check it against your visualisation but adds insights you may not otherwise gain. It is relatively straightforward to publish a spreadsheet online using Google Docs (see Closer look: How to publish a spreadsheet online, below).

Mashing data

Wikipedia defines a mashup as 'a web page or application that uses or combines data or functionality from two or many more external sources to create a new service.' Those sources may be

Closer look How to publish a spreadsheet online

Google Docs is a free website which allows you to create and share documents. You can share them via email, by publishing them as a webpage, or by embedding your document in another webpage, such as a blog post. This is how you share a spreadsheet:

1. Open your spreadsheet in Google Docs. You can upload a spreadsheet into Google Docs if you've created it elsewhere. There is a size limit, however, so if you are told the file is too big try removing unnecessary sheets or columns.
2. Look for the 'Share' button (currently in the top right corner) and click on it.
3. A drop-down menu should appear. Click on 'Publish as a web page'.
4. A new window should appear asking which sheets you want to publish. Select the sheet you want to publish and click 'Start publishing' (you should also make sure '*Automatically republish when changes are made*' is ticked if you want the public version of the spreadsheet to update with any data you add).
5. Now the bottom half of that window – '*Get a link to the published data*' – should become active. In the bottom box should be a web address where you can now see the public version of your spreadsheet. If you want to share that, copy the address and test that it works in a web browser. You can now link to it from any webpage.
6. Alternatively, you can embed your spreadsheet – or part of it – in another webpage. To do this, click on the first drop-down menu in this area – it will currently say '*Web page*' – and change it to '*HTML to embed in a page*'. Now the bottom box on this window should show some HTML that begins with <iframe . . . Copy this and paste it into the HTML of a webpage or blog post to embed it (embedding may not work on some third-party blog hosting services, such as WordPress.com).
7. If you want to embed just part of a spreadsheet, in the box that currently says '*All cells*' type the range of cells you wish to show. For example, typing A1:G10 will select all the cells in your spreadsheet from A1 (the first row of column A) to G10 (the 10th row of column G). Once again, the HTML below will change so that it only displays that section of your spreadsheet.

online spreadsheets or tables; maps; RSS feeds (which could be anything from Twitter tweets, blog posts or news articles to images, video, audio or search results); or anything else which is structured enough to 'match' against another source.

This 'match' is typically what makes a mashup. It might be matching a city mentioned in a news article against the same city in a map; or it may be matching the name of an author with that same name in the tags of a photo; or matching the search results for 'earthquake' from a number of different sources. The results can be useful to you as a journalist, to the user, or both.

Why make a mashup?

Mashups can be particularly useful in providing live coverage of a particular event or ongoing issue – mashing images from a protest march, for example, against a map. Creating a mashup online is not too dissimilar from how, in broadcast journalism, you might set up cameras at key points around a physical location in anticipation of an event from which you will later 'pull' live feeds. In a mashup you are effectively doing exactly the same thing – but in a virtual space rather than a physical one. So, instead of setting up a feed at the corner of an important junction, you might decide to pull a feed from Flickr of any images that are tagged with the words 'protest' and 'anti-fascist'.

Some web developers have built entire sites that are mashups. Twazzup (www.twazzup.com), for example, will show you a mix of Twitter tweets, images from Flickr, news updates and websites – all based on the search term you enter. Friendfeed (friendfeed.com) pulls in data that you and your social circle post to a range of social networking sites, and displays them in one place.

Mashups also provide a different way for users to interact with content – either by choosing how to navigate (for instance by using a map), or by inviting them to input something (for instance a search term, or selecting a point on a slider). The Super Tuesday YouTube/Google Maps mashup, for example, provided an at-a-glance overview of what election-related videos were being uploaded where across the USA (Pegg, 2008).

Finally, mashups offer an opportunity for juxtaposing different datasets to provide fresh, sometimes ongoing, insights. The MySociety/Channel 4 project Mapumental, for example, combines house price data with travel information and data on the 'scenicness' of different locations to provide an interactive map of a location which the user can interrogate based on their individual preferences.

Mashup tools

Like so many aspects of online journalism, the ease with which you can create a mashup has increased significantly in recent years. An increase in the number and power of online tools, combined with the increasing 'mashability' of websites and data, means that journalists can now create a basic mashup through the simple procedures of drag-and-drop or copy-and-paste.

A simple RSS mashup, which combines the feeds from a number of different sources into one, for example, can now be created using an RSS aggregator such as xFruits (www.xfruits.com) or Jumbra (www.jumbra.com). Likewise, you can mix two maps together using the website MapTube (maptube.org), which also contains a number of maps for you to play with.

And if you want to mix two sources of data into one visualisation the site DataMasher (www.datamasher.org) will let you do that – although you will have to make do with the US data that the site provides. Google Public Data Explorer (www.google.com/publicdata) is a similar tool which allows you to play with global data.

However, perhaps the most useful tool for news mashups is Yahoo! Pipes (pipes.yahoo.com).

Yahoo! Pipes allows you to choose a source of data – it might be an RSS feed, an online spreadsheet or something that the user will input – and do a variety of things with it. Here are just some of the basic things you might do:

- Add it to other sources
- Combine it with other sources – for instance, matching images to text
- Filter it
- Count it
- Annotate it
- Translate it
- Create a gallery from the results
- Place results on a map.

You could write a whole book on how to use Yahoo! Pipes – indeed, people have – so we will not cover the practicalities of using all of those features here. There are also dozens of websites and help files devoted to the site. However, below is a short tutorial to introduce you to the website and how it works – this is a good way to understand how basic mashups work, and how easily they can be created.

Mashups and APIs

Although there are a number of easy-to-use mashup creators listed above, really impressive mashups tend to be written by people with a knowledge of programming languages, and who use APIs. APIs (Application Programming Interfaces) allow websites to interact with other websites. The launch of the Google Maps API in 2005, for example, has been described as the 'tipping point' in mashup history (Duvander, 2008) as it allowed web developers to 'mash' countless other sources of data with maps. Since then it has become commonplace for new websites, particularly in the social media arena, to launch their own APIs in order to allow web developers to do interesting things with their feeds and data – not just mashups, but applications and services too. The API Playground (apiplayground.org) is one website which was built to allow journalists to play with a selection of APIs in order to see what they do.

If you want to develop a particularly ambitious mashup, it is likely that you will need to teach yourself some programming skills, and familiarise yourself with some APIs (the APIs of Twitter, Google Maps and Flickr are good places to start).

Closer look Using Yahoo! Pipes to create a sports news widget

Signing up

First you'll need to go to pipes.yahoo.com and register. If you already have a Yahoo! or Flickr account you may be able to use that.

Aggregating feeds into one

1. Log on to Yahoo! Pipes and click on *Create a pipe*. You should be presented with a 'graph'-style page.

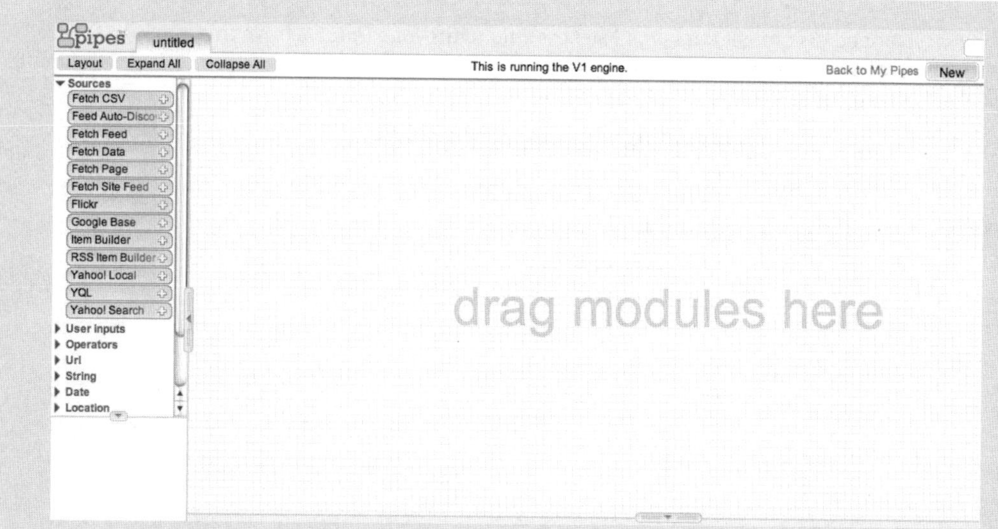

2. On the left column are a number of 'buttons' called modules. These are arranged within different categories, the first category being *Sources*. In the *Sources* category there should be a module called *Fetch Feed*. Click and drag this on to the graphed area.

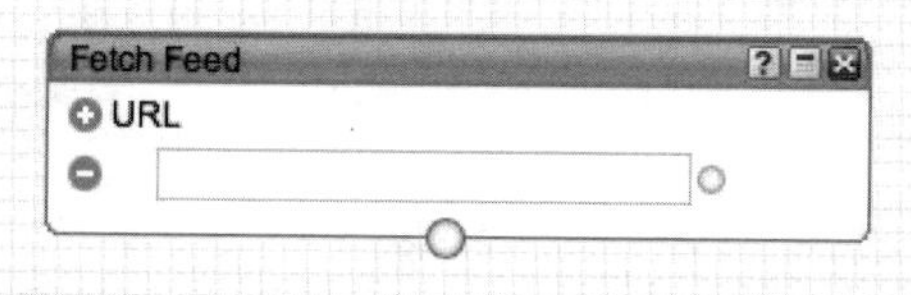

3. Find the URL of an RSS feed you want to aggregate – in this example we'll use the RSS feed for BBC Sport's coverage of Bolton Wanderers (right-click on the RSS icon and copy the link – it should look something like feed://newsrss.bbc.co.uk/rss/sportonline_uk_edition/football/teams/b/bolton_wanderers/rss.xml). Paste the URL into the *Fetch Feed* module input box.

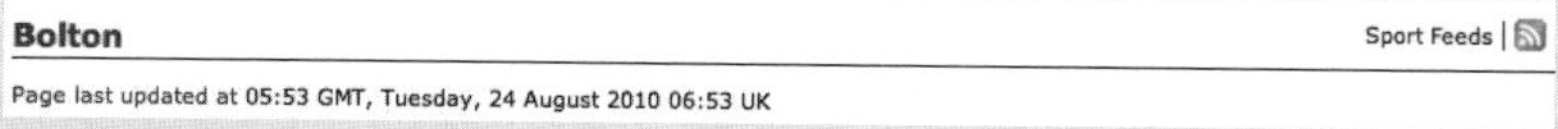

4. To add extra feeds, click on the plus (+) icon next to the URL and further input boxes will appear. Find the RSS feeds for Bolton Wanderers coverage on other news websites and blogs, and add these in each new box.

5. Finally, you need to connect the *Fetch Feed* module to the *Pipe Output*. To do this, click on the circle at the bottom of the *Fetch Feed* module and drag it to the circle at the top of *Pipe Output*. You should now see a pipe appear connecting the two.

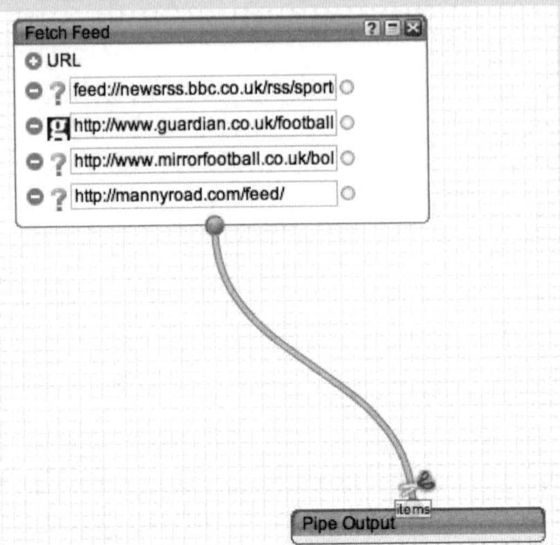

6. Click on *Pipe Output* to see the results at the bottom of the screen.

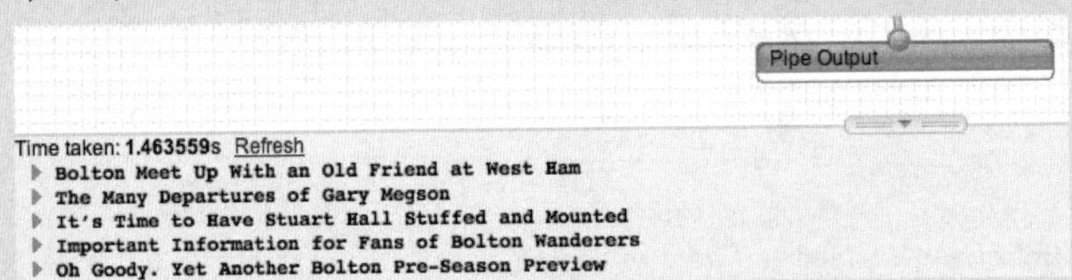

7. That's it. Click *Save* (top right), give the pipe a name, then click *Run Pipe* . . . at the top of the screen. If the results are displayed as images click *List* to see the text version.

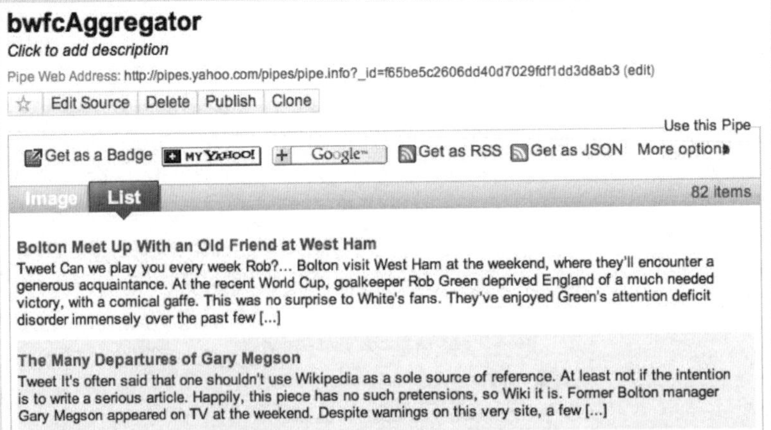

8. Finally, you need to be able to publish the results elsewhere. To do this you need the new RSS feed that has been generated. Along the top of the results you will see various options. Click on the orange *Get as RSS* button to get the RSS feed for the output of this pipe. Copy the URL of that feed

to use in an RSS widget in your blog (see How to blog, Chapter 6, for more on widgets). You can also click *Get as a Badge* to get some HTML that can be put on any website to display results more attractively.

Notes: When you use more than one feed, Yahoo! Pipes will 'cluster' them together by feed rather than by date. To order the results by date, use the *Sort* module under the *Operators* category, connect it to *Fetch Feed*, and *sort by item.pubDate* in *descending* order.

If you want to aggregate feeds after filtering, etc. you can use the *Union* module under *Operators* category.

Filtering feeds

1. Follow steps 1–4 for *Aggregating feeds*, above.
2. On the left column in Yahoo! Pipes are buttons, called modules. These are arranged within different categories. Expand the *Operators* category. There should be a module called *Filter*. Click and drag this on to the graphed area.
3. You need to connect the *Fetch Feed* module to the *Filter* module. To do this, click on the circle at the bottom of the *Fetch Feed* module and drag it to the circle at the top of *Filter*. You should now see a pipe appear connecting the two.

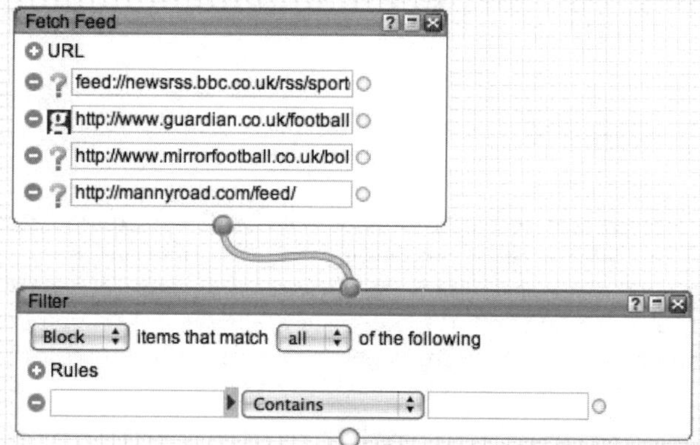

4. Using the settings in the Filter module you can choose to filter the aggregated feed by blocking items (articles) with certain words, or only allowing items with certain words to come through. You will need to choose from the drop-down menu which field (e.g. 'title' or 'category') you want to be the subject of the filter.
5. Finally, you need to connect the *Filter* module to the *Pipe Output*. To do this, click on the circle at the bottom of the *Filter* module and drag it to the circle at the top of *Pipe Output*. You should now see a pipe appear connecting the two.

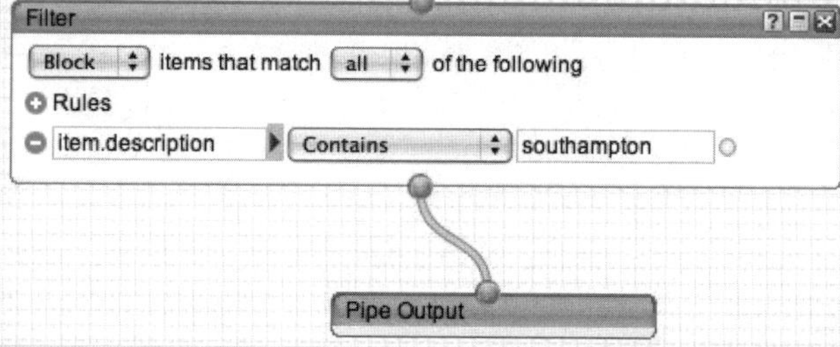

6. Follow steps 6–8 for Aggregating feeds, above, to finish.

All of the above screenshots were created using YahooPipes, http://pipes.yahoo.com/pipes

Note: You can use the *Unique* module instead to filter out several versions of the same post (e.g. when you're using feeds from search results on different engines).

You can see the pipe created above by going to http://bit.ly/ojbkpipeseg – click *Clone* to add it to your own pipes where you can see how it works and adapt it for different purposes.

Closer look Taking it further – resources on programming

If you want to explore programming in more depth there are resources available specifically for journalists. Hackety Hack is a tutorial for learning Ruby on Rails which comes with its own programming environment. Scraperwiki is a website that provides an environment for writing programming scripts in Python so that, again, you don't have to deal with the difficulties of setting one up on your own computer. The site also includes tutorials. More broadly, Help.HacksHackers.com is an online community where journalists and technologists come together to solve problems.

It is always worth attending some events to meet programmers – try searching a site like MeetUp for groups near you interested in a particular programming language.

Closer look Anatomy of a tweet

Plate 6 shows the code behind a simple Twitter update. It includes information about the author, their location, whether the update was a reply to someone else, what time and where it was created, and lots more besides. Each of these values can be used by a mashup in various ways – for example, you might match the author of this tweet with the author of a blog or image; you might match its time against other things being published at that moment; or you might use their location to plot this update on a map.

While the code can be intimidating, you do not need to understand programming in order to be able to do things with it.

Summary

There is a quiet movement taking place in journalism: a generation of journalists who grew up with computers are using them to help do better journalism.

Charles Arthur, a *Guardian* technology journalist, says:

'When I was really young, I read a book about computers which made the point – rather effectively – that if you found yourself doing the same process again and again, you should hand it over to a computer. That became a rule for me: never do some task more than once if you can possibly get a computer to do it.

'I got into data journalism because I also did statistics – and that taught me that people are notoriously bad at understanding data. Visualisation and simplification and exposition are key to helping people understand.

'So data journalism is a compound of all those things: determination to make the computer do the slog, confidence that I can program it to, and the desire to tell the story that the data is holding and hiding.'

Mary Hamilton from the *Eastern Daily Press* says: 'I love coding when it works well, I love that moment of unlocking something or creating something new and useful. I find it oddly exciting, which is probably why I carried on doing it after the first couple of times.'

The Times' Jonathan Richards sees the flood of information online as presenting 'an amazing opportunity' for journalists, but also a challenge:

'How on earth does one keep up with; make sense of it? You could go about it in the traditional way, fossicking in individual sites, but much of the journalistic value in this outpouring, it seems, comes in the form of aggregation: in processing large amounts of data, distilling them, and exploring them for patterns. To do that – unless you're superhuman, or have a small army of volunteers – you need the help of a computer.

'I "got into" data journalism because I find this mix exciting. It appeals to the traditional journalistic instinct, but also calls for a new skill which, once harnessed, dramatically expands the realm of "stories I could possibly investigate . . ."'

Mark Donoghue makes three connections between journalism and computer science, and how they are able to help each other:

'Journalism taught me how to ask questions. Computer Science taught me the importance of asking the right question.

'Journalism taught me how to communicate. Computer Science taught me how to think.

'Journalism taught me how to identify problems. Computer Science taught me how to solve problems.'

As journalists we are living in an era of information overload. Data journalism gives us the skills to find the inaccessible information that our competitors might overlook; the understanding to find the stories and people behind the numbers; and the ability to make those stories understood by users.

These are all traditional skills – with the difference that we have new, powerful tools to use in their practice.

In addition, data journalism offers a way to engage users with the news in ways that print and broadcast journalism could never do. We can present it in ways that allow different people to look at it in different ways. We can create mashups that update the picture in real time. And we can give users access to all of our data and invite them to help shed light on it.

It is a newsroom without walls: there will be better programmers out there, better designers, people with a better understanding of statistics, or who can access information that we can't. All of these people will be potential colleagues in the pursuit of journalism – and joining online communities of support will be as important in your development as reading books on the subject matter. Your role could be as simple as finding some information and raising a question, as *The Guardian* datablog does – or mashing up one source of data with another to provide useful insights. The story – as ever, with online journalism – never ends.

This chapter has touched on disciplines as diverse as statistics, advanced search techniques, information design, research methodology and programming. Knowing a little bit about all of these areas will be useful – but you should continue to read more about them as you progress in your experiments.

And the key thing *is to experiment* – see what data you can find, and what insights you can find within it. Play with visualisation tools and compare the results. Mix different sources of data together to see what happens. And think how this might be useful as you pursue stories and try to find ways to help users understand complex issues. Be curious. Be creative. The chances are that the results will stick out a mile from 99 per cent of everything else on the subject – and what's more: you'll enjoy it.

Activities

1. Submit a Freedom of Information (FOI) request to your local authority, NHS trust or police force using the website TheyWorkForYou.com. FOIs are best for requesting documents or statistics. You could, for example, ask how much they spent on PR in the past three years, or to see any policy documents relating to dealing with complaints. Use WhatDoTheyKnow to see what other FOI requests have been submitted to that body – and the responses. This will help you formulate your own.
2. Create a simple data mashup with Google Public Data Explorer. Pick any set of data and then select a number of elements to compare (for example, different countries).
3. Use the advanced search techniques outlined in this chapter to find a useful spreadsheet on your local council website.
4. Look at a piece of research that has been released recently by the government or a pressure group. How was the information gathered? How big – and how representative – was the sample? How long a period did the research cover? If any of that information is missing, try to get hold of it – and if they won't provide it, ask why.
5. Put a recent speech by a politician into Wordle and create a word cloud. What does it imply about the politician's priorities, or the point they're trying to make?

Further reading

Blastland and Dilnot (2007) *The Tiger That Isn't,* UK: Profile Books.

Brooke, H. (2010) *The Silent State,* UK: William Heinemann.

Fry, B. (2008) *Visualizing Data,* USA: O'Reilly.

Huff, D. (1954) *How to Lie With Statistics,* UK: Penguin Business.

Meyer, P. (2001) *Precision Journalism,* USA: Rowman & Littlefield. The previous edition is available free online at: www.unc.edu/~pmeyer/book/.

Wong, D. M. (2010) *The Wall Street Journal Guide to Information Graphics,* USA: W.W. Norton & Co.

Blogs

OUseful.Info *blog.ouseful.info*

Information is Beautiful *www.informationisbeautiful.net*

Flowing Data *FlowingData.com*

Google Maps Mania *http://googlemapsmania.blogspot.com/*

Tripwire Magazine: 75+ Tools for Visualizing your Data, CSS, Flash, jQuery, PHP, *www.tripwiremagazine.com/2009/12/70-tools-for-visualizing-your-data-css-flash-jquery-php.html*

Chapter 6

How to blog

This chapter will cover:

- What are blogs?
- Closer look: Breakdown of a blog
- Blogging as a genre
- Why blog?
- Closer look: Is blogging journalism?
- Beginning your blog
- Closer look: Which blog service should I use?
- Closer look: Taking it further - plugins and widgets
- Blogging beyond text: from moblogs to tumblelogs
- Closer look: Twitter jargon
- Microblogging and Twitter
- Closer look: Major moments in journo-blogging history
- Blogging and Really Simple Syndication (RSS)
- Closer look: Making money from blogging

Introduction

Blogging has undergone a tremendous transformation over the past few years. From publishing pariah to saviour of journalism, it is now a rare news organisation that does not use blogs. Where once editors asked 'Is blogging journalism?' they now ask 'How can we make the most of our blogs?'

Blogs are tremendously flexible – ideal for quick updates, while also well suited to in-depth analysis; used for personal reflection, but also for impersonal lists of useful links; and able to be based on images, audio, video or text.

Successful journalism blogs have emerged from every quarter, from the BBC's Robert Peston, whose award-winning financial blog broke the story on the crisis at Northern Rock, to the initiatives of local newspapers like the *Birmingham Post*, which invited leading figures to use their website as a platform for expert analysis on local issues.

For budding journalists, not having a blog is like a budding musician refusing to play gigs without a record deal. As Neil McIntosh, Head of Editorial Development at *The Guardian*, put it, on his blog: 'If you enter the jobs market without one, no matter how good your degree, you're increasingly likely to lose out to people who better present all they can do, and have the experience of creating and curating their own site. If a brilliant graduate didn't have a blog, but still made interview, I'd be asking, politely, why not . . .'

In this chapter we'll look at what makes a blog a blog and the wide range of types of blog, and offer advice on maintaining a successful blog. We'll also look at blogging's newest form – the microblog, and its best known brand: Twitter.

What are blogs?

The technology of blogging is barely a decade old. There are various candidates for the 'first blogger' (including some who pre-date the World Wide Web) and the first 'blog', but the key change came in 1999 when the first blogging services emerged which allowed anyone to create a blog without knowledge of HTML.

Before that point most blogs were simply lists of links to other useful sites – a feature that remains central to blogging to this day. As well as linking frequently within individual blog posts many blogs feature a static 'blogroll' in their design: a list of links to other blogs the author finds useful, typically displayed in the outside column.

But with the adoption of blogs by a wider, non-technical user base there came what blog historian Rebecca Blood (2000) calls a 'cult of personality' phase, where authorship, experience and opinion came to the fore, and the 'diary' form of the 'web log' became prominent.

However, as blogs developed in sophistication as a content management system and distribution network, and the medium attracted publicity, people with more professional objectives – including freelance journalists, academics, marketers, activists and independent publishers – started to see the potential of the medium, and it took another direction.

Commercially run blogs, and blog networks were launched. Some – such as Boing Boing, Perez Hilton and the Huffington Post – quickly reached readerships larger than most news websites. Others acted as showcases for their authors' careers in public speaking and consultancy, columns and book deals. Figures such as author Robert Scoble, cartoonist Hugh MacLeod and marketer Seth Godin found a global audience for their work thanks to the distribution networks of the web.

At the same time, the practice of 'blogging' started to outgrow the blog platform itself, becoming a key feature of social networking services such as MySpace and Facebook. Users were invited to post blog-style updates on what they were doing or thinking, or to share interesting links or media. Celebrity bloggers such as Lily Allen used these social networks as tools not just for distributing and promoting their music, but as a platform for communicating directly with audiences, a development that was to have significant implications for the journalists who previously acted as middlemen in that process.

Most recently, the same service has been core to new 'microblogging' services like Twitter, video services such as Seesmic and 12seconds, and audio platforms such as AudioBoo, services that have been adopted in increasing numbers by journalists, organisations and public figures.

As a result, 'blogging' has increasingly become 'publishing' on the web, but with some key generic qualities that journalists ignore at their peril.

Closer look Breakdown of a blog

As blog platforms have become increasingly sophisticated, creators have developed a range of features, from the ability to categorise and 'tag' content to a range of 'widgets' that allow you to pull content from your presence elsewhere on the web. Not all blogs have all of these features, but as both a publisher of a blog and a user it is useful to know what they are and what they do.

Posts

Posts are what a journalist would call articles, or what a diarist would call entries. They are the main content of blogs, updated regularly. One common mistake that people make when writing about blogs is to confuse the term 'blog' with 'blog post'. The blog is the publication; the post is the individual article – people typically *start* blogs and *write* posts so it is incorrect to say that someone 'wrote a blog about' something when what you mean is that they wrote a blog *post*.

The homepage of a blog will typically show the most recent post at the top, while each post will have its own 'permalink' – a page where it can always be found and where comments can be seen and added.

Pages

The other main content of blogs can be found on 'pages'. A typical blog has just one page: the About page, which gives details on the blog's author, history, subject matter, etc. Some blogs will have other pages such as editorial or ethical policies, recommended reading, gallery, etc. Pages are different from posts in that they are not frequently updated. Content from pages is also not shown on the main homepage, but instead linked from it.

Blogroll

A blogroll is a list of other blogs the author likes. It may simply be labelled 'links'.

Subscribe

Often accompanied by an orange button with 'RSS', 'XML' or 'atom', this allows readers to receive updates from the blog through an RSS reader. See the section in this chapter on RSS for more information.

▶

Tag cloud

Most blogs allow you to 'tag' each post with relevant keywords, such as the names of organisations, people, places or topics referred to – for instance: 'Manchester', 'Microsoft', 'Barack Obama', 'snow'. Tagging your posts makes it easier for people to find them and easier for search engines to know what your post is about.

A tag cloud displays the tags used in your blog in a big 'cloud'. Those used the most often will be largest. The tag cloud serves two basic functions: first, it provides an instant graphic representation of the sorts of subjects you cover in your blog; secondly, it allows people to click on individual tags to access a list of related blog posts. In other words, it is a different way to explore your content.

Categories

Categories are similar to tags, but with the main difference that they are specific to your site. Whereas tags tend to refer to keywords within a post, categories tend to refer to themes, subjects and series. Examples of categories would include: 'Match reports', 'Computers', 'Politics', 'Tutorials', 'Behind the scenes'. Most blog services allow you to create a number of categories for your blog posts and add to them as you go along. A category list on a blog is primarily a navigational device that allows people to access related content on your blog.

RSS feeds

Many blogs display 'feeds' that pull content from other places where the author publishes online, such as their Twitter updates, latest photos or latest videos. Some also display feeds from blogs or news websites that they think their users might find useful. These will typically be labelled with the name of the website. For more information on how to do this yourself, see the section in this chapter on RSS.

Archives

Another way to navigate the content of a blog, this allows users to look at entries from a specific month or date.

Widgets

In addition to all the above, blogs can feature a number of 'widgets' that perform additional functions from simple static text (such as a biography of the author or a list of popular posts) to translation, donations and online shopping.

Blogging as a genre

If we are to try to define blogging as a genre, it is first, and perhaps above all else, conversational. It is social. It is networked. Two key features to a blog are links and comments. Fail to include either, and you risk talking to yourself. Jeff Jarvis (2007) describes this particularly well in a blog post where he talks about a BBC journalist he met:

> '[She] was troubled, bearing weight on her shoulders from having to fill her blog and manage her blog. To her, the blog was a thing, a beast that needed to be fed, a never-ending sheet of blank paper. I turned to her and said she should see past the blog. It's not a show with a rundown that, without feeding, turns into dead air. Indeed, if you look at it that way, you'll probably write crappy blog posts . . . I blog when I find something interesting that I've seen

> and I think, "I have to tell my friends about that." You're the friends. So yes, I said, it's just a conversation. And reading – hearing what others are saying – is every bit as important as writing. It was as if scales were lifted from her eyes and weight from her back: She's just talking with people.'

Secondly, blogging is typically incomplete, open and ongoing. It is about process, not product. It is about a shared space.

For example, simply republishing print articles or broadcast journalism on a blog is derisively referred to as 'shovelware', indicating the lack of care with which content is 'shovelled' on to a medium for which it was not produced.

While blogs – which often contain strong opinions – may seem like a natural platform for opinion columns, for example, there are subtle differences in writing a good column for print and writing for a blog. The key difference is that, while printed opinion columns often leave little room for response, blogged opinion typically does the opposite, seeking to start a debate rather than wrap one up.

The open and conversational nature of the medium means that journalists are increasingly using their blogs to post about ideas for articles, seeking users' suggestions for angles and information. The journalist may also blog an early draft version, asking for readers' input, and responding to it. When the published or broadcast version goes live on the news website, the journalist might post a simple link to it on their blog as the latest stage in its production. Some publish an 'uncut' version, too, without the limits of word counts or airtime, or full transcripts of interviews in case users can pick up things the journalist might have missed (Bradshaw, 2009). As one reporter wrote:

> 'On hot-button stories where our readers are asking a lot of questions, we post updates every time we make a phone call. For example, [a company] declared bankruptcy, and the new owner wouldn't take the previous owner's gift cards. Our readers were peeved and hounding us to do something. The corporate folks weren't saying anything, so we didn't have any new information to report. Because we didn't have any new info, we didn't write anything in the paper. But on our blog, we would post updates at least daily to tell people when we left a message and if we had heard back yet. We eventually scored an interview with the new CEO and posted it in its entirety on our site. Another reporter saw it and called us. We swapped info. Our readers also post links to other stories on the topic from other news orgs.'

In short, the story is never finished.

Thirdly, blogging is personal and informal – often difficult for journalists who have been trained for years to be objective and removed from their stories. This personal quality has a number of strengths: it allows you to make a closer connection with readers, which in turn often helps build your understanding of the issues that matter to them. It allows you to be more transparent about the news production process, building trust and news literacy. And it allows you a space for reflection, if you choose to use it.

However, the genre of blogging is still developing, and you may choose to ignore all the above as you experiment in shaping the future of the medium.

Why blog?

There are many reasons for blogging – some editorial, some commercial and some professional.

Editorially, for instance, blogging offers a new way for journalists to source leads and to attract useful sources, particularly outside the formal organisations that normally provide material and reaction. Where traditionally a journalist built a contacts book through accessing directories and networking events, blogs turn that process around, making it easy for members of the public to post comments on a journalist's blog (publicly or privately, via email) or make their presence felt through linking to it (most blogs will send you an email when someone links to one of your posts).

Blogs also offer a speedier method of publishing than offered by broadcast and print production deadlines – an ability to get the story out as fast as possible and so make the first claim on it. This is particularly important as the earliest blog posts on any story act as 'hubs' for early reader reaction and new leads. In many cases, free blogging services can publish faster than bespoke in-house content management systems.

Equally, blogs offer extra space for exploring a story further and a platform for other media: images, video, audio and, of course, links.

Robert Peston, the BBC journalist who broke the Northern Rock story on his blog, says: 'I can do two things with a blog: I can get stuff out very quickly; but the most valuable thing about the blog if you work for an organisation like the BBC is that you can put out an amount of detail you can't get in a three-minute bulletin. The great advantage of the blog is that you are constantly out there putting nuggets out that will give you stuff back and allow you to complete the story more quickly.'

Commercially, blogging's greatest attraction has been its ability to improve a news organisation's visibility on search engines such as Google – a process known as search engine optimisation (SEO). Features that improve the visibility of blog posts on search engines include tagging (giving a post 'tags' that identify the content, such as key terms or names) and categorisation, 'pinging' (sending a notification to search engines that a new post has gone live), frequent linking, and search-engine-friendly web addresses. The fact that blogs are generally frequently updated through posts and through user comments also helps.

In addition, blogs improve the distribution of news stories online. Good blogs tend to work within a wider community, linking to other blogs and blog posts and commenting on each other's stories. In the absence of a formal distribution infrastructure on the web, this passing on of stories becomes particularly important in building audiences.

For those organisations that are not commercially funded, blogs offer an important demonstration of transparency and accountability towards the public, an avenue to building greater trust and responsibility. The BBC, for instance, hosts blogs by a number of senior staff explaining the reasons behind their decisions and reflecting on lessons learned in experiments with news gathering and reporting.

Professionally, blogs have become an important way to make yourself visible to employers, not just as a portfolio of work and a demonstration of expertise, but also evidence of your 'pulling power'. A blog with lots of comment activity, for example, demonstrates that you can bring an existing readership to any job – but don't expect an active audience instantly: this takes time and commitment.

As blogs form part of a wider community, they are very useful networking tools, and journalists are increasingly approached with commissions for work by people who discovered them via their blog. After all, when someone wants an expert on something the first thing they often do is to Google it.

Using the blog as a virtual clippings file – 'klogging', or knowledge-blogging – is also a good way to show how well informed you are, while blogs provide a perfect space for experimentation, exploration and creative development in general. This is a new medium, and an understanding of how it works is becoming increasingly valuable.

Besides, it's not just a matter of a personal portfolio: blogging develops and improves your journalism; blogging develops your expertise in a specialist area; and blogging builds contacts and networks in your areas of interest.

Closer look Is blogging journalism?

Is television a form of journalism? Are words on a page a form of journalism? Are sounds a form of journalism? Blogs are a platform. They can contain journalism, just as TV, radio and print can. Many bloggers practise journalism, many do not. To ask if blogging is a form of journalism is to confuse form with content. It is like asking: 'Is ice cream strawberry?'

G. Stuart Adam's (1993) definition of journalism is an excellent one to use when addressing this: 'Journalism is an invention or a form of expression used to report and comment in the public media on the events and ideas of the here and now. There are at least five elements in such a definition: (1) a form of expression that is an invention; (2) reports of ideas and events; (3) comments on them; (4) the public circulation of them; and (5) the here and now.'

If a blog fits that description, you could argue it is journalism.

Beginning your blog: Step 1 – Choose the focus

Successful blogs tend to have a specific and clear focus, one that is narrower than those used within traditional media organisations aimed at mass markets. Blogging about solar energy, for example, is likely to be more effective than trying to blog about 'environmental news'. This is partly because you are likely to have much less competition, but also because with a blog you want an engaged audience with something to contribute, and you are more likely to get that engaged audience by aiming at a specific subject.

1. For student journalists the *niche blog* can be the most effective type as it is a good way of building your profile in a particular sector, along with contacts and knowledge.

   There is, of course, nothing stopping you having a number of blogs covering different niches so that you end up with a network of blogs covering 'environmental news', and this is a common process as journalism bloggers expand their circle of interest and expertise.

   If you cannot choose a niche to begin with, then choose a generic topic and as you gain experience and knowledge you may find yourself leaning towards a particular area – or you may spot a gap in the market. Blogs are flexible enough that you can easily rename them and change the address without losing the content.

2. Another type of blog aside from one based on a niche subject is the *'behind the scenes' blog*. This can provide a useful space for reflection on the stories you are covering, those you would like to cover, and why you made the decisions you did on the angle you took, the people you interviewed and so on. You can use it to post information that didn't make the 'final cut', and raw material such as full interview transcripts or audio, video, images and even spreadsheets. The BBC Editors blogs provide a great example of this type of blog, providing an insight into the working practices of editors and building trust with users.

3. A third type of blog is the *'running story' blog*. This generally takes the form of a diary as the journalist takes on some form of challenge. Examples might include learning to drive or giving up smoking, preparing for a marathon or a wedding, making a significant journey, or even producing a recipe for each letter of the alphabet. *The Sun* runs a number of blogs along these lines. It is also very useful for events that run over a limited period of time, such as an election, sporting event, or even the broadcast of a particular programme. A more feature-based form, this can be very successful but obviously has a limited shelf life.

Closer look Which blog service should I use?

There are several blogging services available. The most popular are Blogger and WordPress but there are dozens of others, including LiveJournal (a social-network-based blogging service), Posterous (which allows you to post entirely by email) and Tumblr (aimed at those who are mainly linking to material elsewhere). Most are free, while some offer added features for a fee.

The most popular services are as easy to use as email: choose a username and password, and a name for your blog, and it is created for you. All you have to do is log in and click on 'Post' (or something similar). You will be taken to a page with a box for a headline and a box for the post (article). When you've finished, click 'Publish' and the post goes live.

Beyond that, each blogging service has dozens of other features, such as including links, images, video or audio, adding tags and categories, altering the design and adding 'widgets'. You'll get to know these as you use the service more and more. Most have extensive help pages telling you how to use these features.

Because of the ease of setting one up, many successful bloggers run more than one blog – for example, to cover different niche topics, or to play to the strengths of the different platforms. Some services allow you to move your posts there from other services if you need to – WordPress, for example, allows you to import all your blog posts from Blogger.com.

Of course, these three broad types are only examples, and you might combine aspects of each – writing a niche blog which includes reflective postings and a running story. Or you might do something entirely different. The key thing is: just do it. You can tweak and improve as you go.

Beginning your blog: Step 2 – Start posting

A 'post' is an individual article on a blog. It can obviously be about anything you like, but there is a number of types of blog posts which have become generic as the medium has developed and can serve as a helpful prompt if you're short of ideas. The following are some typical examples.

Respond to something elsewhere on the web

The easiest and possibly best way to start blogging. Simply link to something elsewhere that you feel is interesting, or (better) that you disagree with. If you make a constructive response to what someone else has posted, for example, you can start a useful inter-blog dialogue. You might add links to evidence that challenges what the original post says, for example. Its most simple form, when you simply post useful links, has been called 'link journalism'.

Suggest an idea

For a story or for a way of doing things. Invite reaction and suggestions – and don't expect people to come to you. Approach people you might otherwise be shy of asking, and invite them to respond to the comments. Ideas can travel very far, so can be really effective in attracting readers.

Interview someone

A straightforward and easy way to create a post. An email interview can work well, but if you can put an audio or video recording on the site this often adds value. If you are interviewing a busy person it helps if you limit your questions or, if you're asking for their advice, specifically ask for their '3 tips on . . .' or '5 things I know about . . .'. You can even turn this into a series of interviews with the same theme.

Blog an event

Attend a relevant event – a conference, meeting, public talk, demonstration, or even just a conversation – and write about it. If you have access to the internet during the event you can even 'liveblog' it by starting a post as soon as you have something to report and adding updates or new posts as the event progresses. Ambitious bloggers can use the liveblogging tool CoveritLive – or you can even stream parts live from your phone or laptop using services like Qik and Bambuser.

Ask a question

This is about turning your blog post into a kind of forum, where the real action takes place in the comments below your post. Good questions tap into conflict or uncertainty within a community – ethical issues, for example, or how to react to change. Asking for examples to compile a list can also offer an easy way for people to contribute. You might also take a topical hook – for example, if someone has said something controversial or unusual and there is no place yet where people are discussing it, you can provide that space.

The question post typically only works once you've established a readership and generated goodwill by contributing yourself on your blog and in comments on other blogs. It can be very effective in collecting useful information from and for a community. Taken further, you can use free online survey tools such as PollDaddy and SurveyMonkey to conduct a larger survey.

Pick a fight

Many bloggers attempt to generate traffic by loudly criticising another (popular) blogger in the hope that they'll respond and generate traffic from their readers. This sort of tactic is often referred to as 'link-baiting'. In other words, if the criticised blogger responds (takes the bait) it generally means links to your blog. If you are to criticise another blogger, it is worth considering if it will be seen as 'link-bait' or a constructive and valuable debate. Done well, a genuine argument between two bloggers can generate insight and bring factions to compromise. You can also pick a fight with a company or brand, and mount a campaign to instigate change, as Jeff Jarvis did with his 'Dell Hell' campaign which forced Dell to change the way it engaged with consumers.

Reflect on something

It might be a decision or choice that you made, a lead for a story, or anything else that happened in the course of your work or even personal life. Why did it happen? What are the implications? What did you learn? Keep it open so others can contribute their experiences or insights.

Do something visual

Take photographs and/or video footage as you travel along a particular route, or as you attend an event or interview. Explain them, ask questions, include relevant links. Or draw sketches and photograph them. This is an easy way to experiment with mobile phone journalism by taking photos with your phone and texting or emailing them to a web service such as Flickr, Facebook or Posterous.

Review something

Try to make it useful – include links to further information, quote from (and link to) other reviewers. This may be about content curation – summing up what is out there – as much as giving your own opinions.

Make a list

Lists are enormously popular on the web, frequently topping websites' 'most shared' lists. It may be anything from '5 ways to tie a knot' to 'the 100 best albums by women'. A good tip for your first post is to make a list of the top 10 blogs in your subject area – a useful task for yourself while also making them aware of your existence.

Write a how-to

In his book *Click*, Bill Tancer notes how one of the most popular types of search query is 'How do I..?' or 'Why do..?' Tutorials also frequently top websites' 'most-shared' lists and can be enormously useful in generating goodwill in your sphere. If you're feeling particularly confident or experimental, video instructions can work extremely well.

Let someone else post

If you find someone with specific expertise or experience, invite them to write a 'guest post' on a particular subject. Even if they already have their own blog, they will appreciate the opportunity to reach a new audience, or to write in a different context.

Beginning your blog: Step 3 – Comment and link

The blogosphere relies on dialogue and community. It is important not only that you look at other blogs in your area (and outside your area), but post comments when you can. This encourages other bloggers but also makes them aware of you and your blog. It makes them more likely to look at your blog, and post comments in return. You should think of your comments on other blogs as part of 'blogging', as they can often lead to fruitful relationships with sources. Indeed, commenting can be seen as akin to a combination of old-fashioned networking and a method of story research that allows you to interrogate the sources. Also, if you don't post comments on other blogs, you can scarcely complain when no one comments on yours.

Obviously, you should try to avoid posting comments that simply say 'nice post' – this can be seen as 'comment spam': an attempt to improve your blog's search engine ranking by posting links in comments. Ideally, you should try to add something to the original post by pointing out a useful link, fact or contact. Alternatively, you can engage on an emotional level by expressing solidarity with what they're saying or trying to do – or, indeed, by disagreeing. A good argument in the comments is a good sign, and most bloggers will appreciate your engaging with the debate (although if you feel it's going nowhere, withdraw gracefully).

If the blog has an option to subscribe to email updates on comments that come after yours, it is worth doing so, so that you can monitor responses to your comment and engage in further conversation. Alternatively, many blogs have individual RSS feeds for comments (see the section later in this chapter for more detail on RSS).

Needless to say it is especially important that you monitor the comments on your own blog and respond to them. Comments will quickly dry up if readers feel you are not listening. Most free blogging services will send you an email when someone comments, but not all in-house news organisation systems do, so if that is the case make sure to check the comments whenever you log into your blog.

It is important not to take comments too personally, and to react in a reasoned and measured manner – quite often the most vociferous commenter will calm down very quickly when engaged with. While at the *Birmingham Post*, for example, journalist Joanna Geary invited their website's most critical commenter into the newspaper to discuss his feelings about the newspaper in a video interview. In the blog post (Geary, 2009) where she published the video she wrote: 'The man I met in reception could not have been further from what I expected – polite, erudite, passionate and engaged in local news. I think it's worth journalists seeing that not all aggressive commenters are always aware how they are coming across. It is not always personal.'

However, there are also many 'vandals' and 'trolls' who post comments that are intended to provoke a reaction. Knowing when to respond and when to ignore is a delicate art. You know your blog is successful when other readers respond to defend you.

For the same reason that comments are important, linking is an integral part of blogging. Whenever you mention an article, blog post, website or report it is essential that you link to it. Not doing so is seen as lazy blogging, and is frustrating for the user, who then has to visit a search engine to find the webpage you've failed to link to.

Some publishers discourage journalists from linking because they see it as taking readers away from their site (and advertising). However, analysis of website performance on the issue (Karp, 2008; Eaves, 2008;) suggests that the more links a site has, the longer users spend there, the more often they return, and the more links the site gets pointing back to it in return. In addition, one of the factors that search engines like Google look for when ranking a webpage is how many links it contains.

It is important to recognise that Google is not alone in making that judgement: users do too. A page with links is worth more than one without. Good links are a key part of the editorial value of online journalism, just as good visuals are part of the editorial value of television journalism. Successful online journalists such as *The Guardian*'s Jemima Kiss know that a good series of links can provide compelling content even when nothing else is added. Kiss's 'PDA Newsbucket' series on *The Guardian* website consists entirely of regular lists of links accompanied by a one-line description, while journalists such as *Mashable*'s Pete Cashmore have built huge audiences on Twitter by regularly posting links to stories they think their audience will find interesting.

Linking also serves a second purpose – notifying the author of the webpage that is being linked to. Most website authors monitor incoming links, and will see the traffic coming from your blog (many blog services even send an automatic email to the author when you link to them). Again, this is crucial in generating contacts and also in bringing people back to the site to respond to what you have said about them or their work.

Likewise, you should yourself be monitoring what webpages are linking to you, and responding when you can. Many blogging services have built-in statistics pages and email updates that allow you to see this and other information, such as what phrases people are searching for when they find you. You can also use web analytics services such as Google Analytics which will provide more information, such as which countries visitors are coming from, and how long they stay on your site.

Closer look Taking it further – plugins and widgets

If you're using WordPress you can choose to host the blog yourself, which not only means you have a more professional-looking web address (that doesn't end in .wordpress.com) but also allows you to install 'plugins' – extra bits of code that extend the functionality of the blog platform.

Some plugins allow users to post video comments, for example, or subscribe to email updates when new comments appear on a specific post. Others allow people to vote on posts, share them with friends, or make your posts more search engine-friendly. There are plugins that allow your blog to have multiple authors, all with different levels of access, or to have templates for posts that have a similar structure. There are plugins that allow you to include advertising easily, or for readers to 'buy you a beer'. There are plugins that will pull content from elsewhere automatically, or suggest other related posts that readers might like on your blog and others. And there are plugins that will change the presentation of the blog when viewed on a mobile phone or printed.

Services like WordPress and Blogger also allow you to include 'widgets', generally in the sidebar. Typical widgets include recent comments, the most popular posts, and a 'blogroll' of links to blogs you like. But you can also get widgets from other sites, such as a widget displaying your latest Twitter or MySpace update, or your Last.fm station, or video from your accounts on other sites. To access your widgets just log on to your blog and look for the 'widgets' section.

All these little touches can improve your blog significantly and give it a more professional (or personal) look and functionality, not to mention giving you an insight into the technical possibilities of news online.

Blogging beyond text: from moblogs to tumblelogs

While this chapter has focused so far on text-based blogging, there are many other forms of blogging that you should consider and experiment with. Photoblogging, for example, involves posts based around photos. In its purest form the blog simply consists of regular photo updates; others add commentary. Most blogging services allow you to upload images, or you can use a photo-sharing website like Flickr.

Moblogging is blogging from a mobile phone. Many mobile phones come with blogging software pre-installed, such as Nokia's Lifeblog, or you can install a blogging application on your phone, such as Shozu. There are also dozens of blogging services aimed at mobile phone users, such as Moblog and Buzznet, which allow you to post via text message or email, among other features.

Video blogging – or vlogging – means simply that, instead of posting in text, you record your post to video. Many vloggers use a video hosting service such as YouTube or Vimeo and 'embed' their videos in their blog (the video hosting service provides some HTML which you copy and paste into the blog post). Alternatively, you can use a video blogging service like Seesmic. See Chapter 8 on video for more information.

Podcasting is blogging using audio (see Chapter 7 for more on podcasting), while Linklogs are blogs that consist only of links, and Tumblelogs are blogs that combine a jumble of links, quotes, video and images to create a scrapbook of personal experience.

Clearly, you can use any of these forms in a standard blog. Many bloggers may post in text for the most part, but occasionally include a vlog post, a photo entry, link to audio, post from a mobile phone, or just share that week's useful links. The blog platform is flexible enough to allow

Closer look Twitter jargon

Twitter comes with its own jargon: an individual post or update on Twitter is called a 'tweet'. If you like someone's tweet you can pass it on – what is referred to as 'retweeting'. A 'retweet' typically begins with 'RT' followed by the name of the user you're retweeting and their message.

If you want to send a message to someone specific, you begin your tweet with '@' followed by the person's username, so for example a tweet beginning '@paulbradshaw' would be directed at me, and that tweet would appear in my 'Replies' page on Twitter. Equally, if you want to refer to someone, you can use the same convention, e.g. 'Talking to @paulbradshaw about Twitter'. For private messages that are not seen by everyone else, you can send a direct message (DM) by starting your message with 'd', for example 'd paulbradshaw How are you?'. You can only send direct messages to people who are following you.

When you join Twitter you can 'follow' as many other users as you like. This means that you see what they are tweeting about. Likewise, others can choose to follow you, and these are called your 'followers'.

for all of that and, indeed, it will enliven your blog if you mix it up a bit every now and then by experimenting with a different form.

Likewise, it is a good strategy to work beyond the borders of your blog, and have a presence on other websites such as YouTube, Flickr, Seesmic, Facebook, LinkedIn, Delicious or Digg, and of course Twitter.

Microblogging and Twitter

The biggest change in blogging in the past few years has been the rise of microblogging and the microblogging platform Twitter.

Microblogging is ultra-short blogging, typically restricted to 140 characters per entry – the length of a standard text message. For this reason it is perfectly suited to headline alerts, mobile phone journalism, short messages and quick publishing from places that have slow or no internet access (you can generally microblog via text message).

Almost all major organisations have a Twitter feed publishing their headlines, and a significant number of journalists use the platform as well. Some news websites, such as *The New York Times*, publish a directory of where you can find their journalists on Twitter, while publications such as *MediaWeek* maintain a public directory of all journalists on Twitter.

For journalists there are advantages to microblogging. Unlike most blogging platforms, services like Twitter allow you to see who is 'following' you (and who they are following), making it part-social network. This makes it particularly useful for making contacts.

Because of its short form it is ideal for posting updates on your work, asking questions and inviting suggestions from readers. And because of its ease of use and flexibility, it is perfect for getting quick updates from others in your field about what is happening, spotting potential stories or finding contributors in particular locations or industries.

Twitter for news gathering

While news brands typically use Twitter as a basic headline syndication service, some individual programme teams such as the Channel 4 newsroom and Radio 4's PM use the medium in a much more conversational way, giving early indications of running orders and guests, providing behind-the-scenes insights, answering followers' questions and inviting contributions.

Journalists' use of the platform tends to be more sophisticated. Twitter users such as the *Liverpool Post & Echo*'s Alison Gow and *The Telegraph*'s Iain Douglas talk about the stories they're working on, ask for help when they need a quick answer to a question, and help others where they can. In between, they might pepper their updates with useful links and personal comments.

The more people you follow on Twitter, the more likely you are to come across a lead or a useful contact. When China experienced an earthquake in 2008, for example, US blogger Robert Scoble – who follows over 20,000 people on Twitter – knew about it before any US news organisation, and began blogging about what was happening.

To begin finding people on Twitter to follow, search Twitter for people you know, or know of, in your field (there are also Twitter directories like Twellow.com). All the major political parties have their own Twitter accounts, for example, as do some politicians. The service is used by people from every sphere of life, including celebrities, sportspeople, organisations, musicians and, of course, journalists and PR people. But beware of hoaxers.

Look at who those people are following and who they're talking to (if a message begins with @ it is directed at the name following the @ sign). You can also use search.twitter.com to search for people who are talking about particular things, or search within particular areas (Twitterlocal will also help you find twitterers in your local area).

Once you've chosen a few people to follow there are other services (such as Twubble, WhoShouldIFollow.com and Twits Like Me) that will suggest new people to follow based on the words in your profile, what you post about, and who you follow.

It is best to start with following a few people and add a few more every day, following conversations, contributing to them, and posting your own experiences and links (as mentioned earlier, a post to Twitter is called a 'tweet'). The only real way to understand Twitter and microblogging is to get in there and see how people use it.

Once you're following a large number of people, it will be useful to create some filters to help manage the incoming information. Although you can use Twitter's webpage to follow people, there are applications which are much more effective if you want to do more.

There are desktop applications (such as Tweetdeck, Tweetie and Seesmic Desktop) which will give you an audio alert when someone replies to you or sends a direct message (DM) and will make it easier for you to forward tweets ('retweet'). Many also allow you to filter your tweets (for keywords for instance) or set up separate groups of Twitter users that you can follow in separate columns. If you're using Twitter on a mobile phone there are mobile-friendly sites like Slandr, Tweete and Twitstat Mobile that make it easier to read, post and retweet on the move.

For more general monitoring of the whole of Twitter, there are web-based Twitter interfaces such as Twitterfall and Monitter that allow you to set up searches and watch them on screen in real time. And there are services such as Twitturly and TwitterBuzz that pick out the most popular links being shared on Twitter at any one time – when a major story breaks this can be a useful way of picking out the useful material.

Twitter for news publishing, distribution and creation

Most news organisations have separate Twitter accounts for different sections, such as business, traffic and sports, but the real advantage is in how specific you can be: you can set up specific Twitter accounts for individual events, stories or issues. Many of these accounts use a service like Twitterfeed or Pingvine, which simply pull any specified RSS feed and republish the first 140 characters of new updates to a Twitter account, with a link to the full article. This is an obvious use of Twitter, but not one that utilises its main qualities: its social aspect and its speed.

Closer look Major moments in journo-blogging history

1998: The Drudge Report breaks the Monica Lewinsky story. While Drudge says his site is not a blog, it demonstrated how the nimbleness of an online operation could scoop the mainstream media.

2001: September 11 attacks: while news websites collapse under the global demand, a network of blogs passes on news and lists of survivors.

2002: US Senator Trent Lott forced to resign after apparently pro-segregationist statements made at an event and initially ignored by mainstream media were picked up and fleshed out by bloggers.

2003: Invasion of Iraq: Salam Pax, the 'Baghdad Blogger', posts updates from the city as it is bombed, providing a particular contrast to war reporters 'embedded' with the armed forces and demonstrating the importance of non-journalist bloggers.

2003: Christopher Allbritton raises $15,000 through his blog Back-to-Iraq 3.0, to send him to report independently from the war, demonstrating the ability of blogs to financially support independent journalism (called the 'tip-jar model').

2004: Rathergate/Memogate: CBS's 60 Minutes broadcasts a story about George W. Bush's National Guard service, and within minutes a section of the blogosphere mobilises to discredit the documents on which it is based. Dan Rather eventually resigns as a result.

2004: Asian Tsunami: more blogs mobilise around a disaster, of particular significance for video blogging.

2005: July 7 bombings, London: mobile phone image of passengers walking along a Tube tunnel posted on MoBlog and *The Sun*, and goes global from there. A significant moment in moblogging.

2006: The Pulitzer Prize for Public Service cites the blog run by the *The Times – Picayune* in New Orleans during Hurricane Katrina. The flexibility of blogs during a disaster which stopped printing presses and delivery trucks was driven home.

2007: Talking Points Memo blog breaks story of US lawyers being fired across the country, demonstrating the power of involving readers in an investigation, and carrying it out in public.

2007: Dave Winer wins his $2,000 bet (made in 2002) that blogs will rank higher than the *New York Times* for the top five news stories of 2007, demonstrating the importance of blogging in news distribution.

2007: Myanmar protests: the clampdown that followed democratic protests in to the country was seen around the world thanks to blogging, moblogging and social networking sites. Journalists were not allowed into the country. Even after the government cut off the internet, bloggers located outside the country continued to post material.

2008: Peter Hain resigns over donations revealed by UK political blogger Guido Fawkes, who in 2006 also broke a story on an affair by Deputy Prime Minister John Prescott which he claimed lobby correspondents were sitting on.

2008: Chinese earthquake: a key moment for microblogging, as news of the earthquake spreads on Twitter (and Chinese IM service QQ) more quickly than on any official channels.

2008: Collapse of Northern Rock: BBC correspondent Robert Peston breaks one of the biggest stories of the year – not on TV, but on his blog.

As an individual journalist it is better to tweet before you even write the article – ensuring you get the 'scoop' and, equally important, get to the top of Google for a relevant search quickly, as *Birmingham Post* editor Marc Reeves did when he tweeted the arrest of Birmingham City director Karren Brady (she was later released without charge).

Twitter is particularly useful for journalists reporting live: you simply send a text message to Twitter and it is published on your Twitter page. Sky's Julia Reid used it, for example, to post 'minute-by-minute' experiences at Heathrow's Terminal 5, while journalist Robert LaHue used it 'to semi-liveblog a board meeting via texting', and it is often used at conferences and events too (an increasing number of conferences display tweets live on a big screen). If you feel limited by text there are also services that allow you to post images, audio and video to Twitter, such as TwitPic, Audioboo and Twiddeo.

However, Twitter becomes really impressive when you tap into its social, conversational nature – or combine the RSS feeds from a number of twitterers.

Shawn Smith, for example, used it to create the Michigan Twitter Network, which follows more than 1,300 Michigan twitterers. He says: 'We've gained about 200+ followers and use [another] account to send breaking news alerts and also poll users'. In Spain, ADN.es used it to follow voter reactions during a televised presidential candidate debate on TV. During the Mumbai terrorist attacks the BBC included a live feed of Mumbai tweets, and there have been numerous other experiments with using Twitter to monitor traffic congestion and voting intentions.

Ultimately, like blogging, Twitter is simply a platform – the really interesting stuff starts when you try something completely new.

Blogging and Really Simple Syndication (RSS)

Any journalist operating online should understand RSS. RSS stands for Really Simple Syndication and simply means that the content of a website can be syndicated and read anywhere else, by creating an RSS 'feed'.

It is similar in many ways to the newswire system, which allows news organisations around the world to receive a feed from news agencies such as Reuters or Associated Press. The key difference is that it doesn't cost anything to subscribe to a feed, or to produce one. In fact, almost every blog has an RSS feed built in. You don't have to do anything as a publisher to create one.

Subscribing to RSS feeds

One of the basic tools in any online journalist's toolkit is the RSS reader. This piece of software – which can be web-based or on your desktop – allows the journalist to subscribe to a number of RSS feeds and read them all on a single page, rather than visiting each site individually to check whether they have been updated.

There are dozens of RSS readers, but probably the most widely used is Google Reader, which presents the first-time user with a tutorial explaining how it works.

Where to find RSS feeds

The simplest way to find an RSS feed in readers like Google Reader is to click on 'Add a subscription' and search for it. A search for 'BBC Bolton Wanderers', for example, will bring up the RSS feed for all Bolton Wanderers stories on the BBC, as well as a few related blogs.

To subscribe to a feed and receive updates in your RSS reader, just click the 'Subscribe' button under the relevant result.

Alternatively, you can click on 'Add a subscription' and type the web address (URL) of the site you want to subscribe to. The reader will detect any RSS feeds on that page and either subscribe to it, or present a number to choose from.

If the RSS feed you're looking for isn't found, then you will have to find it and enter it manually.

Links to RSS feeds are often indicated by an orange icon like the one shown here.

RSS feed icon

However, if you click on one of these icons you're likely to get a page of impenetrable code, or an error message from your browser. This is because, unlike RSS readers, many browsers don't understand how to read RSS. If you need to copy an RSS feed link, then, it is best to right-click on the RSS feed image and select 'Copy link' or something similar.

Once you've copied the address of the RSS feed you can paste it into your RSS reader's 'Add a subscription' box to subscribe to it.

Note that many sites offer a range of RSS feeds from general news to specific sections and specific stories. You can also often find RSS feeds for all comments or comments on specific stories. Press offices and websites for the media increasingly offer RSS feeds too.

It is not just news websites and blogs that offer RSS feeds. You can get an RSS feed for any individual user of Twitter, for instance, as well as a feed of their favourite tweets. If you use Twitter yourself you can go to your profile page and get an RSS feed of the updates of everyone you follow, or an RSS feed of any @replies sent to you.

Video services like YouTube and Vimeo are riddled with RSS feeds. Feeds you can subscribe to on YouTube's homepage include the top-rated videos, top favourites, most viewed, most discussed, recently updated and recently added. But these are most likely to be too generic to be of journalistic interest. More usefully, if you go to an individual user's page on YouTube you can subscribe to a feed of just their videos; and on an individual video's page you can subscribe to a feed of related videos.

There are RSS feeds all over image-sharing services such as Flickr, from a specific user's photos, to your friends' photos, through to all public photos, as well as forums, comments and photo pools.

Social bookmarking services also have lots of RSS feeds. Delicious has feeds for recent bookmarks, for the most popular bookmarks, or for recent bookmarks with a particular tag (e.g. 'Birmingham' or 'recycling'). You can subscribe to a feed of an individual user's bookmarks, or of their bookmarks with particular tags or combinations of tags. Also, if you are using Delicious yourself, you can create a network of other users and subscribe to a feed of everything they are bookmarking.

Finally, event listing services like Upcoming and Eventbrite also have RSS feeds, so you can subscribe to a feed of events in any local area.

All of this is not just useful in terms of receiving updates yourself, but also because you can republish any of the above RSS feeds on your blog as a widget.

Using RSS feeds as a publisher

As a publisher the first thing you need to make sure is that your RSS feed is clearly visible. In WordPress, for example, you will need to log in, go to the Widgets section, and drag the 'RSS Links' widget on to your sidebar.

More creatively, if you do the same with the 'RSS' widget you'll see a box appear where you can put any RSS feed. This allows you to display headlines in your sidebar from any RSS feed.

Closer look Making money from blogging

Many people start blogging with dreams of making lots of money, and the vast majority end up disappointed. Although some blogs are profitable, and some bloggers make small amounts of money, they are very much in the minority: it is very, very hard indeed to make money from blogging alone.

Advertising can make you money as a blogger, but you will need thousands of visitors every month before you can even generate enough ad revenue to pay for a week's food. Ad services bloggers can sign up to a range from Google's AdSense, which pays notoriously little, to ad networks and tools such as Addiply, which allows advertisers to buy advertising on your site directly. Affiliate schemes (where you mention products with a link to an online shop and take a cut every time someone makes a purchase) can add to that, but again it takes large numbers of visitors to make it profitable.

Most bloggers benefit from their blog indirectly: through payments for public speaking, consultancy work, book publishing or freelance journalism. Some organise events. In short, if money is your motivation, you will need to be adaptable, entrepreneurial, hard-working – and very, very patient.

Summary

The growth of blogging is a fascinating development in the history of journalism – and it is by no means over. Histories of new media indicate that it typically takes around 30 years before new technologies reach maturity – and blogs have barely finished their first decade. Just as mainstream and alternative publishers have adopted and adapted the form, and new technologies such as Twitter have transformed its possibilities, we can expect 'blogging' to continue to develop as people and organisations innovate with the platform – including commercialising it – and technologists develop new platforms with new possibilities for blogging.

You are in the rare position of being able to contribute to that development, just as early users of radio, television and print helped develop the languages of their media with innovations such as the package, the close-up, and the inverted pyramid. Blogging's first decade has taught us lots of lessons: the platform is especially suited to informal, conversational and incomplete forms of journalism, and has important potential for professional development, commercial advantage and editorial improvement. We have seen particular types of journalism blog becoming generic – such as the 'link blog', which consists entirely of links, the niche blog covering a topic too narrow for a mainstream publication, and blogs that reflect on the inner workings of our craft so that we might make a better job of it.

Blogging journalists have learned that successful blogging means looking further than the blog itself – to community and conversation: commenting on and linking to other blogs. And they have learned to link their blogs to their presence elsewhere on the web, from photo and video sharing websites to social networks and Twitter. In print and broadcast we left distribution to the paperboys and schedulers – but online it is our responsibility to distribute ourselves; to be social networkers.

Finally, new blogging platforms like Twitter have introduced a whole new set of options allowing us to more easily follow what people are talking about, access eyewitnesses and experts, and publish instantly from hard-to-reach places.

Blogging's first decade has taught us lots of lessons, but there are as yet no rules. Blogging is, above all, simply a platform for you to do what you wish with. It is a perfect place for experimentation, to discover what works – and what doesn't. Start a blog – now. And try something you haven't tried before.

Activities

Brainstorm ideas for the following

- A blog in a specialist area – does anything else cover this? Could you pick a more specific niche?
- Five posts for a 'behind the scenes' blog that reflects on your work as a journalist
- A 'running story' blog – what challenge could you accept?

Use a blog search engine to find ten blogs in your area

Post comments on those blogs. Make contact with the authors – they will probably have a presence on a social network such as Facebook, MySpace or Twitter. Write a blog post talking about your experiences of joining that community – what can they teach you? Who has been helpful?

Start a Twitter account and use it to do the following

- Conduct an interview via 'tweets'
- Post updates on your progress with a story and invite answers to questions
- Cover a live event

Further reading

Blood, R. (2006). *Weblogs: A History and Perspective, Rebecca's Pocket*, 07 September 2000, 25 October 2006, http://www.rebeccablood.net/essays/weblog_history.html

Geary, J. (2009) 'An Interview with an anonymous blog commenter', March 3, 2009, http://www.joannageary.com/2009/03/03/n-interview-with-an-anonymous-blog-commenter/

Gillmor D. (2004) *We the Media: Grassroots Journalism by the People, for the People*, USA: O'Reilly Media.

Rosenberg, S. (2009) *Say Everything: How Blogging Began, What It's Becoming, and Why It Matters*, USA: Crown Publishers.

Argo Project: Dark Secrets of Blogging: http://argoproject.org/blog/?tag=dark-secrets

Chapter 7

Podcasts and audio slideshows

This chapter will cover:

- What is a podcast?
- Closer look: Why are podcasts so popular?
- Audio formats and kit
- Ideas and planning
- Closer look: Tips for perfect audio
- Interviews and discussions
- Editing
- Publishing
- Audio slideshows

Introduction

Podcasts allow everyone, not just journalists, to broadcast or blog out loud. Before the web, journalists who recorded interviews were aware that much of the value of a story had been left on tape or cut in the transcription process. Radio journalists instinctively know that the value of audio storytelling is often in who is saying what and how they are saying it as well as the environment in which they are saying it. The intimacy and the authenticity of the 'voice' often get lost in print but can be found on radio – and on the web via audio clips and podcasts.

Online audio in the form of a podcast can be downloaded on to an MP3 player and can come in many forms – interviews, discussions, news packages, blogs, information guides, sport, comedy and music. Podcasts allow people to listen on demand when and where they want to, whether it is direct from their computer or via an MP3 player as they make their way in to work. They can be a compelling, episodic feature on a website, a stand-alone audio story, a debate, a video podcast or vodcast, part of a package or subscription service which allows them to listen on a daily, weekly or monthly basis. The portable nature of the podcast means people like to listen when it is convenient for them – on the bus, in the car, jogging, at work. And they can always rewind at the push of a button.

Millions now access music via a service such as iTunes. Downloads have spurred consumer habits and digital dexterity. Initial scepticism about audio on the web subsided after the popularity of podcasts grew in the mid-noughties following Apple's inclusion of a podcast directory in its iTunes store. Online journalists soon found readers wanted to listen in. Audio clips could be embedded into a story alongside pictures and text, as part of an interactive feature, and sites could live stream audio so people could listen online. More recently, audio has become integrated with social media sites such as Facebook and Twitter: published and 'shared' with a single click – finding the listener rather than the reverse.

The choice of podcasts continues to expand and most of them are still free. Whether listeners will want to subcribe and pay for them in the future is part of the digital debate about how web services can pay their way. The phenomenal success of Ricky Gervais' comedy podcast on guardian.co.uk, which was initially free on the website, was soon translated into a commercial success via iTunes. Digital journalists might not have his Hollywood status but can still learn lessons in terms of providing fresh, original audio.

Source: Alamy Images/David J Green

What is a podcast?

A podcast is a digital audio file that can be distributed over the internet. The term is a hybrid of 'iPod' and 'broadcast' but you do not need an iPod to play a podcast. Any modern computer will allow you to download a podcast, and any portable MP3 player will play them. Radio shows are often available in this format but podcasts can cover any topic, are not restricted in terms of style and length and can be created by journalists and non-journalists alike. They can be posted directly to a website but also made available via subscription to an RSS feed. This allows subscribers to check their RSS reader for new podcasts in the same way they might subscribe to text-based content. For example, a radio station might create a

Closer look Why are podcasts so popular?

Iain Hepburn

'Go back a couple of years, and there was a godawful advert for Radio 1, featuring all the DJs at the time on some weird, computer-generated glowing neon platform. Among them was Colin Murray, who said of music: "I listen to new stuff, and it goes in there (indicates ear) and it goes in there (indicates other ear), and as long as it makes a connection there (indicates heart), I play it".

'That's why podcasts have been so successful.

'Audio is an incredibly raw, visceral medium. It's intimate, yet capable of achieving untold scale, because it relies on a connection with the listener's brain. Be it a show about music, movies, parenting or politics, for a podcast to work it has to connect the listener on some level. This isn't the same as radio, where you can have it on as aural wallpaper in the background and forget about it if needs be. People actively choose to seek out and listen to podcasts. So there must be some kind of engagement, of connection, with the audience member that they want to listen.

'It could be as simple as the sort of blokey banter you'd get down the pub with your mates, or a presenter you really like. It could be a subject matter you find fascinating. Whatever it is, it's a niche – the listener's niche. And these days we're forever being told that niche platforms are the way forward.

'As with most aspects of the media, the modern internet has democratised the sharing and production of information. The days when radio, like video and writing, was the preserve of mainstream broadcasters and journalists is long past. The widely available tools and platforms allow anyone to make their own radio show. If you look at the most successful and popular shows on iTunes, they're rarely from a mainstream outlet – shows such as the Football Ramble or Answer Me This loom large over the charts compared to pods from the *Guardian* or the *FT*.

'That's not to say those pods don't have legitimacy – far from it, they're equally finding a niche audience and giving a voice to some of the names previously only seen in bylines.'

Iain Hepburn, Digital Editor of *Scottish Daily Record* www.iainhepburn.com

weekly sports podcast, upload it to their website, give it an RSS feed and make it available independently to directories such as iTunes or PodcastAlley.com so that listeners can get automatic updates.

Audio formats and kit

Online journalists can use audio in a number of ways:

- as a stand-alone story (such as an interview);
- embedded clips to enliven and break up text-based stories;
- as part of a picture story or audio slideshow;
- as a podcast which people can download;
- as an audio 'stream' (listened to via the internet without downloading it).

However, first you need to understand formats as this may influence your choice of kit.

Once an audio file has been created it needs to be saved in a compressed audio file format (this is normally done when you click 'Save' or 'Export' in your editing package, and select a file type). The 'compressed' bit means that it will load faster when it is published on the internet (and it takes up less space on your device). The MP3 format is popular with journalists and end-users familiar with audio player programs such as Real Player, iTunes and Windows Media. Other formats available include WAV, AIFF, MPEG-4 and WMA.

For journalists who like a 'belt and braces' approach it is a good idea to save recordings in a WAV file. This is a larger, uncompressed file but it is much faster and easier to edit. You can save your WAV master copy and export your edited version as an MP3 file.

What kit do I need?

With so much equipment on the market the decision may come down to budget and how much audio needs to be recorded. A beginner needs to keep it simple: a digital recorder (make sure it saves files as WAV, WMA or MP3) with at least 20 hours of storage capacity and a USB port to transfer files.

Most have an in-built microphone but to guarantee good quality audio you need to hear accurately what you are recording and editing. A microphone and headphones are essential – while you are interviewing someone you might not be aware of a clicking noise or a door slam but it will become very apparent in the editing process. The cheaper the recorder, the more hiss and hum on your recording if you don't use a microphone.

Most digital recorders have the basics such as a record, play, stop, rewind and delete button, and allow the user to set the date and time. At the more professional end of the spectrum they can also allow the journalist to separate audio clips and determine the correct sound levels. Audio is stored on the hard drive of the recorder and transferred when you plug it into a computer although some recorders use memory cards which also need a memory card reader to transfer files to the computer.

A good recorder will allow you to attach an external microphone but there are also hand-held wireless mics which are useful when conducting more than one face-to-face interview. A wireless lavalier mic, commonly used during video presentations, can be clipped on to a jacket and dispenses with the need for a hand-held mic – particularly useful when the person being recorded is demonstrating something or is on the move.

Micropodcasting: an easier way to capture and upload audio

For those new to audio the easiest way to start is by experimenting with micropodcasting – short segments of audio recorded via a mobile phone, ideal for blogs. There are several tools, depending on what kind of mobile phone you have, which you can download and which allow the user to upload micropodcasts to sites such as Audioboo and Posterous, distributed via Twitter, Facebook and other social media.

Audioboo is a free application popular with iPhone users (and also available on Android phones). It allows five minutes of audio to be recorded via your phone which you upload to your account (other features are available on Pro accounts). Recording a 'boo' takes only a few minutes and blog services such as WordPress have plugins which allow you to embed your micropodcasts into posts. It is a good way to practise interviews, record particular sounds and 'find' your podcast voice while keeping content short and sharp within the restricted time period.

Some established journalists have become vocal fans of micropodcasting, including the BBC's Rory Cellan-Jones, Tim Bradshaw of the *Financial Times*, and BBC London, which uses it widely (hear examples at http://audioboo.fm/BBCLondon949). It lends itself particularly well to short off-the-cuff interviews, personal reflections on something you've just seen or reported on, and even simply ambient sounds that give an aural impression of the place you're reporting from – such as street sounds, chatter, or the clanking of an old machine.

An interesting idea for regular micropodcasts can work well, too. Chris Marquardt uses the service to provide regular photography tips, while Mary Hamilton spends her walk home from the newsroom recording a podcast about her day. One person came up with the idea for 'First Pages' (http://audioboo.fm/tag/firstpages) – inviting other users to read out the first page of a book they particularly like.

Christian Payne, a mobile journalist who regularly uses Audioboo, feels there are no hard and fast rules on what makes a popular 'Boo'.

> It all depends on what audience you want to engage. 'On the whole I find short soundbites are more welcomed than long ones. If you have to edit the podcast, a top "n" tail should be more than enough for a micropodcast. It should all be about ease of posting and the immediacy of it going live. A non edited piece of audio sounds more intimate and less premeditated "programmed".'

Christian also feels the unpredictability and flexibility of the medium can be its strength:

> 'More importantly than anything (in my opinion) I feel a micropodcast should be and could be anything from one episode or boo to the next. It is the element of "anything could happen next" that keeps me subscribed to the boos I listen to. I want to be taken to new places, though not on any scheduled flight – more of a magical mystery tour.
>
> 'We have production studios in our pockets and they go with us everywhere. Why create a studio environment when there are so many great places/sounds/conversations/situations and moments to share?'

Ideas and planning

A podcast can be about anything at all. It can be an interview, a series of vox pops, a discussion, a guide, expert advice or just a way to blog out loud. It can be pegged to a news piece or be an online extra as part of a package of links about the same subject. It can vary in length from a couple of minutes to an hour. The best way to get ideas is to think about what your target audience would like and the stories and issues that interest them. Try out ideas on friends and family – and ask readers to send you comments and feedback. And make sure you listen to lots of podcasts from a range of sources with a critical ear before setting out to create one.

Play to your strengths and to the interests of your potential listeners. For example: BBC Manchester has a News on the Run feature updated at 6 am every morning which gives a heads-up on news, sport, money, entertainment, traffic and weather for people to take to the gym. Telegraph.co.uk provides reviews, interviews and music in its weekly entertainment podcast The Cut.

Once you have come up with an idea ask yourself:

- What does the listener get out of this?
- Who would subscribe to this?
- Would it stretch to a weekly podcast feature?
- How long should it be?
- How much preparation and research is needed?

Closer look Tips for perfect audio

- Set off with a clear set of objectives – a shopping list – which will make it easier to edit. If you head out without a clear idea of what you want you'll come back with far too much audio and risk missing the point of the piece.
- Strong audio clips featuring good quotes stand out a mile but make a note while conducting interviews to save time before the edit.
- Always ask for feedback, whether it's a package or a report.
- Take time to listen to how other journalists produce podcasts.
- Aim to be original, and to stay out of your comfort zone.
- Don't be afraid of mistakes – just make sure you learn from them.

Sian Grzeszczyk, Correspondent for BBC Radio Coventry and Warwickshire

Once you are satisfied with the answers to these questions you need to think about practicalities such as equipment and the environment you will be recording in. Always test your equipment before going out in the field and just before you start to record. And make sure you have pressed the 'on' button to record – it might sound obvious but when under pressure this is the most common mistake. Some media outlets have their own studios but those without that luxury need to make sure recording is done in a designated quiet area. Out and about, environmental noise such as the sound of traffic or wind can detract from the quality of audio, so be selective about the type of microphone you use and the location. Remember to always carry a notepad and pen – note names, places, spellings and 'killer quotes' that you might want to use as a taster audio clip.

Interviews and discussions

Podcasts can have a relaxed, accessible style but when it comes to interviews the journalistic rules of good research and accurate, fair questioning apply. It is not necessary or advisable to give an interviewee a list of questions (the result will be stilted and sound rehearsed) but you can give them a general idea of topics to be covered. If they are particularly nervous of being recorded, you might give them a quick trial run for the first question. Be clear about the narrative of your story and the order of your questions while following up on answers that beg further investigation.

When recording an interview:

- Keep control of the microphone.
- Don't rustle papers.
- Keep eye contact with your interview subject.
- Keep questions short – try not to ask 'closed' questions that will elicit 'yes' or 'no' answers.
- If they get tongue-tied or make a mistake, record that segment again.
- If you want to keep out of the interview, don't interrupt, mumble, sigh, laugh out loud or say 'ok' or 'mmmmm, I see'. These can be edited out but it makes the process more time consuming.

Listen to:

- Media Talk at guardian.co.uk/audio
- The Cut at telegraph.co.uk/telegraphtv
- The Game at timesonline.co.uk/podcasts
- Best of Today at bbc.co.uk/podcasts
- Gadgets and technology at stuff.tv
- The Economist at economist.com
- Answer Me This at answermethispodcast.com
- Hillsborough: Twenty Years On at realradionorthwest.co.uk
- Hackney Podcast at hackneypodcast.co.uk
- The Onion at theonion.com/audio
- Slideshows at guardian.co.uk/audioslideshows
- More podcasts at podcastalley.com
- and via your mobile phone at twitter.com/podsformobs

For discussions, be clear about the rules of engagement. These can be lively, engaging podcasts, such as *The Guardian*'s weekly Media Talk, but they are also difficult to produce and can lead to a 'zoo radio' effect with participants talking over each other and raising their voices. Be clear about who is hosting the talk and introducing guests, what subjects will be covered and the general length of answer you expect from guests to prevent them monopolising the discussion. It is advisable for the host to agree a signal such as a raised hand to indicate to someone that they need to come to the end of their sentence.

While it is not necessary to follow a script like a live radio show it is a good idea to make notes and craft an introduction, cues to different subjects and lines that would help to round up the podcast. Always remember the listener and talk to them directly. Ask them to share their reactions and ideas across relevant online platforms: your site, forums, blog, Facebook page, Twitter account, or anywhere else. This should be a two-way process: online feedback could give you ideas for the next podcast. Name those who have contributed responses and seek out and engage with listeners – this will guard against podcasts that sound indulgent and smug.

Editing

Before editing your podcast it is worth reviewing all your audio and checking any notes you made along the way. It is essential you do this first, particularly if you have several audio projects on the go or if you have left a gap between the recording and editing process.

Several software programs are available to journalists. The most popular include Audacity®, GarageBand and Adobe Audition. Audacity is a free software program which is easy to install and good for beginners. It allows you to record directly from your computer – which is a good place to start for those with little experience who want to practise basic skills such as recording, deleting, cutting and moving around audio clips. Audacity is a drag-and-drop program which can import WAV, AIFF, AU, IRCAM and MP3 files and works with Windows and Mac computers. It also comes with a series of step-by-step tutorials for the novice. GarageBand (for Macs) is for the more experienced podcaster and offers more features such as the ability to add music and special effects.

Once you have connected your recorder to your computer, keep copies of your audio files in one folder. When you import your files into a program such as Audacity you will get what is called a 'timeline' which indicates the sequence of your audio and tracks that contain audio clips. There are many tools to allow you to add, overlap and fade between clips. When you are starting out it is a good idea to follow a linear narrative – editing, cutting and pasting your clips in order. You can always leave gaps at the beginning and at the end if you want to add anything such as an introduction, music or another type of clip. If you make a complete hash of it, start over again – that's why you need to keep a copy in your folder.

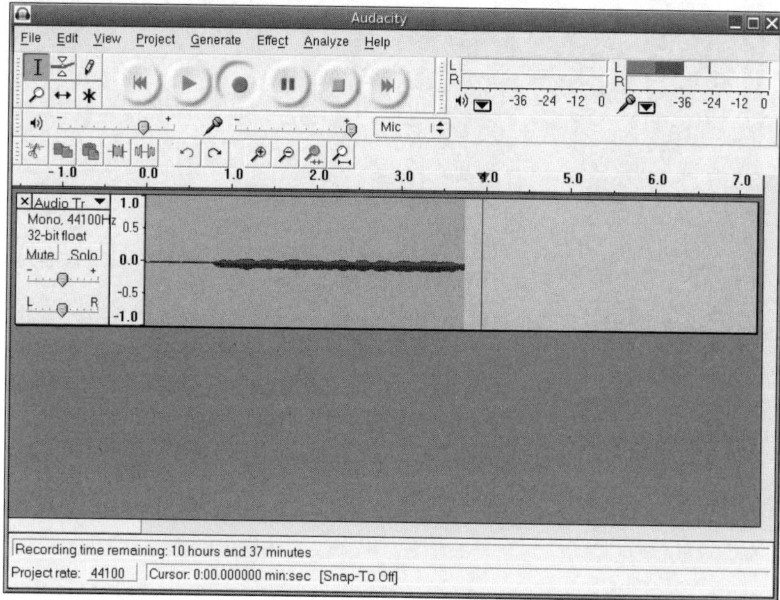

Recording with Audacity

Audacity software is copyright 1999–2011 Audacity Team

When editing, remember the following advice:

- Cut with care – be fair and balanced.
- Don't cut the context of a quote.
- Don't cut the character of the piece – a pause or a stumble may be telling.
- Cut out blips such as coughs, hisses and interjections from the interviewer.
- Select the introductory audio to give meaning to the piece; don't puzzle the listener.
- If music is used, make sure it does not intrude on audio or is likely to annoy the listener.
- Most music is copyrighted in some way. Make sure you know what sort of copyright covers the music (music over 100 years old, for example, may be copyright-free; other music is available for non-commercial use). Try asking an up-and-coming band for permission to use a clip of their music – you can link to their site or MySpace.
- 'Sell' your audio online with good headlines and explanatory text.

Publishing

To publish audio on the web you need to save it in an audio file format such as MP3. In Audacity, for example, you can export the file as an MP3 file and upload to the web host, which will give you the URL address (but first you have to install something called a LAME encoder to complete this process). Most content management systems and blog software will allow you to upload your audio file which will then embed it in an audio player.

Audio and video via the BBC iPlayer

Source: bbc.co.uk/iplayer

If you use Posterous, for example, you can simply email your audio to post@posterous.com and it will be published on your blog as an embedded audio player.

A podcast needs to be made available via an RSS feed so that listeners can subscribe to it and are alerted to fresh content. Blogging software such as WordPress has tools to enable you to do this and there are free services such as podbean.com to which you can upload your podcast and get an RSS feed address. If you're using a blog you can also use Feedburner to create a podcast feed from the blog's RSS feed.

Think creatively about the title and description of your podcast – make it short and snappy if it is a regular podcast and remember to use descriptive keywords to help people find your podcast via search engines. You are then ready to submit your feed to directories such as iTunes, Zune and Podcastalley.com. Another option is SoundCloud, which allows you and others to add comments and other information.

Audio slideshows

Pictures accompanied by sound can be a compelling feature on a website. Audio slideshows can come in different forms: examples include Martin Argles' commentary on his 'behind the scenes' photographs taken for *The Guardian* during the 2010 UK election, and a series called One in 8 Million by nytimes.com, which used the form for stories about individual New Yorkers from rookie cops to mambo dancers.

Slideshows need to combine the best of photojournalism with the intimacy of audio reportage and allow the viewer to consider the images and voices without being distracted. A good example is a report at www.latimes.com/wounded which charted the progress of US soldiers on their return from Iraq. The first person testimony is complemented by pictures and allows the reader to take in a lot of information that might have been lost if they were diverted by video.

A strong subject is crucial to a good audio slideshow. Typically this will be someone with a powerful or fascinating personal story or, less often, a group of people whose collective experiences bring a subject to life. Vox pops, however, do not make very good audio slideshows.

Not all slideshows need audio. A striking set of pictures without a narrative attached to them has value as a picture gallery and is popular with readers, often garnering high traffic figures to a site. For example, a flower show will have stunning images but little in the way of a story. A story with history and context will need explaining and therefore commentary from a journalist or from the subjects in the story.

Exercise

Compare and contrast the treatment the BBC website gives to nature photographs submitted by readers and its slideshow on the Bloody Sunday killings in Northern Ireland which uses archive images and audio (search under slideshows at bbc.co.uk).

Also look up audio slideshows on YouTube, the video sharing site, for ideas and inspiration. Many of these have been submitted by people who are not journalists but are nevertheless of high quality.

Slideshow checklist

Journalists can take their own photographs and gather audio or work on audio in conjunction with a photographer. Pictures may also come from a number of sources including readers' submissions, or the subjects of audio slideshows themselves.

Once you have an idea consider the following aspects:

- Are the pictures likely to have visual appeal (the slideshow will suffer if images are weak or 'samey')?
- Remember pictures of people sell a story, portraits, close-ups.
- Capture ambient sound for atmosphere (use this to introduce and punctuate your package).
- Is there a strong narrative with a beginning, middle and end?
- Ask the subject to include your question in their answer – for instance, if you ask 'When was the first time you . . .?' their reply might begin 'The first time that I . . .' This allows you to let the subject tell their own story without including your questions.
- Think about what might be the first and last image.
- Are captions needed to give further information?
- Avoid over-use of literal imagery – e.g. showing a picture of money when the subject mentions 'money', etc.
- How long should it be? – three minutes is a good average to aim for.

Software for slideshows

Before the editing process, gather all your material and select the strongest images. Listen to the audio – you may need to go back to your first batch of pictures to select another image to illustrate a point.

There are many software programs available to create a slideshow including Final Cut, Windows Movie Maker and Apple iMovies. There are also online services like Vuvox and Flixtime. Many journalists use Soundslides because it is easy to use and lets them add headlines, captions and credits – and you don't need expertise in creating HTML and Flash files. You have to pay for it and download it from soundslides.com which has step-by-step tutorials on how to create a slideshow and embed it on your website.

Edited audio needs to be saved as an MP3 file before it can be imported into the program and photos need to be saved in a JPG file format. Soundslides puts your pictures on a timeline the same length as the audio and allows you to arrange them in order and decide the pace – remember the viewer needs time to take in what they are seeing and hearing. The program creates a folder which you can upload to your site or blog.

Narrative considerations

When you listen to a number of audio slideshows you will notice certain recurring structural characteristics. Often the package will begin with a few seconds of background noise ('wild track') to 'set the scene' before the subject introduces either themselves or the key narrative event that the audio slideshow is about. Imagery may mirror this – an establishing shot of the subject's environment followed by an image of the subject or event.

The story then begins in earnest, and when the first part is completed we may pause to shift focus for the second part, with an accompanying change in background noise. Further shifts in time, space or narrative might be accompanied by other sections of relevant audio and imagery. Eventually the narrative will end – typically with a strong quote and the background audio fading out.

These are not of course rules – and with confidence they are there to be broken – but they can serve as useful guides when starting out.

Summary

Podcasts and audio clips on the web are new story-telling techniques which add another dimension to multimedia journalism. Podcasts have become popular because of their portability and provide a challenge for journalists to create content that readers will want to subscribe to. They can be topical, informative and cover a variety of subjects and themes.

Creating audio needs time, patience and practice, especially for beginners unfamiliar with producing stories with sound using a variety of software programs. The journalistic principles of accuracy and balance apply in the editing process and it is important to get feedback from colleagues and listeners. Podcasts add value to a website as a stand-alone element or as part of a package of stories, but it is important to remember that they can be independently accessed from directories such as iTunes, so loyalty to one podcast may not translate to loyalty to a particular website. Conversely, a fan of your podcast is much more likely to check out your blog or site.

Audio stories can have elements of opinion, humour and music. It is important that journalists listen to podcasts by non-professionals or citizen journalists for new ways to present content. Reading out a column is not enough and can sound stilted and frankly old-fashioned. The challenge for journalists is to create compelling, original content and not be afraid to cut themselves out of the story completely and let people tell their own story.

Activities

1. **Visit a big event such as a music festival or demonstration**.
   - Interview participants.
   - Ask for tips on how to survive a festival.
   - Think about capturing the atmosphere through different clips of sound.
   - Get permission to record live music.
   - Prepare for the event beforehand by checking out the area and identifying good places to capture sound and images.
   - Capture images that will work well in a slideshow – close-up, colour, variety.
2. **Blog out loud**.
   - Give your reaction to a big news event.
   - Reflect on how news organisations are reporting it.
   - What did they get right? or wrong?
   - Don't record from a script but make notes of items you want to discuss.
3. **Create a series of micropodcast guides to your area.**
   - Research your local area.
   - Do weekly reports on local attractions, restaurants, bars and nightlife.
4. **Create your own online radio show.**
   - Sign up to www.blogtalkradio.com with a group of friends.
   - Listen to top-rated shows such as Mediabistro.
   - Come up with a title and a topic, such as sport, fashion, travel, music.
   - Record your show – and aim to get a special guest interview each week.

Further reading

BBC Editorial Guidelines, www.bbc.co.uk/editorialguidelines
Herrington, J.D. (2005) *Podcasting Hacks*, USA: O'Reilly Media.
Hudson, G. and Rowlands, S. (2007) *The Broadcast Journalism Handbook*, UK: Pearson.
Mills, J. (2004) *The Broadcast Voice*, UK: Focal Press.

Chapter 8

Video

This chapter will cover:

- What is online video journalism?
- Closer look: Story formats
- Quantity vs quality
- Closer look: How video journalists have covered the war in Afghanistan
- Kit and editing formats
- Editing software packages
- Closer look: How I shot the BP oil spill story
- Ideas and planning
- Shooting video
- Closer look: Tips for online video journalism
- Editing and publishing
- Closer look: Areas journalists should consider when posting video
- Closer look: Watch

Introduction

Video is not only integral to online storytelling – it is evolving as a form of online journalism in its own right. Journalists can write their story and embed video alongside it, or they can choose to produce video first and enhance it with text, pictures and links. They can upload it to their site, their blog, video sharing sites such as YouTube, and social networks such as Facebook. And it is not just journalists who produce video; anyone with a good mobile phone can shoot and edit video.

There is a wide audience for online video journalism. According to The Pew Internet and American Life Project more than half of US adults have used the internet to watch or download video. Its survey for 2009 found that news was the second most popular category after comedy. Consumers now expect to catch up with the news online, share and comment on video clips and search for eyewitness accounts from those who were first at the scene, whether they be trained journalists or citizen journalists.

Faster broadband connections, cheaper cameras, free editing software and the rise of sharing sites such as YouTube and Vimeo have spurred video production. Advances in technology mean quality has improved from a couple of years ago when images were blurry and choppy. Mobile phones and a new generation of light, cheap, hand-held devices give journalists the agility to respond quickly to breaking stories. Journalists use video to record events and interviews, and they can broadcast their blogs as vlogs (video blogs). They can borrow techniques from television journalism – and they can explore new techniques for a new medium, developing online video journalism further for platforms from laptops and phones to electronic readers such as the iPad.

Video can be a powerful means of communication whether it is shot by a professional or by a bystander. It can be the story or be used as part of a package of stories. A short piece of video embedded in text allows everyone to read a story, get the context and make up their own mind. Video obtained by *The Guardian* and released on YouTube, for example, showed the moment when Ian Tomlinson – who died during G20 protests in London – was assaulted by a police officer. It contradicted official reports of the moments leading up to his death and was a crucial piece of evidence in the subsequent investigation. Meanwhile, the news blackout in Iran following protests in 2009 did not stop individuals from blogging and uploading video to the blogosphere and across social networks such as Facebook. And while streamed coverage by mainstream news outlets of Barack Obama's inauguration were among the most watched events online, there was also demand to watch the unedited version of the US election by thousands of vloggers, such as those at www.jackandjillpolitics.com. Whether they are producing, commissioning or tracking video, the challenge for journalists is to use it effectively.

Online video journalists often work on their own reporting, filming, editing and uploading. They need to keep an eye on the story and be tenacious, focused, prepared and practical. They have to have the people skills to persuade others to go in front of the camera. Some work in teams and have colleagues to help them edit their stories but most of them work on their own.

What is online video journalism?

Online video journalism should not be thought of as 'television on the web.' Or, indeed, as a lesser form of storytelling, low on broadcast quality, self-consciously 'hip' or amateur in execution. While the content and format can be similar to traditional forms of broadcasting – whether it be news reports or interviews – it can also encompass innovative and creative ways of storytelling, a more documentary style or be a platform for opinion in the form of a video blog.

Video captured by a mobile phone might not be slick by broadcast television standards but should be judged on its merit. The viewer of eyewitness footage of disasters is not going to complain that a television crew could have done it better. Indeed, it is often the rawest, unedited coverage that has the most visceral impact on the viewer. Compare the YouTube footage of the death of Iranian protester 'Neda' with the same footage being replayed on broadcast news, for example: although the images are the same, broadcast production dilutes their impact.

At the other end of the spectrum, in highly edited online video you will often find long-form journalism not seen in broadcast media, with production techniques that owe more to film than to television. It seems that successful video online relies on immediacy and speed (raw footage) or quality and length (edited narratives), and not on studio broadcasts or television packages.

Good quality video is now easy to produce. Equipment has become more portable so that journalists do not need a crew. Videos can be published or streamed and distributed instantly to websites so that people can comment on them. They can be made available through an RSS feed, so users can subscribe to receive updates when a video is added.

Online video is, for some, a distinct form of storytelling that is intimate and interactive. For many video producers it is a chance to be more experimental, innovative, creative and investigative. While video can be seen in HD on a big screen and streamed online on a television it is still invariably an intimate medium. Unlike television, which is often watched in company, online video is usually watched while sitting at a computer or holding a phone or iPod.

For David Dunkley Gyimah, one of the first online video journalists in the UK, video journalism signals a revolution, an advance on television news production. His award-winning short documentary, *Video journalism – the UK Solojo Breakthrough* (view a clip at www.viewmagazine.tv) explores the early days of video, and is worth watching to find your feet in the medium.

Some journalists want to distance themselves from television altogether. 'Online video should not ape TV,' argues John Domokos of *The Guardian*. 'For a start, you have to imagine how the person in front of a computer is searching for it and looking at it – it might be in a small frame. It's a much more intimate environment. You have to grab their attention very quickly, in a few seconds.'

The pioneering video journalists of the 1980s and 1990s were the first to use lightweight cameras. Their template for storytelling was to get as close to the stories as possible, and to the people in them. This translates well online. One of them, Kevin Sites, a freelance reporter and so-called backpack journalist, travelled to war zones filming and transmitting his own reports to US networks. He has embraced the online medium, reporting on the Iraq conflict and collaborating with Yahoo! for Kevin Sites in the Hot Zone where his video reports and pictures can be viewed.

John Domokos

Many websites have adopted a documentary, feature style for their video output. The Lens section of nytimes.com is a multimedia section comprising video and photojournalism. Stories such as Soldiers in Crisis – about suicides in the US military – and Car Theft Secrets show the breadth of subjects video can cover.

Closer look Story formats

Video is used in various forms and formats online such as:

- news clips – often provided by agencies, mainstream broadcasters and sites such as YouTube;
- embedded video – a video player 'embedded' in a text article that enhances the story, e.g. a charity parachute drop;
- part of a news package – a video that could have narration, interviews, pictures and graphics to illustrate the story;
- guides – a 'how to' video, popular with magazine websites;
- vlogs – blogging to camera;
- streaming – live webcasts of events. Go to ustream.tv, Qik or Bambuser for free live streaming services;
- shows on internet channels such as Current TV;
- documentary features – see Vimeo's Documentary Film site for examples (vimeo.com/documentaryfilm);
- graphics, animation, video mashups and montages.

Local newspaper sites often prefer newsier angles focused on events, people and sport. The *Liverpool Echo* and the *Yorkshire Evening Post* have video covering football and horseracing. The journalists themselves can sometimes be the focal point in video blogs – as long as they have something interesting to say and a visual kicker. For example, cinema critic Mark Kermode does a twice weekly video blog for the BBC while the journalists at *Stuff* magazine blog about gadgets they are testing. The magazine industry in particular has taken strongly to video, with most large publishers having their own TV studios and many magazines posting video to branded video 'channels' on their own site and on YouTube. Video journalists need to think hard about which stories merit moving pictures and they need to be confident they have the right equipment and know how to use it properly. This needs a lot of practice.

Quantity vs quality

Many newsrooms in the last few years have grappled with commitment to investing in video, choosing to send untrained journalists out using point-and-shoot cameras with video. While the story idea might have been strong the quality inevitably varied, giving an impression of amateurism. For some local news sites video was about getting journalists to read the news from their desks rather than going out of the office to get stories. Professionally trained broadcasters who looked at online video produced by print journalists could be justifiably withering in their criticism of content that was an uncomfortable hybrid of regional television news and home movie.

Better, more affordable technology has raised standards in terms of quality. Grainy images and scratchy audio are now unacceptable. However, video journalism has become much more varied in scope as journalists – and non-journalists – experiment with the form. Photographers in particular, such as Sean Smith of *The Guardian*, are well versed in what makes a telling image

Closer look How video journalists have covered the war in Afghanistan

Watch *Vice* magazine's video series about Afghanistan at its site vbs.tv (you can get a flavour of its reporting style by its tagline 'Blowing the ass off the rest of the internet since the last decade').

Now compare it with a report from Helmand by Vaughan Smith at: frontlineclub.com/blogs/vaughan/, which was shown on Channel 4 News, and Sean Smith's story for guardian.co.uk at: www.guardian.co.uk/profile/seansmith, and Patrick Barth's video report on rescue units at: patrickbarth.com/film/dustoff-afghanistan/

All these video journalists have taken different approaches. Analyse these videos and ask the following questions:

1. Who tells the story?
2. What is the point of the story?
3. Why do you think they took this approach?

and have brought their own style to the form, while individuals such as Lauren Luke – whose YouTube makeup tips led to a regular spot in *The Guardian* – have demonstrated how well an informal, intimate style can build big audiences.

Kit and editing formats

Journalists can produce video with a digital video camera, a computer and editing software. It is also possible to capture video on the hoof using a mobile phone or phone-sized digital camcorder such as a Flip or one of the Kodak Zi series. If you are thinking of getting a new mobile phone for capturing video, look at factors such as image resolution, battery life and internet connectivity (if you are planning on streaming or uploading footage from the phone).

A basic camera will record, play back and have functions such as automatic focus. Those who want to produce work of a consistently high standard in terms of quality should also think about microphones, headphones and tripods – as well as a high resolution camera or high definition (HD) camera which will give a sharper image. Later versions of the iPhone, for example, allow the user to film in a form of HD, download software, edit packages and upload directly to YouTube.

There are many options when it comes to cameras, from the latest generation of HDSLRs (high definition single-lens reflex cameras) to pocket-sized cameras such as the Flip, which is popular with journalism students and reporters who want to capture interviews. Digital cameras record on to internal hard drive, tape, mini disc and memory card. Many of them have in-built features such as lights, microphones and the ability to shoot still pictures but the quality is variable. Make sure that the camera selected can be fitted with extra kit.

The following should be considered when producing high quality video for an online audience:

- An external microphone – there are various mics but start with one that clips to the camera. For interviews in a studio environment use a lavalier microphone. Some cameras come with AV (audio visual) in and out, but don't be fooled into thinking all AV sockets will allow you to record with a microphone.

- Headphones – always check audio levels (and they are a good reminder to 'listen' as you concentrate on shooting).
- Tripod – to keep the camera steady start small with something like a Gorilla tripod. The Flip camera comes with its own mini-tripod (you can even get an attachment for your bike).
- And . . . remember to pack lens cover, extra batteries and memory cards . . . and to switch on the camera!

Editing software packages

Popular editing programs are Windows Movie Maker, iMovie, Final Cut Pro, Final Cut Express, Avid Media Composer and Adobe Premiere Elements (or Pro). Movie Maker (on a PC) and iMovie (part of the bundle with Mac computers) are free video editing software and good for beginners. Many television journalists use Avid while Final Cut Pro is popular with documentary and independent film makers. These require more expertise as they have more effects and functionality.

The key factors to consider when deciding which software to use are what kind of computer you use, budget, expertise – and the kind of video journalism you will be producing. Video uses up a lot of memory and so you will need additional storage (portable hard drive) plus a high processor speed.

I'm just a beginner – what's the easiest way to get started?

Don't panic. Before you do anything, start recording video using your phone. Have some fun even if it is just taking some footage of your cat. Try not to bump into any walls. Then get someone to record you as you do a piece to camera, perhaps as an extra for your blog. Try to film yourself by holding the phone at arm's length, pointing at you. Knowing where to hold the camera is a skill in itself that you'll need to have learned if you ever come across something newsworthy and need to do a quick piece to camera.

Closer look How I shot the BP oil spill story

'I was on my own for the duration of the BP project. I started researching the story about two weeks before I went over there. I planned for seven or eight films on a variety of subjects around the impact of the spill. Most of these came off with the exception of the widow of one of the men killed in the initial explosion who declined to be interviewed. The fishermen who were unconcerned about the possible contamination of their fish were a lucky find who happened to be there when I was interviewing the sports fisherman about his loss of trade.

'When you are working on your own you need to prepare meticulously before you leave for the shoot. I phoned and emailed everyone to make arrangements but kept days and times flexible so I could move stuff around and get interviews I hadn't planned on. I never storyboard my work, I prefer to write interview questions which I then use to structure the video content.

'You have to leave adequate time for editing the footage you have shot. All eleven videos were shot, edited and published over the eight-day period I was in Louisiana so I was shooting during the day and editing at night. You have to be persistent and determined as only you know how hard you've pushed for a story so skiving is easy but you'll know if you did it.

▶

'It can get very stressful and lonely when you are on the road putting it all together on your own so have a support network of friends and family you can call/email to complain or celebrate during the shoot.

'As for kit, I used a Sony V1 with shotgun mic and wind shield for the majority of the filming. I also used Sennheiser EW 100 radio mics and a Handex camera-mounted light.

'I usually use a Sony A1e which is a much smaller camera but it takes more time to set up and as I knew I would have a car for the duration of this job (a luxury I don't usually have) I knew I could leave the camera set up with mic and lamp mounted. The most important thing for me with kit is make sure it's yours and take care of it. Don't add new bits of kit or change settings on an important job, test everything before you leave the office.

'Also make sure you have at least one Plan B: a second radio mic or a wired lapel mic, for example, as well as a spare bulb for the lamp – it will go eventually. What works well online is compelling or unique footage that is either very well shot or offers incredible access or both. Or it's strippers and puppies. It's tricky to say what works well online since online is changing all the time. It used to be a very 'lean forward' experience where short, funny videos were best but now you can have YouTube routed to your TV and Sky package, sent to your Xbox so online and offline are merging.

'I'd just stick to the same principles that make journalism interesting. Find a story, find an angle and then work hard investigating that story and presenting it for your audience to see.'

Alastair Good, Video Journalist,

Get used to the medium and see if you are comfortable in front of the camera. Upload your first videos to a free host such as YouTube and embed them on your blog (YouTube has an embed button which gives you the code to copy and paste on to your blog. If you are using WordPress you can use a shortcode instead – go to en.support.wordpress.com/shortcodes to find out more).

View your videos online, get your colleagues to comment on them and read your feedback from others. Even if you do not specialise in video this exercise will help you understand the process and help you communicate with others should you have to commission video.

Ideas and planning

Once you have an idea for a video, ask yourself: who would want to watch this and why? The story might be good but it might be better served through text, stills, audio or a combination of all three. Think about practicalities such as resources and time. Think about images that can be used and how they will propel the story. Some news organisations have their own studio to record interviews and news bulletins. But if your website shows news bulletins using video are you adding any value to a story that is already broadcasting on 24-hour rolling television news channels?

Interviews can be a compelling feature if the subject or person is interesting or if there is an element of exclusivity about the video. Q&A-style questioning of officials is unlikely to elicit good video although specific responses used as clips in a package might add balance. Remember that intimacy works particularly well online and if the issue is appropriate and the subject is willing it may be better to let them tell their story themselves rather than putting yourself between the story and the viewer.

Features and news packages need research and planning. It is not necessary to storyboard your feature in the prescriptive way of a film director so that each and every shot is prefigured (unless you are planning to invest time in a documentary-style piece). Stories have a habit of changing and developing. However, think about the people, the places, the action and still shots you might want to use. Before setting out make a checklist and consider the following aspects.

- What's the story?
- What pictures will I need? – think about locations and shoots.
- Can you shoot the story on your own? – think about transport.
- Have you packed the right kit and tested it?
- What kind of environment are you going into? Think about terrain, weather, lighting, safety.
- Have you researched interviews in advance and made appointments?
- Plan ahead – video stories take more setting up than print. For instance, you can't film a story about forestry in a series of lumberjacks' and activists' offices. You have to arrange to meet them in a forest.
- Have you permission to shoot video? Think about government buildings, public spaces such as schools, or copyright material such as music that may be playing in the background.
- Permission slips – you will need contributors to sign a form giving permission to publish or broadcast their interview.
- Parental consent – needed for interviews with children.
- Identification – court reporting rules apply to video.
- Think about balance, right of reply and visual libel. This is an easy trap to fall into when you juxtapose images with voiceover without thinking how the two fit together. See Chapter 11 on law for more.
- Think about third-party footage. The preponderance of cameras now means that you may find useful footage from other people – or even from a CCTV camera. Google 'Man stuck in lift 40 hours' for an example of how one story was brought to life by using CCTV footage.

Shooting video

It is not enough to switch the camera on and start shooting. You might capture hours of material but find in the edit that you have badly framed shots, no close-ups, jerky footage and invasive ambient sound. Think about the different elements of the story you need.

In other words, shoot to edit. For example, you might be covering a protest by parents at the closure of a local school. A shot of people chanting with placards or of people marching only tells one part of the story. Think about the composition of visuals that will tell the story and give it context: footage of the school and its location, close-ups of individuals and their placard messages, interviews, a shot which shows how big the demonstration is and the reaction of bystanders. Is the protest holding up traffic? Are there police?

The next step is to know how to frame video.

There are three shots that you need to practise and become familiar with. Keep the camera still and always get these three shots before doing moving shots.

- Wide shot – stand back and establish the scene.
- Medium – move closer in to the point where people can be easily identified.
- Medium close-up – used for interviews, usually just head and shoulders.

Source: iStockphoto/Damir Cudic

Medium shot

Then there is the rule of thirds, used in photography. Imagine each shot is divided vertically and horizontally into thirds. Avoid placing your subject in the middle of the shot. For example, if someone is being interviewed they should be off-centre and their head below the top line so they don't look like they are being squeezed into the shot. You also want to avoid the impression of someone staring at you directly, which is off-putting. There needs to be room between the person being interviewed and the direction that they are looking. Give them 'lead room' by positioning the camera to one side.

For those starting out, the following recommendations also apply.

- Use the autofocus and autolighting function on your camera.
- Use a tripod – this is key to professional-looking video (but not necessary if, for example, you stumble upon a news story and setting up a tripod would mean missing key footage).
- Avoid sweeping shots left and right (or panning) – too much movement is distracting.
- Avoid too much zooming in and out for the same reason.
- Capture movement in the frame; don't be tempted to create movement by moving the frame around.
- Don't follow a wide shot with another wide shot: use a variety of angles.
- Try to ensure that subjects enter and leave the frame rather than you following them.
- Remember that close-ups work well online.
- Leave yourself at least 10 seconds of tape at the beginning and end where the shot does not move. One of the first rules of editing is not to cut on a shot that is still moving.
- Remember to choose a shot, press record and film it, then stop recording and set up for the next shot. Inexperienced camera operators tend to leave the camera rolling and end up with hours of useless footage.

Source: Flickr/Michael Hernandez

Rule of thirds

There are many techniques used by experienced television journalists and video producers who have developed the skills and invested in the equipment to create professional videos. Beginners should keep to these basic rules for online video because out in the field they will also be responsible for carrying their equipment, taking notes of names and contact numbers, and moving to where the story is.

Once the basics have been learned, video producers should consider experimenting with the following: a piece to camera (for example, a video piece for a blog) and shooting cutaways (often used in interviews, when there is a shot of the interviewee's hands or sitting room, for example). You should also get into the habit of shooting enough supplemental footage that illustrates the story or point a person is making. It is easy to make mistakes in a stressful situation particularly when you are on your own with no-one else to rely on.

The following are common pitfalls for even the most experienced video producers.

- Forgetting to turn the camera on;
- choosing the wrong environment, e.g. a dimly lit office or in front of a bright light;
- umming and aahing while interviewing – remember to keep quiet;
- allowing interviews to go on too long – keep interviews short and to the point with open questions which prompt your interviewees to give decent responses;
- letting the interviewee make time-specific references which may not make sense later – don't be afraid to brief the interviewee to avoid that type of reference;
- videoing someone in front of distractions, e.g. traffic or a poster with easily read text;
- letting the interviewee grab the microphone.

Closer look Tips for online video journalism

1. Always have a camera with you.
2. Be clear about what the story is, and what your film is doing.
3. Show, don't tell, and don't try to ape TV formats.
4. The internet is an intimate medium; get close to your subject, allow them to tell their story, instead of using soundbites.
5. Be fair to your characters and subjects.
6. Speak to real people, use real voices, rather than talking heads.
7. Try to get real life happening in front of your camera, instead of set-up shots and GVs (general views).
8. Be ruthless with your edit, keep it short and tight, and take advice from people who weren't on the shoot.
9. Watch quality documentaries and keep up with what others are doing.
10. If you're starting out, upload to YouTube, video blog, and share on social networks.

John Domokos, Video Producer, guardian.co.uk

Editing and publishing

The footage you have captured on your camera is unlikely to have a linear narrative and will contain a mix of footage that needs to be edited together. Editing software programs for video have non-linear editing systems allowing the journalist to cut, move and delete video and audio to construct the story. But first it is a good idea to look at all the raw footage and decide what elements are needed to construct a story with a clear beginning, middle and end. This can be a time-consuming process – don't be tempted to start editing straight away. You may have forgotten a particular sequence, or the significance of a quote might not have been clear at the time of recording.

Editing your video

Start by looking at the footage. You may have more than an hour's worth which you need to edit as a three-minute video. You may have several hours of footage from which you want to construct a 15-minute feature. Either way, save yourself time by going through the footage and logging the clips you want to use. This process is called a rough-edit.

Log the clips by giving them catchlines (labels) and create your log by hand or electronically (most software programs allow you to do this). Note the 'in' and 'out' points (the precise time) of each clip by looking at the digital time display on your video camera. Be selective about your clips and choose establishing shots, a range of close-ups and mid-shots and have a mix of short, killer quotes and longer, more descriptive elements from interviews. Try to be disciplined. You may need to drop footage of an interview if two people make the same point.

Import and edit

Once you have connected your camera to your computer you need to import your video to your selected software program. Movie Maker and iMovie have a drag and drop, cut and paste system which allows audio, music and titles to be added. They also have a timeline where clips are added to create a narrative and where you can layer video and audio clips so that, for example, you can add ambient sound.

Editing using iMovie: news vox pops

Source: Used with permission from Microsoft

Decide what order you want your clips to go in and cut and paste them on to the timeline. You can look at your clips frame by frame, cut them and split them in two.

Think about pacing – you need to draw in the viewer while getting to the point. Online audiences tend to have a shorter time threshold in which they view a story online because they have the facility to click to something else. Keep the pace lively and keep in mind the length of your video.

For example, a shot lasting 30 seconds in a three-minute video is generally far too long as you may find that the story gets squeezed or becomes incoherent. This is a tough area to make rules about – the content should dictate the style and length. Consider transitions if you feel clips are at the right length but seem jerky when put together. The software program you use will give you options for transitions such as dissolves and fade in and fade out. Don't be tempted to use the more elaborate transitions that do things such as turning the image into a rotating cube: remember that the focus is the story, not your knowledge of editing software.

How long should it be?

One advantage of producing for the web when compared with television is that there is no rule about length – you don't have a schedule to worry about. Often a one- to three-minute video can tell the story or enhance accompanying text and work well with news items. For a more feature-based story, aim for about ten minutes if it is your first foray into video reporting. It may not seem long to you at first but think about how much footage you will have to shoot and edit on your own. More importantly, think about the viewer: is there enough of a story arc to keep them interested? For stories that lend themselves to a more documentary style, consider breaking up your feature into parts to make a series of videos.

Adding audio

Many online video journalists like to dispense with voiceovers where the journalist introduces a piece or adds running commentary. They prefer to let the visuals of the story, the narrative of the video and the people in the piece tell the story. The argument is that voiceovers hold up the story (because people want to see action not talking heads) and that their use is too much like broadcast television (this is a stylistic preference).

For some, the idea of the journalist appearing in the video, holding a microphone and standing outside a building is old-fashioned and clichéd. These are devices that evolved to allow television journalists to tell stories that did not suit the moving image, but had to be told visually because, after all, this was television. Of course, unlike television journalism, in online journalism you don't have to use video to tell the story – and if you are resorting to holding a microphone outside a building you should be asking yourself the question: might this story suit another medium better?

However, there is nothing to prevent a journalist recording a separate piece of audio to run with the video if it helps to give context and add meaning to the story. This can be recorded on to the video camera itself or separately using a microphone attached to your computer. Don't be tempted to add loud music to add to the dynamic of the piece or music with lyrics that will detract from the message. It is likely to be copyrighted and the listener might not like your taste. Remember to get permission if you use music and other copyrighted material. If you do need to add music there are many websites where you can download copyright-free music for free – and upcoming musicians are good sources of free music if you feel it adds to the story, but make sure you give them a credit.

Clever use of audio or natural sound can make your story much more evocative. Don't show a picture of a baby crying in a feeding situation without letting your viewer hear the sound. This is known as letting your package breathe. And try not to show pictures of people talking if your voiceover prevents the viewer hearing what they are saying. This is known as goldfishing.

Creating titles and credits

Your program will allow you to create titles and credits which you can type and place on the video. Interviewees should have their name and title clearly displayed, set left or right, at the bottom of the screen. Be sure to use credits for byline purposes and for commissioned material such as archive footage and music. Check the size of the text – it can appear very small online. As with transitions, resist the temptation to choose more elaborate caption designs. Keep the typography and colour simple – and the focus on the story, not your telling of it.

Publishing video

Video files need to be compressed into a file format that works online. MOV is popular among journalists but there are other formats such as MPEG and MP4 and AVI and FLV. Most multimedia organisations allow journalists to upload video files so that they appear in what is called an embedded video player which allows the viewer to click on the player and stop and start it as they wish. It will also show them the time and length of the video and give them the ability to pause the video and set the volume for the audio. An easy alternative is to upload video directly to a video-sharing site such as YouTube, which accepts all of the above file formats and many more besides. Once you have uploaded your video you can post it on sites or a blog using an embeddable video player. Take a look at other video sharing sites as well such as Vimeo, Metacafe, Viddler, DailyMotion and VidiLife.

The compression process can leave your crisp video footage looking blurred, so experiment to see how compressed it needs to be. High definition (HD) is becoming the norm, but it too will need to be compressed and it also uses up considerably more memory (HD comes in more than one size).

Closer look Areas journalists should consider when posting video

- Video works best with short, explanatory text and headlines with keywords that make them searchable. Tag them.
- Promote your video through links in text on similar subject stories.
- Promote by having links to video on homepages and section pages.
- Newspapers and magazines can promote video in print as an online extra.
- Television news programmes can direct viewers to 'full' versions of video online following the version that was edited for broadcast.
- Upload to several video-sharing sites. Many schools block YouTube, for example, but not services such as SchoolTube.
- Make videos available as an RSS feed. RSS feeds are automatically generated for most video-sharing sites – find out what your RSS feed is in case you need to use it to syndicate your videos elsewhere.

Closer look Watch

- Alastair Good's videos at: www.telegraph.co.uk/journalists/alastair-good
- John Domokos's videos at: www.guardian.co.uk/multimedia
- David Dunkley Gyimah's videos at: www.viewmagazine.tv
- Andy Gallacher's videos at: www.vimeo.com/andygallacher
- Channel 4's documentary site at: www.4docs.org.uk
- David Berman's videos at: www.sitbonzo.com
- Kevin Sites at: www.kevinsitesreports.com
- The New York Times at: www.lens.blogs.nytimes.com
- Compendium of video journalism at: www.kobreguide.com

Summary

Video provides online journalists with a compelling medium to tell a story. Moving images are popular with people who are using digital cameras to record and share their own stories, be they citizen journalists or home movie enthusiasts. This may have taken a little of the mystery out of 'film-making' but it also means the ability to appreciate good video is more widespread.

The transparency of the process challenges journalists to provide stories with value and integrity that rise above infotainment and broadcasting cliché. Online video journalism is evolving and journalists should strive for quality and originality, taking the best of television and film techniques while not being a slave to convention.

The key to good video is the story, the idea, the information and the purpose of the video. Journalistic skills are vital as well as manual dexterity and technical proficiency. Beginners should start small, experimenting with video on mobile phones and watching videos produced by amateurs and professional journalists. Technique is unlikely to come naturally and there will be mistakes on the way. Practice is essential.

Activities

1. **Video a trade show.**
   - Get permission to shoot video at an event such as a toy, gadgets or wedding trade show.
   - Start with establishing shots of the venue and people as they pour in.
   - Take mid-shots of exhibits, displays.
   - Interview exhibitors and customers using close-ups.
   - Find the most popular stand and video someone testing a product (it could be you).
   - Find out what the themes and trends are and sign off with a good quote.

2. Broadcast your blog.
   - Decide how long your video will be – keep it short.
   - Pick a subject you were going to write about.
   - Make some notes of key elements you want to include.
   - Try not to read from a script; keep it natural. If you fluff your lines, start again – or carry on and just cut out the mistake in editing (people are used to jump-cuts in online video) or leave it in to keep it raw and informal.
   - Post it to your blog and YouTube – read comments and respond – appropriately!

Further reading

BBC Editorial Guidelines, www.bbc.co.uk/editorialguidelines

Hudson, G. and Rowlands, S. (2007) *The Broadcast Journalism Handbook*, UK: Pearson.

Mills, J. (2004) *The Broadcast Voice*, UK: Focal Press.

Morgan, V. (2008) *Practising Videojournalism*, UK: Routledge.

Burgess, J. and Green, J. (2009) *Online Video and Participatory Culture*, UK: Polity Press.

Chapter 9

Interactivity

This chapter will cover:

- What is interactivity?
- Thinking about control
- What does this mean for journalists?
- Technologies of interactivity: linking
- Closer look: When should I link?
- Technologies of interactivity: interactive maps
- APIs and mashups
- Polls and surveys
- Forums
- Closer look: The 1–9–90 Rule
- Comments on blog posts and articles
- Interactive storytelling
- Closer look: Q&A: Robert Minto, Interactive Editor, FT.com
- Games and interactivity
- Closer look: How do I make my site more interactive?

Introduction

In his 2001 book *Online Journalism*, Jim Hall argues that, in the age of the web, interactivity could be added to impartiality, objectivity and truth as a core value of journalism. It is as important as that.

Interactivity is central to how journalism has been changed by the arrival of the internet. Whereas the news industries of print, radio and TV placed control firmly in the hands of the publishers and journalists, online you try to control people at your peril – not just for social reasons, but hard commercial ones as well.

One of the reasons why interactivity is so central to online journalism is that people use the web on devices (computers, mobile phones, etc.) with cultural histories of utility, very different from the cultural histories of television, radio or even print.

People go online to *do* something. Companies that help with that process tend to prosper online. Those that attempt to curtail users' ability to do things with their content often find themselves on the end of a backlash. The Associated Press, for example, has been particularly criticised for its clumsy attempts to assert its right to 'own' certain stories.

News is, of course, a service. But working in an industry that produces newspapers and broadcasts, it has been easy to forget that, and believe that it is a product. The web is reminding us otherwise.

What is interactivity?

Liu and Shrum (2002, p. 54) define interactivity as 'The degree to which two or more communication parties can act on each other, on the communication method, and on the messages and the degree to which such influences are synchronized'. Put more simply, interactivity is mainly about two things: communication and control.

On the communication side, interactivity means allowing users to communicate with the news organisation, with individual journalists and – crucially – with each other. While many commentators will focus on the arrival of two-way communication between journalist and reader using facilities such as blog comments, Twitter and journalists' emails, it is equally important to recognise the emergence of a three-way communication structure: between journalist and reader, and reader and reader (see Figure 9.1).

Ultimately, the attraction for news websites is the same as their roles in print and broadcast: the ability to gather people with a passion for the same issue in the same place.

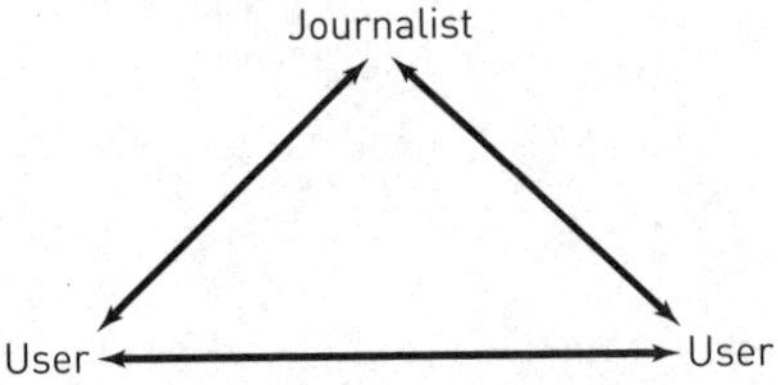

Figure 9.1 Three-way interactivity

Software / Hardware	Time	Space
Output	Hyperlinks, online video/audio, podcast, databases, Flash interactives, PDF papers, Sky+, RSS, Last.fm, mobile phone	Mobile phones, iPods, Wi-Fi laptop, RSS
Input	Blog, podcast, vlog, forum, chatroom, comments, live chats, wiki, YouTube, Flickr, social networking sites, email, SMS	Moblogging, UGC, CJ, Twitter, Shozu

Figure 9.2 Interactivity: a matrix of user control

Source: Paul Bradshaw, onlinejournalismblog.com

Thinking about control

User control can be over *when* someone consumes their media (time-shifting), or *where* (providing podcasts that people can listen to on an MP3 player, for instance). It can also mean control over *input* into a story – everything from allowing comments on a story to letting readers vote on what should be covered. It can also mean control over the news *output*: the BBC's personalised homepage, for example, allows you to move blocks around or remove them, specify what sort of sports news you want, where you want your weather report to focus on, whether you want education news or technology, and so on.

This matrix of control is illustrated in Figure 9.2. It provides a conceptual framework through which you can think about how you make your own journalism interactive.

For example, if you are working on a piece of journalism you might ask:

- How can I give the user control over the space in which this is consumed? Make it downloadable, perhaps?
- How might I give the user control over input? Perhaps by blogging about the idea for the article and inviting suggestions for angles, sources, research, etc.
- How can I give control over output? Allow users to enter their postcode and find out about how the story affects them?

Control over time and space

Where broadcast required the user to be present at a particular time, and print to wait for the next edition, technologies such as video on demand (VOD), personal video recorders (PVRs) such as Sky+ and TiVo, along with podcasts, mobile phones and websites, allow the audience to consume at a *time* convenient to them. The PDF newspaper is another, less successful, development that also allows readers to avoid the dependence on print and distribution cycles.

Similarly, whereas television has normally required the user to be physically present in front of a static set, the spread of mobile phones, MP3 players and portable MPEG players and Wi-Fi laptops allows the audience to consume in a *space* convenient to them. Portable radio and portable newspapers have always had this advantage, of course.

Online journalists need to think about how to play to these strengths. If you are producing 'live' online journalism such as a chat or liveblog, will you make a transcript or recording available for those who cannot view it at the time? If you are publishing audio or video, is it downloadable so that people can view it on a portable device? Is it available through channels such as iTunes?

Control over input and output

With linear media such as TV, radio and print, it is the producer, editor or journalist who structures how content is presented (the output), deciding which quotes to select and what footage to use in order to tell the best story in the time or space available. New media allows the audience to take some of that control. Examples include the following:

- At a basic level, hyperlinks allow the reader to dictate their experience of 'content' through their choice of clicks.
- With online video and audio, the user can pause, fast-forward, etc. – and if it has been split into 'chunks', the user can choose which bit of a longer video or audio piece they experience.
- RSS allows users to create their own media product, combining feeds from newspapers, broadcasters, bloggers, and even Delicious tags or Google News search terms.
- Database-driven content allows the user to shape output based on their input, e.g. by entering their postcode they can read content specific to their area. At a general level search engines provide a similar service.
- Flash interactives allow the user to influence output in a range of ways. This may be as simple as selecting from a range of audio, video, text and still image options. It may be playing a game or quiz, where their interaction (e.g. what answers they get right, how they perform) shapes the output they experience.

In terms of input, again, the old media model was one that relied on the producer, editor, etc. – from selecting what story to cover to which sources to interview, and what angle to take. The audience may have had certain avenues of communication – the letter to the editor; the radio phone-in; the 'Points of View', but the staging, shaping, editing and distribution of that was still up to professional media producers.

The new media model, as Dan Gillmor points out, is one that moves from a lecture to a conversation. This has the following results.

- Blogs, podcasts, vlogs, YouTube, MySpace, Facebook, etc. allow the audience to publish their own media.
- Forums, message boards, chatrooms and comments on mainstream media blogs allow the audience to discuss and influence the content of mainstream media, as well as engaging with each other, bypassing the media.
- Live chats with interviewees and media staff do the same.
- User-generated content/citizen journalism sees mainstream publishers seeking out input from consumers, from emails and texts to mobile phone images, video and audio.
- Wikis allow the audience to create their own collaborative content, which may be facilitated by mainstream media.

- Social recommendation software like Delicious, Digg, etc. allows users to influence the 'headline' webpages through bookmarking and tags.
- A similar but separate example is how page view statistics can be used by publishers to rank content by popularity (often displayed side by side with the editorial view of what are the 'top stories').
- Email. Although we could always, in theory, contact producers and editors by telephone, they didn't publish their numbers on the ten o'clock news. Email addresses, however, are printed at the end of articles; displayed on screen alongside news reports; read out on radio; and of course displayed online – and their most important feature lies in how they lower the barrier to contacting a journalist: sending an email is just easier and cheaper than picking up a phone or writing a letter.

Once again, the issue for an online journalist is knowing how to play to the strengths of these technologies. Are you making it easy for users to input into the journalistic process? Is your production process aimed at a fixed output such as an 800-word article or three-minute radio package, or are you making your material available in other ways so that users can interrogate the areas they are most interested in?

What does this mean for journalists?

For journalists, the rise of interactivity means thinking about how you can give control to your readers – who are now, of course, users. That means giving control over the time and place they use it – so, making content downloadable, for example, or bookmarkable, or emailable. Allowing them to put it on their social networking page. Allowing them to sign up for email or text or RSS updates.

It means putting your content where the user is, not the other way round. This means thinking of places like YouTube, Twitter, Facebook, iTunes and Flickr – in turn, driving new traffic back to your own news site. Many news organisations now have their own channels on YouTube, for example – for the simple reason that most people go there when searching for video. This means it is easier for people to find, and their videos and accompanying advertising are seen by more people.

In an advertising-based business, the key issue becomes how you can make sure the advertising either travels with the content, or the distribution of that content results in increased return visits online and on other platforms. In a subscription-based business, the issue becomes how you make people aware of the great content you have. Some publishers have tried to address this by making content visible to search engines such as Google but not to users, or allowing users to read a certain number of articles before being asked to pay, as the *Wall Street Journal* did. But no one has yet discovered a method that generates the same returns as publishers enjoyed at their peak.

Giving control over the input and output of articles is about a different set of strategies – 'calling out' for contributions when you first start working on a story (usually via your blog, social network or Twitter account); allowing comments on what you've written; creating a space for further development and discussion via a forum or wiki or chatroom. Making your raw material available so others can build on it, or even point out corrections. All of these actions add to the 'package' of journalism that you provide, making it more interactive, accountable, and likely to find its audience.

It means thinking, when relevant, not of linear traditional journalism, but of packages of information that the user can navigate in their own way, from a mix of audio, video, text and animation to database-driven packages that deliver specific results to specific enquiries.

It means thinking of ways to engage the user: could we do a game about this? A quiz? Create a tool? Invite users to pose the questions to our interviewee? Involve them in the investigation from the start?

'Conversation is king'

At its root, most interactivity in online journalism revolves around making stories conversational and social: something that people can share with friends, talk about, play with and talk to. New media commentator Jeff Jarvis puts it this way:

> 'In this new age, you don't want to own the content or the pipe that delivers it. You want to participate in what people want to do on their own. You don't want to extract value. You want to add value. You don't want to build walls or fences or gardens to keep people from doing what they want to do without you. You want to enable them to do it. You want to join in.'

Look closer, and you could argue that the distinctions between conversation and publishing in an online medium are being eroded. Everything that we say is recorded, linkable, distributable. Conversation itself has become publishing. A journalist in this context, then, needs to become a professional conversationalist: a mix of the ideal party guest and the ideal party host, taking part in – and stimulating – conversations in a number of ways:

- Be involved in your communities, online and offline. Comment on blogs, post on forums, correct and update wikis, converse on Twitter, join and contribute to social network groups.
- Open up your own work for others to contribute editorially: include an email address; allow comments. In particular, don't structure your work as a dead end: present it as work in progress on your blog; ask questions and leave them unanswered; acknowledge gaps in your knowledge; invite contributions there and elsewhere.
- Respond to contributions, publicly if possible. This not only shows that you are responsive but prevents others from making the same points.
- You must show explicitly that you are part of the conversation, by linking to sources (who will in turn know that they are being quoted either through alerts or traffic).
- And finally, most importantly: you must listen. This means reading blogs, forums and other media in your sector, and then starting from the beginning again: comment, respond, link, open up.

Figure 9.3 shows one way to look at the whole process.

Figure 9.3 The conversation loop
Source: Paul Bradshaw, onlinejournalismblog.com

25 June 2010 Last updated at 20:05

Budget: What would you cut?

Chancellor George Osborne has delivered his first budget with detail on how he plans to cut the budget deficit.

The Institute for Fiscal Studies estimates that cuts in spending and increases in taxes adding up to £74bn a year are needed to reduce government borrowing to the level it was at before the financial crisis.

So that is your target - use the sliders below to raise VAT or trim spending to see if you can make the necessary cuts in the deficit.

Spending on/tax raised	Equivalent to	Saved (£m)
VAT 17.5% VAT rate	£0 bn tax raised	£ 0m
Welfare 0% % cuts	£0 cut in the basic weekly pension	£ 0m
Health 0% % cuts	0 days' cost of running NHS hospitals	£ 0m
Education 0% % cuts	0 secondary schools built	£ 0m

PLATE 11 BBC Budget Calculator
BBC, www.bbc.co.uk/news/10373060

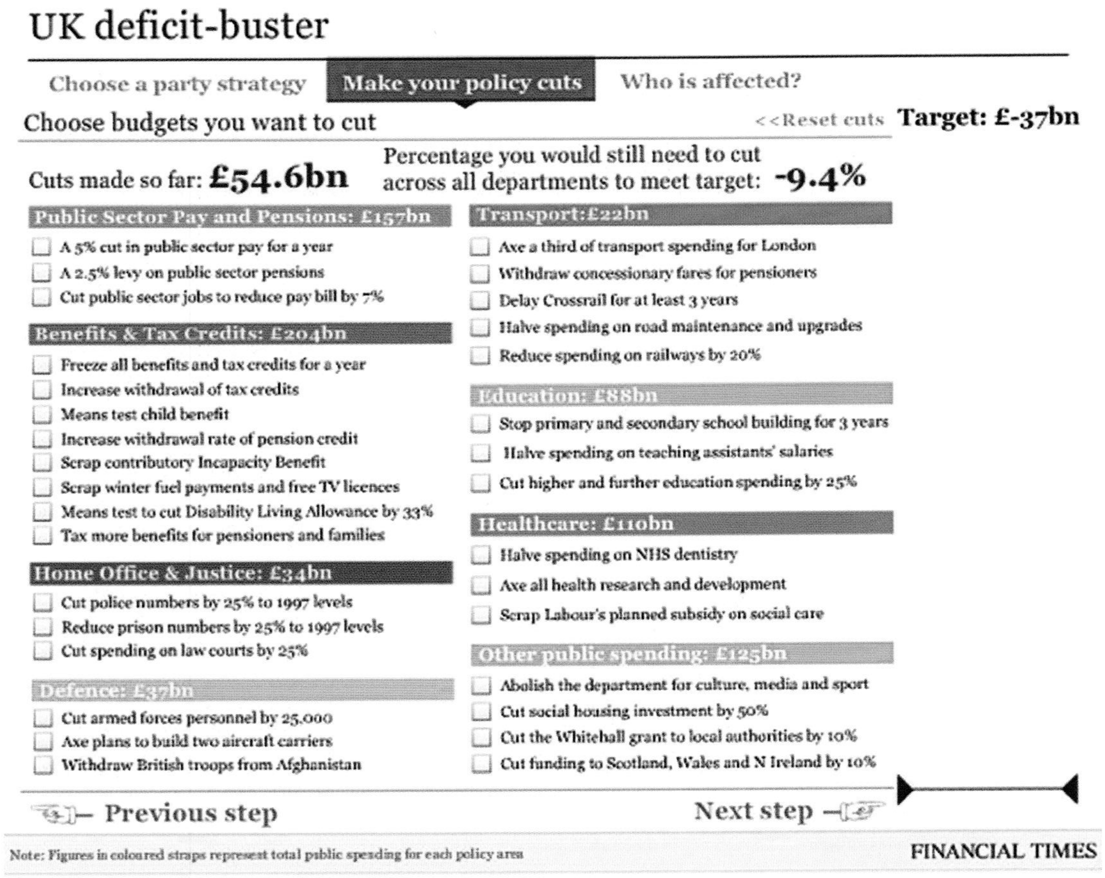

UK deficit-buster

Choose a party strategy | **Make your policy cuts** | Who is affected?

Choose budgets you want to cut <<Reset cuts **Target: £-37bn**

Cuts made so far: **£54.6bn**

Percentage you would still need to cut across all departments to meet target: **-9.4%**

Public Sector Pay and Pensions: £157bn

- [ ] A 5% cut in public sector pay for a year
- [ ] A 2.5% levy on public sector pensions
- [ ] Cut public sector jobs to reduce pay bill by 7%

Benefits & Tax Credits: £204bn

- [ ] Freeze all benefits and tax credits for a year
- [ ] Increase withdrawal of tax credits
- [ ] Means test child benefit
- [ ] Increase withdrawal rate of pension credit
- [ ] Scrap contributory Incapacity Benefit
- [ ] Scrap winter fuel payments and free TV licences
- [ ] Means test to cut Disability Living Allowance by 33%
- [ ] Tax more benefits for pensioners and families

Home Office & Justice: £34bn

- [ ] Cut police numbers by 25% to 1997 levels
- [ ] Reduce prison numbers by 25% to 1997 levels
- [ ] Cut spending on law courts by 25%

Defence: £37bn

- [ ] Cut armed forces personnel by 25,000
- [ ] Axe plans to build two aircraft carriers
- [ ] Withdraw British troops from Afghanistan

Transport:£22bn

- [ ] Axe a third of transport spending for London
- [ ] Withdraw concessionary fares for pensioners
- [ ] Delay Crossrail for at least 3 years
- [ ] Halve spending on road maintenance and upgrades
- [ ] Reduce spending on railways by 20%

Education: £88bn

- [ ] Stop primary and secondary school building for 3 years
- [ ] Halve spending on teaching assistants' salaries
- [ ] Cut higher and further education spending by 25%

Healthcare: £110bn

- [ ] Halve spending on NHS dentistry
- [ ] Axe all health research and development
- [ ] Scrap Labour's planned subsidy on social care

Other public spending: £125bn

- [ ] Abolish the department for culture, media and sport
- [ ] Cut social housing investment by 50%
- [ ] Cut the Whitehall grant to local authorities by 10%
- [ ] Cut funding to Scotland, Wales and N Ireland by 10%

Previous step | Next step

Note: Figures in coloured straps represent total public spending for each policy area

FINANCIAL TIMES

PLATE 12 FT.com: UK Deficit Buster
The Financial Times, http://cachef.ft.com/cms/s/0/abe91fdc-4e08-11df-b43700144feab49a.html#axzz1luwZn0iJ

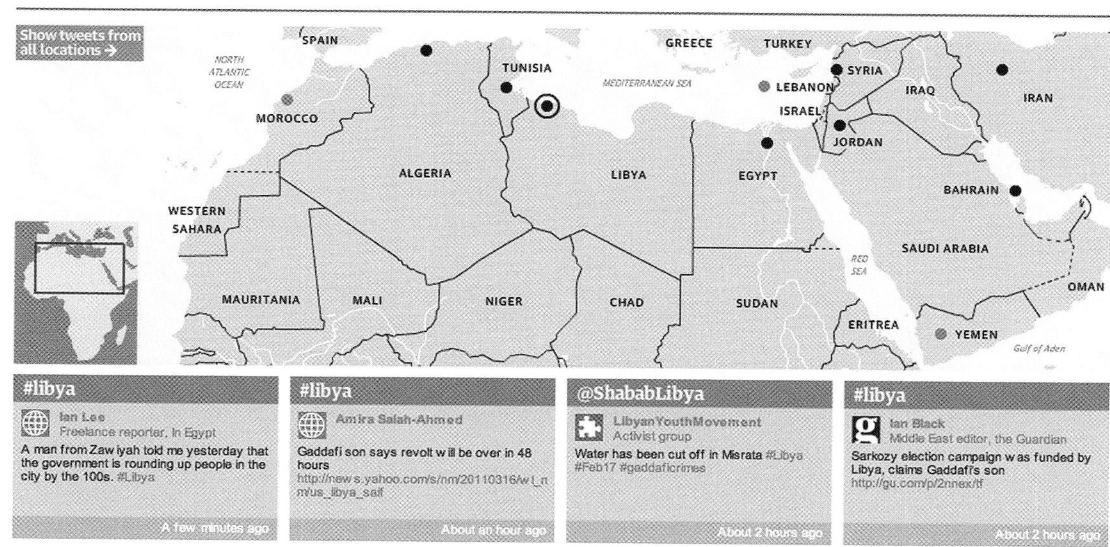

PLATE 13 Twitter network of Arab and Middle East protests – interactive map

Guardian News and Media Ltd, www.guardian.co.uk/world/interactive/2011/feb/11/guardian-twitter-arab-protests-interactive?CMP=twt_gu

The Budget Game

Feb 9, 2009 — You're welcome to play with balancing the 2003 city budget, but we've revised and updated our budget game for 2009. Balance! lets you play with the options on the 2009 budget table.

May 12, 2003 — In an effort to close the city's $3.8 billion deficit, public officials have been playing the usual budget games - laying off workers, raising taxes, and threatening to close firehouses and zoos. Now with our interactive NYC Budget Game, you can play too. You spend the money. You make the cuts. You raise and lower the taxes.

PLATE 14 The Budget Game (Gotham Gazette)
The Gotham Gazette, www.gothamgazette.com/budgetgame/

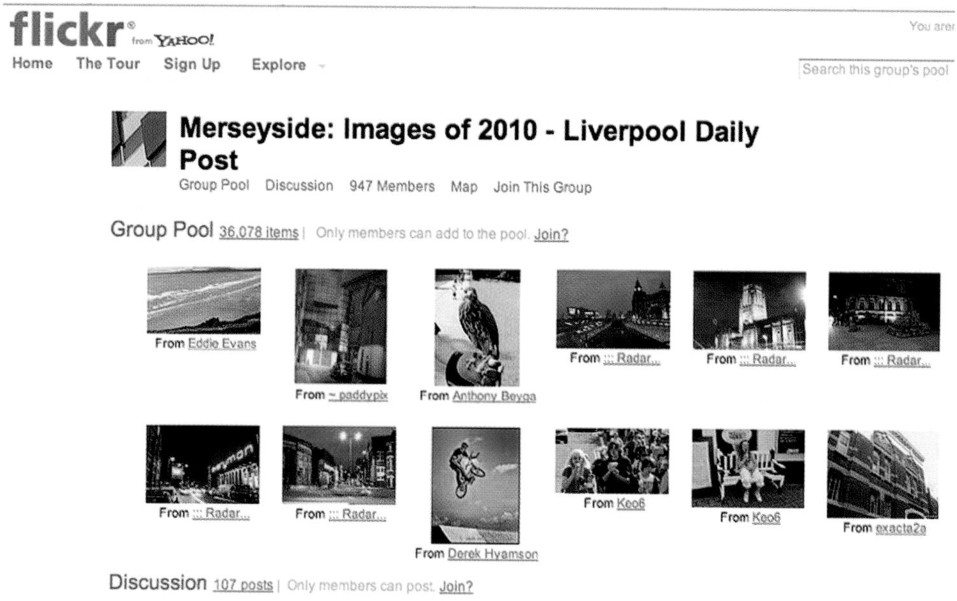

Home The Tour Sign Up Explore

You are

Search this group's pool

Merseyside: Images of 2010 - Liverpool Daily Post

Group Pool Discussion 947 Members Map Join This Group

Group Pool 36,078 items | Only members can add to the pool. Join?

From Eddie Evans

From ~ paddypix

From Anthony Beyga

From ::: Radar...

From ::: Radar...

From ::: Radar...

From ::: Radar...

From ::: Radar...

From Derek Hyamson

From Keo6

From Keo6

From exacta2a

Discussion 107 posts | Only members can post. Join?

PLATE 15 Liverpool Daily Post and Echo Flickr Group
Trinity Mirror Midlands Limited, http://img.skitch.com/20100827-f2kc3uwged95tcfasjg43p8xkp.jpg

FirstPerson on msnbc.com

Hot topics
Barack Obama
Afghanistan
Mexico
China
Pakistan
California
msnbc.com home

Browse
Video
Photos

Marketplace
Watch Movies
Netflix-Try for free
Progressive
Get car insurance

FIRST PERSON

Your place in the Gulf

The Gulf Coast is host to memories, vacations and livelihoods. Click to see reader images of their special places that are threatened by the oil spill from Galveston, Texas to the Florida Keys. View

Are you on the scene?

What did you see?
Send us your video, photos or personal report through the form here.

Top features

Send us your Saab stories, pictures
FirstPerson: Send us your stories and photos of you and your Saab. Old photos welcome! We will publish a selection of the best photos and comments.

Send us your weather images
Share your best travel photos
Are you a gamer? Share your photo!
TODAY's looking for the cutest cats!

PLATE 16 MSNBC's citizen journalism website First Person
MSNBC Interactive News, LLC, http://img.skitch.com/20100827-cumip8b9djnaip2d6rteggi2xa.jpg

SATURDAY
11th July 1998

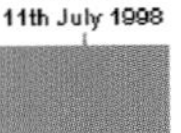

BBC ONLINE

Saturday

INTERVIEW

If you're new to the BBC Homepage, click here

Online

BBC Homepage
BBC Site Map

Main Sites

News
World Cup 98
Weather
World Service
Education
beeb @ the BBC
BBC Worldwide
BBC Across The UK

Services

Web Guide
TV Listings
Radio Listings
Online Channel
BBC Ticker
Feedback
Search
Help

Inside the BBC

Jobs at the BBC
The BBC and You
Copyright

TODAY ON THE WEB

Movies
Radiation-breathing giant lizards, city-stomping apes, three-headed dragons and men in rubber monster costumes - as the summer blockbuster Godzilla nears its release date, check out the cheerful, tacky world of the Monster Movie.
Visit the Movies website

Today's other recommended sites:
Home Truths
Nose around the nooks and crannies of the weekend.
CBBC
Packed with fun and all your favourite programmes.

A selection of top BBC sites | Go

CHOICES

Science and technology sites
Evolution Website - 4,000 million years crammed into one website.
Tomorrow's World - Welcome to the Future.
Sky At Night - Developments in astronomy with Patrick Moore.

The Book Case
Relax in our online reading room.
Wannabe a pop star?
Take the TOTP star personality test.
Blue Peter
Here's one we made earlier.

Grabbit Rabbit
Let's see you catch those carrots!
The Generation Game
Cuddly toy? Toaster? Take a turn on the conveyor belt.
Goodness Gracious Me
How English are you?

Antiques Roadshow Quiz
Made to measure for fashion folk - this week's questions are on costumes and accessories.

SERVICES

BBC Ticker
Have the latest headlines running on your screen while you work, play or browse.
BBC Online Channel
The very latest news, weather, sport, finance, travel and leisure for IE4 or Netscape 4.
BBC Shop
Come and have a browse around the BBC shop.
BBC Tickets
See BBC shows live, for free.

Web Guide
BBC reviewers select the best websites from around the world. Check out today's features and choices.

- Dictionary.com
- Mind the gap
- What's new on the Web
- Your Choice
- Jonathan Agnew's favourite Web sites

TELEVISION & RADIO

ON NOW
BBC1
Joins BBC News 24
BBC2
Space: Above and Beyond

ON NOW
RADIO 1
RADIO 2 Jeff Owen
RADIO 3 Through the Night
RADIO 4 As World Service
RADIO 5 LIVE Up All Night

HIGHLIGHTS
The Pop Zone
More Loverly Than Ever: The Making of My Fair Lady
Pride and Prejudice

HIGHLIGHTS
Private Passions - Amanda Holden
Talking Comedy
Sport on 5

We've put your questions to Kirsty Wark, now read the interview and email us any questions you have for Dale Winton or Craig Doyle.

MAIN SITES

NEWS
London blasts 'narrowly foiled'
New move in marching crisis
Damages award in church sex case
Landmines Bill whips through Commons
Abiola autopsy doctors arrive

SPORT
Coulthard speeds at Silverstone
Last gasp for B&H final
Southampton to announce Hughes move

WEATHER

1.00am
London
16°C
select city | go

EDUCATION
South Africa 2000
What's it really like to live in South Africa?

WORLD SERVICE
World Lectures
Speakers from around the world discuss the new Millennium
How to tune in.

beeb @ the BBC
True Brit
Warm up for the British Grand Prix with TopGear.

HELP

New to the BBC homepage? Let us show you around.

Make the BBC my homepage? Here's how.

BBC UPDATE

Melvyn Bragg leaves Start The Week for new BBC series
See your dreams become reality
Birthplace of the Beatles on BBC

BBC

PLATE 17 1998 version of bbc.co.uk
BBC, www.bbc.co.uk

THE TIMES | THE SUNDAY TIMES | TIMES+ Log in | Contact us Search

THE TIMES

News | Opinion | Business | Money | Sport | Life | Arts | Puzzles | Papers | Tuesday, October 5 | London | Max 18C

Latest News SocGen rogue trader Jérôme Kerviel told to pay €5bn damages

Marriage tax break pledged in child benefit row

Philippe Naughton and Sam Coates
October 5 2010 9:40AM
Ministers are pledging to introduce a tax break for married couples before the 2015 election, it emerged today as criticism grew of the plans to axe child benefit for higher rate taxpayers from 2013. Just 24 hours after announcing that child benefit for 15 per cent of families would end, government sources briefed that the tax break plan would go ahead despite doubts raised by the coalition agreement between the Conservatives and the Liberal Democrats. David Cameron, facing a backlash over the child benefit plan, hinted this morning that an anomaly which penalised families where one

SocGen rogue trader told to pay €5bn

Servant 'was beaten and murdered by Saudi prince'

Briton wins Nobel Prize for Physics

Two Manchester-based scientists who discovered a new form of carbon that is promising to

LATEST NEWS

Two-day diet can cut risk of breast cancer Dieting just two days a week can help to reduce blood levels of hormones linked to disease

Two arrested as historic pier destroyed The Victorian pier in Hastings has been 95 per cent ruined after fire swept through structure

Councils in legal challenge to school building axe Waltham Forest, Luton and Nottingham City councils will take on the Education Secretary

Car bomb explodes in Londonderry A car bomb exploded behind a bank causing substantial damage but no injuries

Services plunge

Mental Health
Are we no longer embarrassed about anything?

Travel
The Times guide to six perfect city breaks for autumn

PLATE 18 Timesonline.co.uk 2010 redesign launch for new subscription model
The Times Online, www.thetimes.co.uk/tto/news/

THE HUFFINGTON POST

THE INTERNET NEWSPAPER: NEWS BLOGS VIDEO COMMUNITY

January 18, 2011 | Log In | Sign Up

f Connect twitter

FRONT PAGE | POLITICS | BUSINESS | MEDIA | ENTERTAINMENT | COMEDY | SPORTS | STYLE | WORLD | GREEN | FOOD | TRAVEL | TECH

LIVING | HEALTH | DIVORCE | ARTS | BOOKS | RELIGION | IMPACT | EDUCATION | COLLEGE | NY | LA | CHICAGO | DENVER | BLOGS

FROM AP: The nation's weather... 2 minutes ago

SEARCH

DISARMING STATEMENT

Veteran GOP Senator Voices Support For Assault Weapons Ban

PLATE 19 The Huffington Post homepage
The Huffington Post, www.huffingtonpost.com

As a journalist, doing all of these things gives you four advantages:

1 Your work will be informed by user contributions, and better for it.

2 You'll be more likely to be 'there' when a story breaks – and to understand the context.

3 As you talk about your work, and involve users in it, you will be distributing it as well. If your motivation is commercial, replace 'conversation' with 'distribution'. Nothing works better online.

4 Nobody likes a tourist. You'll be building the trust and social capital needed for other users to give you the information that you need – or to help you find it.

Without the help of your community, without an effort to engage in conversation, your work will be one-dimensional, as flat as the paper it used to be printed on.

Technologies of interactivity: linking

Probably the most fundamental example of interactivity is the simple act of including links in an article. In an age when everything from press releases and public statements to events and government reports is published online, there is no reason not to help users by linking to those whenever they are mentioned. Failing to link often results in a frustrated user experience for the reader, who has to leave your site to perform a Google search instead. Providing a link adds extra depth to your journalism, gives the reader more control over how they experience the 'story' and a reason for the user to keep returning to your site.

There are also strong commercial reasons for linking. An article with a lot of links will be more highly ranked by Google, for example, and there is evidence that sites that link out get linked to more often in return (Eaves, 2008). Indeed, one of the most successful news websites of the last decade – the Drudge Report – is made up primarily of links.

Closer look When should I link?

As an online journalist you should be linking habitually. Here are just some of the occasions when you might link to a source:

- If you refer to a report, link to it.
- If you mention a statistic of any kind, link to the source where it came from. If you cannot find it, you should be asking why.
- If you refer to an event, link to a previous article reporting on that event.
- If you refer to an issue, and your website has a subject page devoted to that issue, link to that (articles on *The Guardian* website do this automatically).
- If you refer to a particular concept (for example, scientific, engineering or mathematical), link to somewhere that the reader can find out more.
- If you refer to any website or blog, link to that website (unless there are ethical or legal issues in doing so). Readers get particularly frustrated if a story is about a website but they are not able to easily click through to that site.

- If your article is one of a series, you should link to previous instalments – and return to update the piece with a link to the next part once it has been written.
- If you are reporting on a particular product, link to the official page for that product, as it will often provide extra detail on product specifications that some readers will find useful.
- You might also link to any organisation or person mentioned in your piece, but you should be guided here by how useful that link is likely to be to the user. If the article is about a new car and you mention Ford, are they really likely to want to go to Ford's website? Or just the page about the car you are reporting on?
- You should also add links to resources you've used in writing the article.
- Broadly speaking, once you've written an article ask yourself: what might the user want to know or read now? Are there concepts they will want to explore? Products they need to know more about? Events that need explaining? Personalities they may not be familiar with?

Technologies of interactivity: interactive maps

Maps have become a familiar part of the news language online due to a number of advantages:

- They provide an easy way to grasp a story at a glance.
- They allow users to drill down very quickly to relevant information local to them.
- Maps can be created very easily, and added to relatively easily by non-journalists.
- Maps draw on structured data, making them a very useful way to present data such as schools tables, crime statistics or petrol prices.
- They can be automated, updating in response to real-time information.

News organisations have used maps in many ways. Brenda Burrell of the BBC's Future Media & Technology unit says:

> 'We use maps to help explain news stories, add context, background information or provide another way of viewing content around the story. Examples include simple locator maps; maps that show additional layers of information; image-mapped satellite images; and interactive maps, which tend to come in two main types on our site: firstly thematic maps created using public data or data obtained by Freedom of Information requests. These often work best over time – one good example shows the rise in the number of jobseekers during the recession. Secondly, mashups – combining dynamic "Google"-type maps with user comments, video, audio, pictures, text reports. We use these to display comments (which can be themed "yes", "no", "don't know", etc.) or BBC news content as it relates to specific events or disasters like G20 or the Italian eathquake.'

James Thornett, Development Manager, Interactive, for BBC Nations & Regions, points to user research which suggests that most of the audience 'still see a map as a route-finding device, an answer to "show me how to get from A to B" or "tell me where this building is", whereas news has long been consumed in a linear fashion, "Give me the big story of the day, what's the second most important item, and so on". Mapping functionality is also quite complicated for a lot of web users and you cannot rely on the audience easily understanding how to pan, zoom, scroll a map, or cope with the differences in graphical pin-points, hover panels, embedded audio/

video content. Web users generally want to get at information quickly, particularly time-sensitive journalism content, and any design or interface barriers that prevent this can be quite a turn-off.'

Maps have enormous potential for storytelling but you should be careful to make sure that they are the right medium for both the story and its audience, and that the user is not left frustrated when trying to use them.

Image maps

In addition to traditional cartographic maps, it is possible to use images of anything as a 'map' that you navigate in the same way with your mouse, clicking on particular areas to bring up relevant detail. Examples have included the route of a race or river, a building's floorplan, a timeline, line or bar chart, or even a group photo. In one excellent example, NPR took a picture of health lobbyists attending the hearing of a new health bill (www.npr.org/news/specials/2009/hearing-pano). Users could click on individual people to find out more about them – and were also invited to identify others in the picture. Similarly, *The Guardian*'s Interactives section often includes diagrams where you can roll over different areas to find out information about different aspects of the process or story.

A few years ago you needed to have skills in Flash or Dreamweaver to create an image map. However, a number of web-based tools (e.g. Vuvox and FineTuna) have since been launched that allow you to create these more easily and provide a different way to interrogate an issue which grabs the user's attention.

Mapping public data

In the USA there has been a rich history of mapping crime statistics online, stimulated enormously by Adrian Holovaty's ChicagoCrime.org, which he later developed into EveryBlock, a website which doesn't just map crime but also planning and alcohol licence applications, filming, news stories, street closures and restaurant inspections. EveryBlock pulls in information from a range of sources and displays the results based on the zip code you enter, giving you a picture of everything happening local to you.

In the UK the most significant mapping of public data has been around elections. *The Telegraph* election maps, for example, pull from a database to provide links to specific statistics and reports when a user clicks on a particular area of the country.

Working with the public

Interactive maps need not be generated from in-house knowledge alone – inviting users to contribute across all your platforms can be a key ingredient in fostering interactivity. For example, when motorists started contacting the BBC about problems with their cars following visits to petrol stations, journalists decided to ask viewers, listeners and website visitors if they had experienced similar problems. As responses poured in, the corporation was able to gather data from viewers and website visitors and to compile a map of cases richer than that held by any motoring organisation or transport department. That data allowed them to pinpoint the particular petrol stations where the problems had originated, and kicked off an investigation by Trading Standards which found that contaminated fuel was the cause.

Similarly, during floods in its area, BBC Radio Berkshire used maps to show which were the worst affected areas, and what people were saying, along with data about the location of emergency services, forming an important source of information for both residents and their relatives during the crisis (see Plate 10).

On a regional level the *Manchester Evening News* plots information from users about congestion and roadworks on its travel map; and the *Hartlepool Mail* has used its readers' contributions to map pot holes and derelict areas of the town. On the less serious side, newspapers have used maps for sightings of an unusual bird, to identify where readers are living around the globe, and to map sightings of unidentified flying objects.

How to involve users in mapping

There are three broad approaches to mapping contributions from users. The first is to process every contribution manually – taking emails, phonecalls, comments and texts and entering them into the map yourself. This has clear advantages in being able to verify the information and keep the map working properly, but obvious disadvantages in the amount of time it requires for a journalist and how long it takes for the map to be updated.

A second approach is to publish the map in an editable format – that is, allow anyone to edit the map directly. This obviously has the advantage of not requiring any further work from the journalist other than checking the map regularly and correcting any mistakes. However, it does require a certain level of technical competence from users, and if you're editing a Google Map, which at the time of writing allows users either total control or none, you will find users accidentally editing each others' entries and the title of the map itself.

The third approach is to part-automate the process in a way that addresses the weaknesses above. You can, for example, set up a Google Map so that it displays data from a Google spreadsheet. Publishing that spreadsheet and allowing users to edit it will likely result in more contributions, fewer errors, and easier correction (if anyone vandalises the spreadsheet you can easily 'revert' to previous versions). You can also create a Google Form for that spreadsheet, which you can publish on a website for users to fill in by answering a few questions. This makes it even easier for users to enter information and prevents them editing others' input – although it may mean duplicate entries from different people entering the same information.

Ultimately, as the BBC's Brenda Burrell explains: 'We have learnt that we should proceed with caution – maps are not always the best interface for exploring content as there can be a lot of clicking involved and not all users find mashup-type maps that intuitive. So as journalists we need to consider where they will add value, rather than using them because we can.'

Geotagging and the semantic web

Both the rise in mapping and a rise in people accessing news on mobile phones have created a demand for 'geotagged' (or geocoded) news. Geotagging a news article means adding geographical information to it – usually, latitude and longitude – in a way that makes it easy for search engines and news distribution platforms to understand what area that news article refers to.

In practice, this means that if you are on a mobile phone with GPS technology you can search for 'restaurant reviews near me' or 'crime stories near me'. Likewise, if you were looking for a new house you could easily find stories about the local schools, or plans for new buildings. Many search engines take into account the searcher's own location when bringing up search results, so including geotagging in news stories would also increase the likelihood of your content being found by a local searcher.

Most news organisations are exploring geotagging in some capacity – in many cases, changing their content management systems so that journalists can add such information in. Some have used this information to launch 'hyperlocal' parts of their news websites that allow users to read stories specifically about a particular postcode.

At the same time, organisations such as Reuters have developed technologies that add geolocation data to stories after they have been written – using semantic web technology to look for place names in the article text and disambiguate them, understanding that the 'Birmingham' referred to is the UK's second city and not the place of the same name in Alabama, USA.

The weakness of the latter approach is that it can only work on the information contained in the article, which may not be specific enough. Meanwhile, journalists geotagging their own articles need to be aware of the privacy and legal implications in, for example, identifying the specific house that a criminal lives in. Normally postcodes in the UK are vague enough for this not to happen, while licensing arrangements mean that Google Maps' mapping of UK postcodes varies in accuracy.

APIs and mashups

An increasing number of news organisations are allowing people to create 'mashups' of news content that allow users to interact with news in different ways. A mashup is a webpage or website which combines information from more than one source to create something new – such as combining a feed of the latest stories with a map to allow people to see at a glance where the news is coming from. The chapter on data journalism goes into much more depth on what is involved in a mashup, but the key thing from the point of view of interactivity is allowing users to interact with your content on a technical and creative level.

One of the earliest experiments in allowing users to mashup news content was the BBC's Backstage project (backstage.bbc.co.uk), which provided various content and feeds for developers to combine with other sources in interesting ways. Projects created by users include an automated 'podcast' of BBC World News text as synthesised speech, a tool to download, merge and index video clips, and a service which combines the BBC's top stories with those that users are actually reading.

Since then, National Public Radio (NPR) and the *New York Times* in the USA and *The Guardian* (Plate 7) in the UK have all launched APIs (application programming interfaces) that allow developers to experiment with their content in similar ways. Early experiments have seen users create a map of *New York Times* property articles, and a website which matches *Guardian* science articles with reports from a scientific journal. However, a news organisation need not have created an API for its material to be 'mashable' – a simple RSS feed (see Chapter 6 on blogging for more on RSS) is enough to allow users to filter or combine content to create a new 'mashup'.

All of these experiments add value to news content and provide new ways for users to interact with it – particularly undervalued archive content – not to mention tapping into otherwise expensive development expertise for the relatively marginal initial cost of developing the API. In some cases, it also provides new potential for selling advertising by giving new life to old content or bringing it to new audiences.

For more on mashups and mapping data, see Chapter 5 on data journalism.

Polls and surveys

Polls and surveys are an old tool for journalists – often derided for their tendency to be methodologically flawed and to provide superficial 'news'. More recently, PR companies have relied increasingly on 'surveys' of varying quality and reliability to get their clients into the news. All surveys should be treated with caution and you should read up on survey methodology before conducting one with any serious intent.

Online, polls and surveys are extremely easy to create, with numerous web services to help you create one with a few clicks, such as PollDaddy and SurveyMonkey. Once you've created a poll with these tools you will be presented with a simple link to the survey form that you can include in your article, or a few lines of HTML which you can copy and paste to your webpage. Some also offer the facility to publish directly into Facebook, Twitter and other social networks.

Clearly, publishing a poll online allows people to campaign for a particular result. Opening voting for winners of a competition, for example, will inevitably lead the candidates and their supporters to try to round up support for their success, while interest groups and campaigning organisations will often seek to skew the results of surveys that could influence public policy. This problem is sometimes called 'freeping' after the website Free Republic, which directed its users to swamp some online polls with their votes. On this basis short polls and surveys are best used as a piece of entertainment on a site or for topics that are unlikely to attract that sort of campaigning, such as insights into what people do rather than what they think.

Monitoring mentions of the survey and the webpages that people are coming from to visit your page can also alert you to any campaigning. One easy way to do this is to use a tracking service such as Bit.ly – this primarily allows you to shorten a URL (web address) but if you create an account with the site you can see where the URL is being published online and how many people are clicking on it there.

Longer, more general surveys, however, can have more success. One of the most innovative users of online surveys has been the *Lancashire Evening Post*, which started hosting a monthly 40-question survey on a range of issues in 2008. The breadth of the survey enabled it to avoid some of the problems identified above while providing the basis for more in-depth exploration in specialist supplements and more extensive interactivity online. Surveys on issues such as local transport were presented in the context of responses from local transport chiefs and used to inform transport policy.

Forums

Amidst all the gloss of Web 2.0, the relatively old technology of forums – also called messageboards – is often overlooked, and yet forums remain extremely popular among users. Many niche magazines have forums which are far more active than the core magazine website – and than some news websites too. In many cases the first place to look for news on any local event is not the news website forums, but the local football club's forum, which will contain discussions ranging far beyond sport, while there are many important discussion spaces online such as TripAdvisor and Money Saving Expert. These can be used to interact with users at any point in the news process from looking for leads through to post-publication feedback.

The main advantage of forums lies in their simplicity. The lack of explicit top-down management allows people to get on with conversations regardless of the topics set by journalists. That said, journalists can support activity on forums by supplying material for conversation, which is one reason news websites often have reasonably healthy forums.

In some cases news organisations will host live events on their forums such as live chats with celebrities, public figures or experts. *The Guardian*'s Careers site, for example, hosts a regular careers chat with invited experts, which it promotes to users so that they have their questions ready. The resulting exchange of questions and answers is then written up in a more traditional article for the website. In addition, they will often email experts who have taken part in a particular chat if there is a relevant question on another forum they can contribute to. This community management is incredibly important in ensuring the health of your forums.

If you are to host a forum you need to decide whether to make users register to post, and how to moderate contributions. It helps if you have a moderation policy which sets out clearly what is considered acceptable in your online community – look at the forum or community policies

Closer look The 1–9–90 rule

In 2006 website usability expert Jakob Nielsen published a report on 'participation inequality' – in a nutshell, the fact that on any given website the majority of users will not participate in any way. The report summarised: 'In most online communities, 90% of users are lurkers who never contribute, 9% of users contribute a little, and 1% of users account for almost all the action.' This became known as the '1–9–90 rule'.

It is worth noting that this does not mean that 90 per cent of all internet users do not participate – just those of any particular website (in contrast, research suggests that a majority of internet users have contributed to a website in some form).

The implication for journalists and news organisations is that you should only expect 1 per cent of your audience to participate in any given project. For every blog comment there are likely to be 99 passive readers; for every image upload another 99 users just looking; and so on. To get significant participation in a project you need a significant audience.

of any other media organisation for ideas. You may also want to consider whether to appoint particularly active users as moderators or administrators. Many forums show how many posts a user has made, which is often used as a marker of their standing in that community. Some forum communities include cliques of users who will turn up their noses at contributors who have not 'served their time' in contributing. It is important to understand these community dynamics.

Web expert and professor Clay Shirky – who is worth reading further if you are interested in online community – puts it particularly well in this speech he made to the BBC (2002):

> 'The relationship between the owner of community software and the community itself is like the relationship between a landlord and his or her tenants. The landlord owns the building, and the tenants take on certain responsibilities by living there. However, the landlord does not own the tenants themselves, nor their relations to one another. If you told tenants of yours that you expected to sit in on their dinner table conversation, they would revolt, and, as many organizations have found, the same reaction occurs in online communities.'
>
> 'Community is made possible by software, but the value is created by its participants. If you think of yourself as owning a community when you merely own the infrastructure, you will be astonished at the vitriol you will face if you try to force that community into or out of certain behaviours.'

In other words, as an online journalist you should be led by the community rather than the other way round, and remember that it is a conversation, not a lecture.

Comments on blog posts and articles

News organisations allow comments on articles and blog posts for a number of reasons. The hard commercial one is that it leads users to spend more time on a site both contributing and reading comments – which is good for advertising. The editorial reasons include engagement with an audience and the opportunity for users to help correct mistakes in an article – or add new information or angles. As Yochai Benkler (2006) puts it:

> '[This] does not mean, however, that deliberative journalism should reduce all discussion to common sense. Rather, the perspectives of "ordinary people" should be allowed to transform the analytical distinctions of established experts as well as define new questions.'

Blogs often include systems that notify you of any new comments on your blog. News website content management systems, however, often lack this feature – or instead notify the person responsible for the website rather than the individual journalist, so you may have to make a special point of checking comments on your articles or putting systems in place that will notify you.

As explained in Chapter 6 on blogging, comments are fundamental to the success of any blog, and this means engaging with them wherever possible. If you are lucky enough to receive lots of comments and you cannot engage all the time, then try to engage with the early comments to demonstrate your engagement and address issues early. Interestingly, although research has shown a minority of users are interested in commenting, a larger percentage see the ability to comment as important – and the feature appeals most to those who described themselves as not interested in news, i.e. the very readers news organisations should be most concerned about (Kelly, 2009).

At some point you will receive abusive or critical comments. How you deal with these is very important. The first rule is not to respond emotionally. As a journalist you should be prepared to deal with critical responses in a constructive way, and steer the debate away from descending into pointless abuse.

In practice, this means picking out the core points to a person's criticism and ignoring the personal attacks. If there are valid points, acknowledge them – and, most importantly, if there is an error in your article, correct it and acknowledge it in the comments (and the body of the article if possible). This can pay enormous dividends for you and the news organisation, leading to increased pageviews, more comments, and general goodwill as the commenter spreads the news about your positive reaction to their points.

Ignoring the comments is not a constructive approach and can either lead to comments being bogged down in personal attacks, or in users not contributing because they feel their voice is not heard – or both.

Some users, however, post abusive comments just to get a response – what is referred to as 'flaming'. The key is to recognise whether that is the case – and you will learn from the history of that person's comments. In the initial stages a good rule is to respond to the first comment but if they insist on trying to steer the debate back in a personal direction, or it's not adding anything to the debate, then say as much and politely withdraw. If you have a healthy commenting community you will notice that other users will deal with the commenter as well.

It is also worth noting that comment threads on blog posts can be extremely healthy without the constant input of the journalist. A sign of a successful blog is when users can engage in conversations with each other in the comments. If that is happening then the blog has become a platform not just for publishing but for genuine discussion.

In some cases news organisations will close comments on a particular article or blog post – sometimes on highly contentious issues such as immigration which are likely to lead to racist comments, but most often for legal reasons, i.e. the article is about an ongoing court case and there is a large risk of comments being made that are in contempt of court. You need to be aware of your organisation's policy on these issues.

Interactive storytelling

A number of news organisations have had big hits with 'clickable interactives': multimedia narratives that cover a story from a number of angles to create a rich user experience. Typically, these combine video coverage, audio slideshows, timelines and Flash animation to allow the user to choose how they explore the story, but any interactive or multimedia elements might be included. Research suggests that users spend more time on your page when information is presented in this format (DiSEL, 2005) and also recall more process-related information. In contrast, users appear to recall slightly more basic factual information when information is presented in normal HTML (Ruel & Outing, 2004).

The Washington Post's interactive feature 'Being A Black Man' (Plate 9), for example, explores the broad issue of 'what it means to be a black man in today's society' and features video interviews with people from a variety of backgrounds and careers; a poll for users to vote in; image maps; audio slideshows; and a comment feature.

Because of the quality and depth of such pieces of work, they often attract large numbers of views from around the world, over a long period of time. However, the resources involved in their production mean that subjects must be chosen carefully both for their mass appeal and longevity as a news story. Issues covered by *The Guardian* (www.guardian.co.uk/interactive), BBC (news.bbc.co.uk/1/hi/in_depth/interactives/default.stm) and the *Financial Times* (www.ft.com/uk/interactive) – which all have sections dedicated to interactive features – range from climate change and women in the boardroom to the Middle East conflict and a world wine map.

Laura Ruel and Nora Paul (2007) say that interactive presentations work best when you want users to spend more time with the presentation; describe the experience as 'enjoyable;' recall more of the information; recall your brand; and feel entertained. Static presentations, on the other hand, work best when you want users to 'click to' all of the presentation's materials; and perceive the site navigation as easy.

They also present a checklist of seven questions to ask when considering producing a story as an interactive. They are:

1 Does the story concern elaborate or unfamiliar processes/procedures? (Yes – 1 point)

2 Is the level of interest in the topic high enough that people would be willing to figure out story navigation? (Yes – 1 point)

3 Does the story have value beyond the first few weeks? Is it likely to be a topic in the news again? (Yes – 1 point)

4 Is entertaining the audience more important than simply informing? (Yes – 1 point)

5 Is it important that the audience be able to recall specific facts from the story? (No – 1 point)

6 If the story is told in separate components, is it essential that all the components be viewed by the audience? (No – 1 point)

7 Do you hope the audience recalls where they saw the information? (Yes – 1 point)

If you get five or more points, they say, you should 'strongly consider an interactive story approach'.

Sometimes a simple calculator can make a successful interactive feature: the *New York Times*' 'Is It Better to Buy or Rent?' (www.nytimes.com/interactive/business/buy-rent-calculator.html?_r = 1), for example, allows you to compare the costs of renting or buying equivalent homes based on a range of factors.

A more complex example is the *Financial Times*' UK Deficit Buster, which invited users to make different decisions on how to cut the country's deficit. The user could choose which political party's strategy to adopt, make their policy cuts, and then find out what the implications of those cuts might be. The interactive tool used exclusive data from the Institute for Fiscal Studies, was featured on the front page of the newspaper and affected the news agenda that day. The *FT*'s Rob Minto says the interactive took two days to create: 'It was actually relatively simple once you had the data'.

However, one of the potential disadvantages of clickable interactives is that they can become out of date if new information is not incorporated. Some ways to address this include allowing comments so users can post updates, incorporating a live RSS feed from sources elsewhere which are updated (e.g. blogs, the news site itself, or a social bookmarking account), or pulling from a live database which itself is updated. Either way, you will need to plan for the long-term maintenance of the interactive, including manual monitoring and corrections.

Although most clickable interactives are created using sophisticated design tools such as Flash and languages such as HTML5 and Javascript, you can also use one of the increasing number of web-based tools that allow you to achieve similar results, such as Vuvox, Dipity and Sprout. The more complex your interactive, the more advanced your technical skills are likely to need to be.

Closer look Q&A: Robert Minto, Interactive Editor, FT.com

Q: Why are interactive features important?

Interactivity is important in the same way that people climb Everest – because it's there. If you can do it, you should. If you don't allow your audience to have a conversation (i.e. comment or participate in some way) they will assume you don't care what they have to say.

The main objection is that comment areas turn into a 'who shouts loudest' competition, which can be an issue. Also, overwhelming numbers of comments mean a debate is hard to follow, and can go rapidly off-topic. But a good debate is a great thing. It's important that writers contribute and respond – simply writing the article isn't good enough, you need to engage with (intelligent) comments.

Q: What kinds of features work well?

Features that work well are ones with a long shelf-life, that people can turn to as a guide or application, that show more than a simple story could convey. The *FT*'s deficit buster is a great example: www.ft.com/deficitbuster which set the news agenda. Other more data-driven features include our feature on sovereign debt: www.ft.com/debt – a country-by-country analysis of debt, and a numbers-driven feature on the competitive areas between Google, Apple and Microsoft: www.ft.com/techgiants. All very different, but they enliven the story and have relevance a long time after publication.

Q: What can go wrong?

Three main things:

1 The so what factor. Lots of work to show something that we all knew anyway.

2 Traffic just doesn't register. Not promoted, not forwarded, no buzz.

3 You're wrong! Comparing datasets that infer causation when it's really correlation. Getting the data wrong.

And there's the tech side of screwing up code in graphics or databases falling over which can set you back, but that's another area altogether.

Q: What skills do you need to have to convey information via maps and graphics?

Statistical rigour, attention to detail, an eye for design, understanding XML and things like that, knowing a great image when you see one, keeping things simple, being open to new possibilities.

Q: Do journalists need to engage with readers? What about snarky comments?

Simple answer: yes. Not following up on a few comments is like starting a debate at a dinner party, and then leaving the room. You wouldn't do it in real life, so don't do it online. Be respectful (where due). Ignore snarky comments, and have a thick skin.

Games and interactivity

'Tell me and I'll forget; show me and I may remember; involve me and I'll understand.'

Proverb

One emerging area of interactivity in journalism is the idea of using games to allow users to engage with issues in the news. Like interactive storytelling, this is a hugely resource-intensive type of journalism and, as a result, rarely used. However, it is not unlikely that the cost of producing a 'news game' will come down enough for these to become more common.

Of course, the idea of a 'game' is a broad one – many news organisations already use quizzes, for example, to liven up their coverage (the BBC produces an annual Oscars quiz on its news website; and many news websites feature weekly sports or current events quizzes). But, as the BBC's Philip Trippenbach (2009) explains:

> 'Where games really come into their own is as a medium for deep explanatory journalism – especially journalism about complicated systems with many inter-relationships, interacting forces and factions ... A video game journalist can construct a model of how things work and interact with the situation being described, and allow the audience to explore the model at leisure.'

The *Gotham Gazette*, which has been a leader in the field of games journalism, has created news games including the 'Ground Zero Planner' (which allows users to 'design the World Trade Center site the way you think it should look') and The Budget Game (www.gothamgazette.com/budgetgame) where you can try to balance the city's budget. *The Economist*'s 'Energyville' game, meanwhile, tasked players with ensuring a city's energy supply in reaction to various financial, environmental and technological changes.

Trippenbach feels games are less useful for telling the facts of what happened in a given past event, but that they have enormous potential to explain how things work. As an example, he suggests a game on the topical issue of illegal immigration:

> 'A game . . . could cast the player in the role of an African migrant trying to get into the EU. The player would have to deal with all aspects of the journey – tough conditions back home, dealing with corrupt smugglers, eluding border controls, obtaining black-market work or fake papers . . . This sort of engagement, if properly designed, would be intensely fun and convey a rich understanding of the complex realities of a difficult issue.'

Academic literature on journalism often highlights how the pressures of print and broadcast formats force journalists to simplify real life into black-and-white narratives with a beginning, middle and end. The potential of games – and interactivity in general – to allow users to explore an issue as if it were a physical space is something that most online journalists should be thinking about as part of their role.

Closer look How do I make my site more interactive?

- Link. It's the most fundamental element of online journalism: whenever you mention a report, a previous story, an organisation or a concept, link to another webpage that gives more information, whether it's on your site or not.

▶

- Make sure the technical basics are covered: comments on all pages (not just articles); as many RSS feeds as is possible – from individual sections, journalists and keywords (tags) to feeds for comments on a particular article.
- Adopt a cultural attitude that sees users as partners in news production, not mere consumers. Help them contribute in any way they can: respond to comments, provide raw material, involve them early on in any story.
- Make any audio, video or maps embeddable by using services which provide that functionality (e.g. YouTube, Google Maps) – or take it to the user.

Summary

Interactivity is a central feature of online journalism as a genre. The best online journalism exploits the potential of the medium to create an experience that allows users to experience the story in the way they want – whether that is at a time or place convenient to them, or in a way that allows them to ask questions of the aspects they don't understand or, indeed, agree with. Journalism that does not allow users to interact with the issues, facts and stories involved risks being seen as flat and frustrating: a disappointing user experience that reflects on the news brand as a whole.

News is a highly social product. As well as serving the information and entertainment needs of consumers, it provides a currency that can be exchanged with friends, family and colleagues to establish a person's place in their community: 'Did you hear about . . .?' 'What do you think about . . .?' Until relatively recently, traditional media companies had a near-monopoly on news. But the rise of the web has brought with it vast competition in who can provide that. For news organisations, then, the game has been raised, and journalists need to adapt in playing to the strengths of a new platform that is interactive, social, and endlessly linked.

Successful online journalism – like successful journalism in other media – engages the user, allows them to connect with others who share their interests, and ultimately empowers them as citizens. And there are developments every month that bring new possibilities for all of these – make sure you explore them.

Activities

1. Draw up a storyboard for an interactive game around a particular issue. Think about the following:
   - What are the issues?
   - Who are the main characters?
   - What are the challenges that they face?
   - What factors do they have to weigh up in making decisions?
   - What sorts of storylines exist around this topic? (History, present, future.)

2. For a particular topic you want to write about, think about how you can give your users control:

   - During *newsgathering*: can you allow users to interact with your ideas generation process? Research? Interviewing?
   - *News production*: how can you produce news in ways that allow users to have more control over it?
   - *Distribution*: how can you give users control over distribution (without undermining your business model – or in a way that adds to it)?

3. Use Google Maps or another mapping tool to create a map of incidences of a particular event, e.g. crimes, failing schools, accidents.
4. Play with one of the online interactive storytelling tools – choose from Vuvox, Fine-Tuna, Animoto, Comiqs, PimPamPum, Sketchcast, Storybird or VoiceThread. Think how it might allow you to tell a story differently – what sorts of stories, issues or fields would suit it best?

Further reading

Bruns, A. (2005) *Gatewatching*, USA: Peter Lang Publishing.
Bruns, A. (2008) *Blogs, Wikipedia, Second Life, and Beyond*, USA: Peter Lang Publishing.
McAdams, M. (2005) *Flash Journalism*, USA: Focal Press.

Chapter 10

User-generated content

This chapter will cover:

- What is UGC?
- Closer look: UGC on news sites
- Why is UGC important?
- Closer look: Five types of content?
- Technology is not a strategy, it's a tool
- Closer look: Live UGC feeds – issues to remember
- UGC: Different audience, different issues
- Working with UGC: the contributors
- Why do people contribute content?
- UGC technologies
- Closer look: UGC and copyright
- Closer look: Hoaxes

Introduction

Depending on which study you read, at least half of all internet users have contributed some sort of content to a website. From uploading photos to a social network or making an edit on Wikipedia, to posting comments on a blog or starting a blog themselves, the internet provides countless ways to communicate, make connections with others, share and express yourself.

In the news industry this enormous variety of creativity, opinion and communication is often referred to as 'user-generated content' – or its more common, abbreviated form: UGC.

It is a phrase generally disliked for its ugly commercial framing, and the way it downplays the editorial value of 'content'; yet, for better or worse, and despite numerous suggestions of alternatives ('audience material', 'community curated works', 'participatory culture', 'indigenous content', 'entrepreneurial generated content'), the phrase appears to be here to stay.

On news websites UGC has become part of the furniture, whether it's a comment box on news stories, or Your Videos section, to streaming Twitter updates on an event into your website and providing fully-fledged social networks. This chapter explores the reasons for incorporating user-generated content into a news operation, who contributes content online and why, elements to consider in a UGC strategy, and how user-generated content has been used on news platforms.

What is UGC?

There is a long history of audience involvement in news production, from letters to the editor and readers' photos, to radio and television phone-ins, and on-screen texts from viewers.

For many producers and editors, the development of user-generated content online is seen – and often treated – as a continuation of this tradition. However, there are two features of user-generated content online that make it a qualitatively different proposition.

First, unlike print and broadcast, internet users do not need to send something to the traditional media for it to be distributed to an audience: a member of the public can upload a video to YouTube with the potential to reach millions. They can share photos with people all over the world. They can provide unedited commentary on any topic they choose, and publish it, regularly, on a forum or blog. Quite often they are simply sharing with an online community of other people with similar interests. But sometimes they will find themselves with larger audiences than a traditional publisher because of the high quality of the material, its expertise, or its impact.

The bigger the story, the more likely that it will be broken on a user-generated content service before a news organisation's website. News of the earthquake in China in 2008, for example, broke on Twitter even before the US Geological Survey had recorded the tremors.

At other times, UGC will highlight interest in a story that news organisations did not think newsworthy as happened, for example, when US Senator Trent Lott made pro-segregationist remarks at an event and bloggers not only asked for him to be called to account, but also found a history of previous similar remarks.

Because of this, one of the challenges for media organisations has been to find a way to tap into blog platforms, forums, and video and photo sharing websites, rather than trying to persuade people to send material to their news websites as well. For some, this has meant setting up groups on the likes of Flickr, LinkedIn and Facebook to communicate with users on their own territory. For others, it is simply a matter of adapting their working practices so that online sources are monitored alongside more traditional sources.

The second difference between user generated content online and its print and broadcast antecedents is that there are no limitations on the space for it. In fact, whole sites can be given over to your audience and, indeed, are. *The Telegraph*, *Sun* and *Express* all host social networks where readers can publish photos and blog posts, and talk on forums. *The Guardian*'s Comment Is Free website provides a platform where dozens of non-journalist experts blog about the issues of the day. And an increasing number of regional newspapers provide similar spaces for people to blog their analysis of local issues under their news brand, while numerous specialist magazines host forums with hundreds of members exchanging opinions and experiences every day. On the multimedia side, Sky and the BBC provide online galleries where users can upload hundreds of photos and videos.

The term user-generated content itself is actually probably too general to be genuinely useful to journalists. It can refer to anything from a comment posted by a one-time anonymous website visitor, to a 37-minute documentary that one of your readers spent ten years researching. The most accurate definition might simply be that user-generated content is 'material your organisation has not commissioned and paid for'. Unless you are talking in such broad terms it is worth being specific about the type of user-generated content you are referring to – and, more importantly, why you are using it. The rest of this chapter will look more specifically at the different types of UGC, the people who create it, and the strategies news organisations and journalists employ in working with it.

Closer look UGC on news sites

Here are just some of the forms user-generated content takes on news websites:

- Allowing comments on news stories and reporter blogs
- Allowing users to rate stories
- User votes and polls
- Galleries of images submitted by users
- User-submitted video galleries
- Images and video from users making up part of a journalist's report
- Incorporating live 'feeds' from discussions around the web, e.g. 'What people are saying about this on Twitter'
- Groups on Facebook and LinkedIn for the news website
- Flickr and YouTube groups for readers
- News website Nings (a build-your-own social network platform)
- Social networks such as MySun and MyTelegraph where users can blog, post to forums, 'bookmark' favourite articles and post other information
- Liveblogs using platforms like CoverItLive
- Live chats

- Users tagging articles with key words
- Forums
- Reader blogs
- Live Q&As
- Wikis (webpages that users can edit)
- User-generated maps
- Mashups (users mix content from one news site with other content or technology, e.g. mapping)
- Crowdsourcing (inviting users to help investigate something, often by breaking it into smaller tasks that they can complete)

Why is UGC important?

'UGC is not cheap,' said Neil McIntosh, head of editorial development at *The Guardian*, in 2008: 'It's many things, but it's not cheap. It's extremely expensive to nurture it and to make it something worthwhile. My heart sinks when I hear the union [of journalists] saying that journalists are going to be replaced with UGC.'

The costs of UGC include the technical cost of hosting multimedia content, hiring new staff such as community managers and moderators, and training existing journalists to monitor and contribute to UGC. So, why do publishers spend so much time and money in trying to attract, host and monitor it?

For publishers, UGC is commercially attractive. It can help attract more users and keep them on site for longer. It also provides more content against which to sell advertising, although the unpredictable nature of UGC means it often commands lower advertising rates than editorial (Deloitte, 2009).

Secondly, there is clear demand for it: four of the most visited websites in the UK are UGC sites, while research by Deloitte found 51 per cent of consumers were accessing personal content created by others (a figure rising to 71 per cent for those aged 13–24). Research by Nielsen (Ofcom, 2008) into user behaviour shows that people are spending an increasing proportion of their online time on the types of community sites where user generated content is shared, while research by Hitwise into the area found that, when people searched for news events, Wikipedia and YouTube figured more prominently than the sites of mainstream media news companies.

On the editorial side, when a big story breaks – from the Chinese earthquake to the Mumbai attacks – it increasingly breaks on social media websites such as blogs, Twitter, forums, Wikipedia and social networks – the homes of user generated content. As the head of Reuters said of the Asian Tsunami of December 26 2004: 'For the first 24 hours the best and the only photos and video came from tourists armed with 1.3 megapixel portable telephones, digital cameras and camcorders. And if you didn't have those pictures you weren't on the story.' (Glocer, 2006) The head of the BBC's UGC hub, Matthew Eltringham (2009), notes: 'We are increasingly moving the focus of our work into the much wider and wilder world of the web itself.'

In this environment there is an increasing focus on journalists as 'content curators' and community managers. Content curation involves summarising, clarifying and verifying the vast amount of information circulating around particular issues and stories. During the Mumbai terror attacks, for example, BBC journalists had to verify claims being made on Twitter, while a survivor's blog account of the Haiti earthquake found by a *Guardian* journalist was published on its front page.

Community management, meanwhile, means helping communities to engage with the news operation as contributors, collaborators, tipsters and distributors. The BBC's UGC hub has built an enormous database of potential sources from its contributions, while traffic from users of web services such as Twitter and Facebook are accounting for an increasing proportion of visits to news websites. Increasingly, consumers are expecting news to find them rather than the other way round.

The Guardian's Social Media approach statement offers a particularly good summary of how a journalist should approach user-generated content – and provides a useful template for any news organisation's own policy. This is what it says (emphasis in original):

1. **Participation adds richness and perspective** to media objects.
2. As part of our mission to become the world's leading liberal voice, we want to **encourage the world's voices** to come together on our site to discuss or participate in conversations about liberal contexts or issues.
3. In a really social media company, **the role of the journalist becomes more important, not less**. Journalists become curators of contexts and experiences – interactive storytellers, trusted guides and interpreters of fact and experience.
4. **We should embrace, not replace, successful external social applications** (e.g. Flickr, Facebook, Delicious, Youtube, Digg, etc.) and encourage people to use applications they're comfortable with to promote, extend and share our content and their experience of it.
5. **Quality of conversation is more important than quantity**. We aim to inspire, recognise and reward quality contributions. Engagement matters.
6. **Communities and conversations need nurturing after creation.** We need to put in work after launch or publication, though it may use different skills and tools from the work put in before.
7. Not everything will work for a mass audience, but the long tail is important: **we support niche interest communities**.

Closer look Five types of content?

In their study 'ugc@thebbc' (2009) Claire Wardle and Andrew Williams looked at how the BBC dealt with user-generated content and suggested a typology of five types from a news organisation perspective. These were:

1. Audience content (broken down into Audience Footage – of newsworthy events – experiences – case studies – and stories – tip-offs)
2. Audience comments (opinions shared in response to the news)
3. Collaborative content (material produced by the audience with training and support from journalists)

▶

4. Networked journalism (initiatives which 'explicitly attempt to tap into expert communities within the audience to improve the quality of journalistic output')
5. Non-news content (e.g. photographs of wildlife, scenic weather, community events)

They map the tensions between these in Figure 10.1.

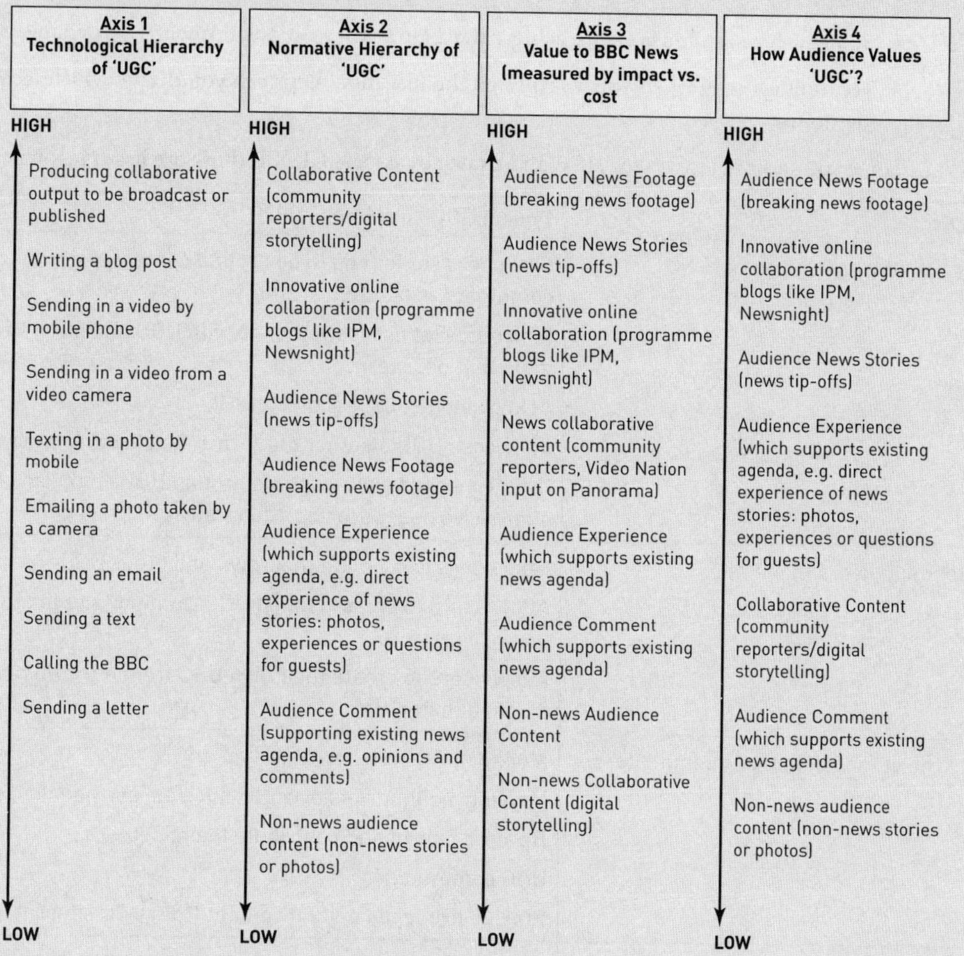

Figure 10.1 Tensions between audience material

Wardle C. and Williams A. (2008), 'UGC@ the BBC: Understanding its Impact upon Contributors, Non-Contributors and BBC News', A research paper for Cardiff School of Journalism

Technology is not a strategy, it's a tool

A common mistake made when first venturing into user generated content is to focus on the technology rather than the reasons for using it. 'We need to have our own social network!' someone shouts. But why? And, indeed, how do you do so successfully?

A useful framework to draw on when thinking about how you approach UGC is the POST process for social media strategy outlined by Forrester Research (Bernoff, 2007). This involves identifying:

- People: who are your audience (or intended audience), and what social media (e.g. Facebook, blogs, Twitter, forums, etc.) do they use? Equally important, why do *they* use social media?
- Objectives: what do you want to achieve through using UGC?
- Strategy: how are you going to achieve that? How will relationships with users change?
- Technology: only when you've explored the first three steps can you decide which technologies to use.

Some common objectives for UGC and strategies associated with those are listed below:

Objective	Typical UGC strategies
Users spend longer on our site	Give users something to do around content, e.g. comments, vote, etc. Find out what users want to do with UGC and allow them to do that on-site Acknowledge and respond to UGC Showcase UGC on other platforms, e.g. print, broadcast Create a positive atmosphere around UGC – prevent aggressive users scaring others away
Attract more users to our site	Help users to promote their own and other UGC Allow users to cross-publish UGC from our site to others and *vice versa* Allow users to create their own UGC from our own raw or finished materials
Get to the stories before our competitors	Monitor UGC on other sites Monitor mentions of keywords such as 'earthquake', etc. Become part of and contribute to online UGC communities Provide live feeds pulling content from UGC sites*
Increase the amount of content on our site	Make it easy for users to contribute material to the site Make it useful Make it fun Provide rewards for contributing – social or financial
Improve the editorial quality of our work	Provide UGC space for users to highlight errors, contribute updates Ensure that we attract the right contributors in terms of skills, expertise, contacts, etc. Involve users from the earliest stages of production

*See the section on live feeds.

Closer look Live UGC feeds – issues to remember

News organisations have experimented with pulling live feeds of user-generated content from websites such as Twitter, Flickr and YouTube. If you do this there are two key risks you need to consider. The first is copyright. When *The Independent* decided to illustrate its online coverage of snow-covered Britain by pulling a feed of any images on Flickr with the keyword 'uksnow', for example, they didn't realise that the stream would include images that some owners had explicitly stated should not be used in commercial media.

A second issue to consider is potentially offensive or spammy material. During the 2009 budget, for example, *The Telegraph* embedded a live feed from Twitter of any messages ('tweets') that included the word '#budget'. The coverage was hijacked by a number of users who posted irrelevant, amusing and abusive tweets such as: 'Well that's the *Telegraph's* #budget twitterfeed boned. What shall we destroy next?' before the feed was taken off the site (Kiss, 2009).

UGC: Different audience, different issues

Journalists are not only expected to know their audience but also how that differs from the population as a whole. Hosting user-generated content complicates this because not only will an online audience invariably be different from the print or broadcast audience, if you have one (transcending national or local areas for instance), but the section of that audience which actively contributes material will be different too. As a journalist it is crucial that you bear in mind the different groups of people you are dealing with:

- People in the country as a whole
- The specific audience for the print or broadcast product (if there is one)
- The audience for the online product
- The audience that contributes user-generated content.

In 2007, for example, according to a MORI survey (Wardle and Williams, 2009), only 23 per cent of the British public had sent in material to a broadcast, print or online news organisation. Just 4 per cent had sent material to a dedicated news website (not to be confused with general UGC sites).

While UGC can be useful in illustrating, complementing or generating stories, it should not be used as a reflection of 'public opinion' or 'the state of the country'. To make such a statement the sample must be demographically representative of the population as a whole, and large enough not to be skewed by small individual differences.

In contrast, some online grassroots protests will be dismissed by their targets, or by others, as not reflecting genuine opposition. Uproar over comments made in an opinion column by *Daily Mail* journalist Jan Moir regarding the death of Boyzone star Stephen Gateley, for example, generated a reaction so strong online that the Press Complaints Commission received more complaints than at any point in its history. Jan Moir dismissed the reaction as 'heavily orchestrated', but analysis of the reaction across Twitter, forums, Facebook, blogs and the *Daily Mail* article itself, indicated no central organisation but rather communication facilitated by the internet between various people who were able to express, show, and react to the article in question at an accelerated rate.

Returning to UGC on news websites, the typical contributor to any news organisation (in any medium) is white (97%), male (54%), between 55 and 59 (31%), employed full-time (34%)

and a non-manual worker (36%). It is worth remembering that internet access and the literacy to use social media are distributed unevenly within society, with figures in 2008 indicating that around a third of adults did not use the internet or had never used it. Internet access is particularly low in the over-65s and people in social grades D and E (semi-skilled and unskilled manual workers, casual workers, pensioners and those on state benefits).

In this context, then, say UGC researchers Wardle and Williams (2009), phrases like these should be avoided:

'We've had lots of emails. I want to read a few of them as they really give a sense of what people are thinking.'

'The audience seems very divided by the look of the texts and emails we've received.'

Working with UGC: the contributors

Working with UGC involves two broad approaches. The first is about having systems in place that make it as easy as possible for potential contributors to create material and share it on your site with you and other users. The second is about moving away from your own news website to where potential sources are communicating elsewhere on the web: forums, social networks, Twitter, blogs and photo, video and audio sharing websites.

Nowadays, you cannot assume that UGC will come to you simply because of the brand of the news organisation; increasingly, the online reputation you have as a journalist, and the relationships you foster with others online, can be vital in gaining access to eyewitnesses, experts and material.

This sort of journalism means cultivating contacts, not just a contacts *book*. It means understanding communities, and sometimes being led by them. It also means creating tools and systems as often as creating stories.

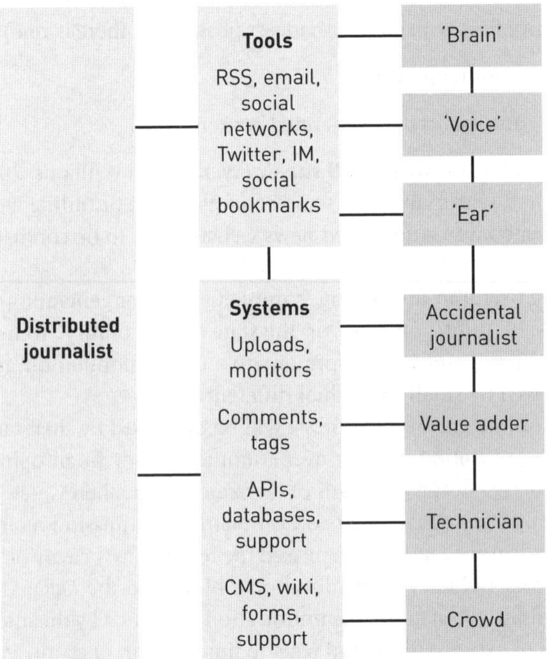

Figure 10.2 Distributed journalism
Source: Paul Bradshaw, onlinejournalismblog.com

The types of contributors that come under the UGC umbrella can vary enormously, from the specialist blogger who has a large audience and high journalistic standards, to members of the public who capture key footage on their mobile phone. Once again, you should think carefully about which contributors you are seeing to involve, and how you might do that.

Finding contributors through monitoring

The first three types of contributor are already active producers of UGC online. As a result, the best strategy to involve them in your news operation is to use monitoring tools such as RSS readers (see Chapter 6 on blogging for more on how to use these) and to make contact with them whenever you can – through comments, Twitter messages, and so on.

The brain: journalists already use experts extensively. Traditionally, these have been accessed through professional bodies and academic institutions. But this often means that these sources are part of a narrow, political elite that can have vested interests. Increasingly, however, online journalists are gaining access to a wider range of voices whose authority comes from many sources, from hands-on experience to simple, well supported arguments.

As an online journalist, you should be monitoring these experts, subscribing to their RSS feeds (see Chapter 6 on blogging for more on RSS feeds), quoting or linking when relevant and commissioning when you need analysis. In this way bloggers such as Royal Mail worker 'Roy Mayall', ambulance worker Tom Reynolds and Baghdad Blogger Salam Pax have all been published in *The Guardian*, while the *Birmingham Post* invited local figures to post on its blogs section.

There is also an argument for leading by example: a distributed journalist who blogs is demonstrating they want to be part of the conversation. Others have employed an 'enthusiast-in-chief' who brings a reputation with them to lead a UGC site – as Yourclimbing.com did when it appointed champion climber Katie Brown to that position.

The voice: Separate from the expert, the 'voice' writes well, compellingly, often wittily or in an entertaining fashion, whether or not they have expertise or personal experience – much as the traditional columnist does. Or they produce compelling imagery, video or audio. There are photobloggers, for example, who produce an ongoing visual record of their local area or culture.

Once again these are people you should be following, linking to and occasionally commissioning from. If you or your publication have set up a Flickr group these are the people you should invite – or indeed approach to lead it.

The ear: someone, somewhere, knows what's going on in a particular community of space or interest. They may filter that to their blog, or Twitter account, or mailing list – or they may simply note what they see in a social bookmarking account (e.g. Delicious, Digg, Stumbleupon). The distributed journalist subscribes to the RSS feeds or mailing list, and supports and encourages this filtering by linking and contributing when they can. A combination of cuttings file, specialist publication and community representative, for a journalist they can provide useful leads in specific areas or a resource for researching a particular topic or field.

Attracting contributors through systems

The second group of contributors tend to be less active producers of UGC online, and are more likely to contribute to news sites. Attracting them to your site rather than to your competitors will partly depend on the systems your site has in place to allow them to contribute.

The accidental journalist: this is the person who stumbles upon a news story – the archetypal citizen journalist – and captures it on a mobile phone, camcorder, or simply with their eyes. You cannot cultivate a relationship with the accidental journalist in the same way as you can with habitual producers – instead, news organisations have to rely on the old-fashioned relationship represented by their brand, reputation and reach.

So, what can the news organisation do? Be available, be a trusted name, and have a budget to pay if you can: amateur video footage of suspected July 7 bombers being arrested, for example, was sold to Sky for tens of thousands of pounds. A spokesperson at the time said the channel judged each offer 'on a case by case basis and would consider paying for footage on rare occasions where pictures have extraordinary editorial value' (Douglas, 2005).

Set up channels of access: include journalists' emails in their reports; provide simple uploading facilities on your website; and invest resources in monitoring submissions both to your own site and to other user-generated content sites like YouTube and Flickr – because the accidental journalist will not always know they have a story. Ensure that journalists know how to get media from a mobile phone on to a computer if a member of the public walks into the newsroom with footage.

Finally, get involved in media training with your community, so that (a) they can spot a story; (b) they produce something of decent quality; and (c) they think of you first, because you're the one who taught them to do (a) and (b). Wardle and Williams' BBC study (2009), for example, notes the success of the BBC's programme of 'intervention-based participatory journalism' which provides training and support to under-represented groups.

The value adder: the value adder is hot on facts, hot on grammar, hot on spelling (but not on style or legal issues, a key role for subeditors). They pick up the mistakes, and they clean up vandalism. They annotate, adding bits of information – comments, useful links, tags (internally if you have a tagging system for users and externally if they use services like Delicious or Digg), or votes on whether a story is 'good' or 'bad'.

Again, systems are key here – for instance, in having a comments facility in the first place; acknowledging and making corrections; allowing tagging and bookmarking. And a culture of openness where feedback is welcomed and value adders are thanked *or* recognised.

The technician: this is the person who takes your stories, classifieds or raw data and does something interesting or valuable with them – for example, mapping them with Google Maps; or comparing editors' choices with what people are actually reading; or creating a Facebook app; or simply suggesting an idea.

In September 2009, for example, independent developers created a mobile phone application that allowed users to download *Guardian* articles to their phone before their daily commute. The popularity of the application demonstrated a demand which led three months later to *The Guardian* itself launching a paid-for application for the iPhone, which instantly became a best-seller. It was because the same newspaper made data on MPs' expenses available that developer and academic Tony Hirst was able to identify which politicians were claiming unusually high travel expenses – and to visualise this on a map.

The technician can add genuine creativity and value to content, but for them to do that you need to open up your systems so that users can make interesting things with your stories, media or data. An increasing number of newspapers including *The Times*, *Guardian* and *New York Times*, for example, now publish 'data blogs' which talk about the raw data behind current stories, often making that data available in basic spreadsheets. Al Jazeera, meanwhile, makes many of its video reports available online with permission for people to re-use for non-commercial purposes. BBC's Backstage project provides a supportive community for developers to do interesting things with the vast amount of untapped potential in the material held by the corporation.

See the section in Chapter 9 on interactivity for more on 'mashups and APIs', and Chapter 5 on data journalism for more on the potential of raw data.

The crowd: the former audience is not just a group of people who can now talk to you. A conversation can only achieve so much. Crowdsourcing – inviting users to collaborate in the process of production (literally: 'outsourcing to the crowd') – offers a way to cover issues and investigate stories that, in some cases, traditional journalism cannot match. It does this by making users part of the news-gathering process.

There are, broadly, two main types of crowdsourcing project: one taps into a diversity of expertise (the engineer, the insider, the accountant) or experience; the other taps into sheer man-power – lots of people doing a small task each, like sifting through one part of a large amount of information, making a request for information, or conducting one interview.

A classic example of the former was the investigation conducted by the Florida News-Press into high charges for connecting new homes to the water supply. Not having the resources to do the whole investigation themselves, the newspaper invited readers to help, and tapped into a wealth of expertise in the area. The second type of crowdsourced investigation is becoming more common: one of its best examples was when Parliament released records of MPs' expenses and *The Guardian* published them on its website, inviting users to look at individual pages and categorise them.

Systems that facilitate that process – like wikis, content management sytems or even simple online forms – are important, but so is developing support structures and identifying the one per cent of users who are regular contributors (see the 1–9–90 rule in the previous chapter).

Naturally, these categories are not exclusive – the brain may have a good voice (so to speak); the 'ear' may add value; being part of a crowd may lead someone to think of filming a newsworthy event when they stumble upon it. Perhaps even more important than either your monitoring tools or systems for users to contribute is a culture that supports users' activities. If you do not involve and encourage users in your news production process, they may contribute content elsewhere where it is easier or more rewarding.

Why do people contribute content?

Research by McKinsey in 2006 suggested that the motivations behind users contributing video to a website fell into a series of categories. The top four were:

- a hunger for fame;
- the urge to have fun;
- the desire to share experiences with friends; and
- a desire for others to benefit from their knowledge.

Notably, older users were more likely to share content than younger ones.

Research into the motivations of Wikipedia users, using a framework from earlier studies of volunteering, found that those motivated by fun and ideology (the belief that information should be free) were likely to make more contributions (Nov, 2007).

Research into photo sharing (Miller and Edwards, 2007), meanwhile, has noted how camera-phone images have been used to tell stories *with* photos rather than (in traditional image sharing) *about* photos.

Li's (2005) research into the motivations of bloggers found the most significant factors to be:

- documenting their own life and keeping in touch with friends;
- improving their writing;
- self-expression;
- to share information;
- feeling part of a community; and
- the appeal of the medium itself (instant, easy, accessible).

John Kelly's report on citizen journalism (2009) identified factors including enhancing one's reputation; gaining exposure; activism; to engender a sense of community; and the joy of creation.

Clearly, news websites offer fame and exposure of a sort to users, but the other motivations are equally important. For example, one of the reasons for the incredible success of Facebook is how easy it makes it to share experiences with friends. Given the choice between uploading their photos to their local news website and Facebook, most users will choose the latter – and the same applies to photo-sharing websites like Flickr or video-sharing sites like YouTube.

If you are to work on a UGC project, then, you need to think about the full range of reasons people upload content and do the following:

- Make it easy for people to share with their friends
- Make it fun
- Provide a feedback mechanism so they know it makes a difference.

The other key element in the success of a UGC project is attracting and supporting the 'alpha users' who contribute the majority of the content. Much user-generated content adheres to a 'long tail' law, with a small number of users responsible for the majority of material and page views, and the majority of users contributing less material which receives less attention. When McKinsey looked at a video-sharing website, for example, they found 3–6 per cent of users were responsible for 75 per cent of the videos; and 2 per cent of users accounted for over 50 per cent of all videos viewed.

A healthy UGC community relies on this active minority to attract the less active majority. Neglect them, and they will go elsewhere, taking the community with them.

UGC technologies: pictures and Flickr

Strong images are an integral element of both print and television journalism, and UGC websites such as Flickr (which allow you to upload photos and share them with family, friends or the world) are becoming a significant source of images for many publishers and broadcasters. In addition, many news websites have extensive galleries of user photos.

Hosting users' photos yourself – as broadcasters such as the BBC and Sky do – allows you to control how they are presented, and to organise and 'brand' that accordingly. However, this obviously requires investment in technology and management.

Using a platform like Flickr – as publications such as *The Guardian*, *Manchester Evening News* and *Liverpool Post* do – avoids these costs and allows you to tap into existing photographic communities. However, it also requires relinquishing control over that content, while there are costs in maintaining and supporting the community (contributing to Flickr group forums, for example, or providing advice), and time spent cross-publishing content on to the news website (including gaining permission).

Of course, the BBC and Sky maintain groups on Flickr too, partly because users who are particularly interested in photography are more likely to post their images there, but also due to its added functionality. Having a group on Flickr also provides a news organisation with an added distribution and promotion channel, another way for users to stumble across your content.

Flickr has been used by news organisations in creative ways. In Liverpool the *Daily Post*'s Flickr group led to the production of a book of photos capturing the city's year as European Capital of Culture. Writing about how the UGC element made the book different from a traditional photography book, Alison Gow explained:

'I think the difference is that the Flickr photographers weren't running to a tight schedule, covering the event for two papers, up against a deadline and with another job to get to. They were immersed in the event, spectator and recorder (sometimes participant); they were capturing the essence of the performance, rather than faithfully portraying an event.

'[It] has offered some clue to new, exciting ways newspapers can work with communities to create something new, lasting and valuable for readers. We could have produced a book of 2008 using staff images only and it would have been a quality publication. But collaborating with the Flickr group to tell the story of a special year feels so much more satisfying and is, I think, a more appropriate tribute.'

Sarah Hartley, who was involved in Flickr-based projects at the *Manchester Evening News*, feels that Flickr and photographic UGC work particularly successfully when focused around a specific theme or event. 'If you're quite specific about what you expect of people it seems to work best. And backing that up by ensuring that those guidelines are kept to.'

The Guardian, whose experiments with Flickr include inviting users to upload their 'message to Obama' (later published as a book), have comprehensive internal guidance on setting up Flickr groups. Written by Meg Pickard, it includes the following advice about setting up and running a Flickr group.

Dos and don'ts of setting up and running a Flickr group

Do this

- Ask yourself: 'Are people really likely to bother participating?' If not, then it's not worth doing.
- Check whether anyone else is already running an identical group – if so, join it, don't duplicate it.
- Make it clear what the group is for – e.g. is there a particular format or type of shot? Remember that, while setting constraints can be limiting, they can also be extremely helpful and make it easier for people to join in or know how to participate.
- Invite people to join the group, but don't spam. Invite people who have a known or proven interest in the topic.
- Participate in the group. Respond to questions, comment on photos and keep looking for good things or people to invite to the collection. Add images yourself whenever possible – good community requires participation, not just a platform.
- Recognise and respond to good or interesting submissions or perspectives, even if you don't feature them on the [newspaper] site.
- Act as a good Flickr member: report issues where you find them and encourage good behaviour.
- Be a good ambassador for the [newspaper] on the foreign turf that is Flickr.com. Behave well and be welcoming, funny, polite and intelligent.
- Above all, always treat Flickr users with respect and fairness.

Don't do this

- Don't create something you wouldn't want to be involved with yourself, or can't really see the point of.
- Don't make a group and then walk away.
- Don't seek to exploit Flickr users or give them any indication that you would want to do so.
- Don't be afraid to remove items from the group pool if they're not appropriate, or remove members from the group if they cause trouble.

UGC technologies: citizen journalism portals

Like 'user-generated content' – for which it is often used as a synonym – the phrase 'citizen journalism' is not widely liked, largely because definitions – and perceptions – of what citizen journalism is differ widely. Bowman and Willis (2003) describe it as the 'act of citizens playing an active role in the process of collecting, reporting, analyzing and disseminating news and information'. Jay Rosen (2008) says: 'When the people formerly known as the audience employ the press tools they have in their possession to inform one another, that's citizen journalism.'

Much citizen journalism activity is covered by the rest of this chapter; however, it is also worth highlighting the specific 'citizen journalism'-branded websites that play a key role in the news environment.

The most successful example of a citizen journalism-based site is OhmyNews, the Korean news startup which boasts tens of thousands of contributors, overseen by over 50 staff. It has been credited with helping elect Roh Moo-hyun as president. The site expanded internationally with less success, and the market has become quite crowded with dozens of other startups launching including AllVoices.com, Backfence, GroundReport, GlobalVoices, Rue89 and the TV network Current.tv. Interestingly, research into 64 of these sites found that, contrary to the typical portrait of citizen journalism, the sites were tightly controlled in terms of what they allowed to be published (Project for Excellence in Journalism, 2008).

In addition to startups, news organisations have launched sister sites to provide platforms for citizen journalism, including CNN's iReport (which began as a TV programme before becoming a website), Fox News' uReport; ABC's i-CAUGHT and MSNBC's FirstPerson.

Many news organisations have also partnered with more general social media sites for large events – such as CNN's partnership with YouTube for two debates; the Canadian Broadcasting Corporation's partnership with Facebook; and MSNBC's partnership with MySpace in recruiting two convention correspondents. The *Huffington Post*, meanwhile, launched offshoot OffTheBus.net with Jay Rosen to cover the 2008 US election campaign with an express brief to focus on the grassroots view (rather than the view from the campaign bus, hence the name). Around 12,000 people participated.

John Kelly (2009) notes a range of research that suggests citizen journalism tends to be 'softer and more focused on personal and community life, more rooted in commentary, and less concerned with day-to-day hard news such as politics and crime'. If you are to attempt a citizen journalism platform or partnership, it is worth bearing in mind its typically softer and managed nature.

UGC technologies: Twitter

The short, instant nature of Twitter lends itself particularly well to news, and since its launch in 2006 it has increasingly been the first place for large news stories to break. Not only that, but, once 'broken', new details often continue to be broken on Twitter – along with rumour and myth. One of the key skills of an online journalist is being able to pick the facts from the noise, and challenge hoaxes (see the section on hoaxes below for more on how to do this). This might be done with the collaboration of an online community with which the journalist has built a relationship of trust.

Steve Herrmann (2008), writing on the BBC Editors Blog about a BBC experiment in streaming Twitter updates from members of the public during the Mumbai terror attacks, said of the experience:

> 'These accounts move more quickly and include a wider array of perspectives and sources, not all verified by us, but all attributed, so that in effect we leave some of the weighing up of each bit of information and context to you.

'[Most of] the Twitter messages we were monitoring ... did not add a great amount of detail to what we knew of events, but among other things they did give a strong sense of what people connected in some way with the story were thinking and seeing. "Appalled at the foolishness of the curious onlookers who are disrupting the NSG operations," wrote one. "Our soldiers are brave but I feel we could have done better," said another. There was assessment, reaction and comment there and in blogs. One blogger's stream of photos on photo-sharing site Flickr was widely linked to, including by us.

'All this helped to build up a rapidly evolving picture of a confusing situation.'

He added that 'there are risks with running accounts that we haven't been able to check', and points to the widely circulated myth that the Indian government had asked for an end to Twitter updates from Mumbai. 'Should we have checked this before reporting it? ... I think in this case we should have, and we've learned a lesson.'

The emerging consensus seems to be that if you are to embed a stream of live twitter updates on your site there should be some editorial filter to ensure it isn't hijacked or filled with spam (typically any word or phrase which becomes a 'trend' on Twitter is attacked by fake Twitter accounts which post spam containing those keywords). After all, users can always go to Twitter.com and use the search facility to see an unfiltered feed of all updates containing that word.

UGC technologies: video and audio

User-generated video shares many of the characteristics and considerations of user-generated photography discussed above. Many news organisations host users' videos on their sites, but many also have channels on video-sharing services such as YouTube. It is relatively easy to embed a YouTube video on a news website, or syndicate a feed of the latest uploads. Also, you can create communities on YouTube (and other video-sharing websites) around a particular theme.

Any use of video and audio UGC should address the same issues faced by the use of content generally. Leah Betancourt (2009), digital community manager at the *Minneapolis Star Tribune*, specifically identifies issues including:

- whether the video meets the publisher's standards of newsworthiness and taste;
- ownership (i.e. copyright);
- verification; and
- being particularly careful when it comes to videos of people in private situations.

In addition to video-sharing websites there are also video *conversation* websites and video *streaming* services. Seesmic, for example, allows users to record a video directly from their webcam and start a conversation. The replies to that conversation are linked together so that you can embed the whole conversation on another website as one 'video'. BBC's Have Your Say used this as a way to invite opinions on a debate and publish the results easily.

Video streaming services like Qik and Bambuser allow users to stream video live from a phone or laptop to the web. This is particularly useful for news events, and allows users to post comments and questions directly to the person filming (these appear on the phone or laptop screen). News organisations reporting on a live event should check whether any of the people attending are streaming using these services.

After the live stream has finished, a recording of the whole stream is still available to view. Again, both the live stream and the archived result can be embedded on any website.

Closer look UGC and copyright

Content that has been uploaded or exchanged online is subject to the same copyright laws as print and broadcast material. Just because someone has uploaded their photo or video to Facebook does not mean that they have given permission for you to republish it on your website, magazine or television bulletin.

You should make sure you look out for – and are familiar with – the Creative Commons licence. This is a licence that any content producer can use to assert who can use their material and on what basis. Visit http://creativecommons.org/about/licenses/ to find out more.

However, those who do not display a copyright licence still own the copyright to their work, and you will need permission to reproduce it.

At the time of writing, the role of audio in user-generated content is relatively minimal. While there are dominant spaces for sharing photos and video, opportunities for recording and sharing audio have been limited. However, the relative ease with which audio can be recorded using smartphones like the iPhone, associated applications (apps) and web services such as Audioboo is beginning to change this.

UGC technologies: tagging and social recommendation

Social recommendation, or social bookmarking, sites such as Digg, Reddit, Stumbleupon and Delicious allow users to recommend articles to others by 'bookmarking' them (saving them to a public webpage which displays everything they have saved). In addition, they can categorise or add 'tags' to the stories so that other users interested in stories on a particular topic can find them more easily.

People use bookmarking sites like these to easily show interesting articles and webpages to others in their online community, or as a way of keeping a virtual 'cuttings file' of material they may want to go back to at another point. If I want to find an article I once read about research on UGC, for example, I would go to http://delicious.com/paulb/ugc+research, while I could suggest the same link to someone if they asked me if I knew of any research on UGC.

The front pages of social bookmarking sites display the articles that have been bookmarked by the most people at that time. If your article is displayed here it will benefit from a boost in visits. As a result, a number of news organisations have introduced features such as 'share this' buttons to make their content more easily 'bookmarkable' – although research (Belam, 2008) suggests there is no relationship between the existence of these features and the numbers of stories bookmarked.

Unsurprisingly, the news agendas of social recommendation sites tend to reflect the interests of their users. One week-long study revealed the following:

> 'The user-news agenda … was more diverse, yet also more fragmented and transitory than that of the mainstream news media. This does not mean necessarily that users disapprove or reject the mainstream news agenda. These user sites may be supplemental for audiences. They may gravitate to them in addition to, rather than instead of, traditional venues. But the agenda they set is nonetheless quite different.'
>
> Project for Excellence in Journalism, 2007

News websites have their own equivalents of these social bookmarking sites: the 'most read', 'most emailed' and 'most commented' rankings that often appear on the homepage. In these cases, the simple acts of readers affect how stories are presented.

The best way to use social bookmarking sites as a journalist is to start bookmarking useful material yourself and see (a) who else is bookmarking them and (b) what else is being bookmarked with the same 'tags' (keywords that you add when you create the bookmark and that help you find it later, such as 'environment', 'Bristol', 'bobjones', etc.).

Another way to use them is to invite readers to use a particular tag when bookmarking interesting material on a specific, and republishing a collection of those bookmarks on their site, as *The Guardian* does with some of its fashion coverage.

UGC technologies: wikis – collaborative journalism

Wikis are websites which allow contributors to add, remove and edit content in a process of collaborative authoring. In addition to these core features users can typically receive updates when an edit is made; look at a history of edits (and easily remove vandalism); and use 'discussion pages' to debate edits.

The best known example is of course Wikipedia, which includes a 'current events' section and is often one of the first places to be updated when a major event occurs. There are also hundreds of other websites that use wiki technology, including many for journalistic purposes, such as Wikipedia's sister site Wiki News, *Wired* magazine's How-to wikis, CNET's backgrounder wikis, and *Trinity Mirror*'s regional wikinortheast.co.uk.

Setting up a wiki is as easy as setting up a blog, with free and premium services available on other websites. If you use Google Docs, for example, you can 'publish' any document as a webpage and allow others to edit it. There is also free wiki technology that can be installed on a news organisation's own website.

Wikis are a particularly useful tool when you want to gather a great deal of information – particularly in an area where the information is too broad to summarise as a journalist – and reach some sort of consensus. They are also useful for repositories of background information – for example, the *San Diego Tribune*'s 'Amplipedia' which allows users to add information about the local music scene. However, when entries concern people rather than things – i.e. biographies – there is an increased likelihood of malevolent contributions that attempt to smear people or hoax journalists, and if you are relying on this information as a journalist you should ensure that you verify it.

Wikis are less successful when the subject matter is opinion, as the *LA Times* found when its 'wikitorial' opinion column experiment was 'forked' into two opposed versions and then closed down within hours due to vandalism. The 'neutral point of view' (NPOV) stance of Wikipedia – which states that opinion has no place in entries – appears to be almost a generic feature of wikis in general.

Vandalism is a recurring issue on wikis, although it is easy to revert to an earlier version before any vandalism occurred. 'Edit wars' are a related problem, where contributors continually overwrite each other's contributions because of a difference of opinion. Attempts to address these issues vary. Wikipedia's own entry on wikis says:

> 'Some wikis allow unregistered users known as "IP addresses" to edit content, whilst others limit this function to just registered users. What most wikis do is allow IP editing, but privilege registered users with some extra functions to lend them a hand in editing; on most wikis, becoming a registered user is very simple and can be done in seconds, but detains the user from using the new editing functions until either some time passes, as in the English Wikipedia, where registered users must wait for three days after creating an

account in order to gain access to the new tool, or until several constructive edits have been made in order to prove the user's trustworthiness and usefulness on the system, as in the Portuguese Wikipedia, where users require at least 15 constructive edits before authorization to use the added tools. Basically, "closed up" wikis are more secure and reliable but grow slowly, whilst more open wikis grow at a steady rate but result in being an easy target for vandalism.'

Walsh (2007) puts forward the following argument:

> 'Even if you don't plan on moderating a community, it's a good idea to have an editorial presence, to pop in and respond to users' questions and complaints. Apart from giving users the sense that they matter – and they really should – it also means that if you do have to take drastic measures and curtail (or even remove) a discussion or thread, it won't seem quite so much like the egregious action of some deus ex machina.'

Wikis also work well when material is 'seeded' so that contributors have something to get their teeth into – but that material also needs to be incomplete in some way so that there are ways for people to contribute. Wikipedia does this particularly well when it signposts an entry as a 'stub' and says it needs work. You might also want to consider inviting a small group of contributors to help populate a wiki to establish the 'culture' of contribution and maintenance before publicising it to a mass audience.

UGC technologies: DIY social networks

Many news organisations host their own social networks, while most have some sort of presence on third-party social networking sites such as Facebook, MySpace and LinkedIn. As previously mentioned, it is important to start with your audiences and find out what social networks they use. LinkedIn, for example, would be appropriate if you have an audience of professionals; MySpace would be appropriate if you are covering music; and Bebo would be relevant if your publication was aimed at a pre-teen audience.

There are also sites that allow you to create your own social network with just a few clicks. Ning is the best known of these and will give you a site with its own forums, live chat facility, user blogs, audio, and the facility for users to upload video and photos. You can even customise the appearance of the site to match your publication's brand. In 2010, however, the site removed its free option so you will now have to pay to use it. Free alternatives include Grou.ps, Groupsite.com, SocialGO and BuddyPress.org.

The advantage of all social networks is the potential to reinforce the sense of community in an audience – an audience that might work as collaborators in the news production process, distributors of your media, and subscribers to your products. This list of roles indicates how delicate it can be to manage and serve that community – making a social network work can take a lot of care, not least in fending off spammers and preventing war breaking out between users with different opinions. There are books on community management which tackle this in depth, and it is worth reading widely if this is a step you plan to take.

Closer look Hoaxes

Any involvement in UGC needs to consider the possibility – or probability – that at some point someone is going to try to pull a hoax. These can range from pieces of satire being mistaken for reality to incorrect 'facts' being repeated, faked images, fake statements, fake websites and fake news events. Falling for one of these hoaxes can lead to huge embarrassment for your employers, and damage to your career.

Wikipedia can be a particular target when public figures die: false information was added to the Wikipedia pages of composers Maurice Jarre and Ronnie Hazlehurst soon after their deaths were announced, and was subsequently repeated by a number of news organisations. In another example, a 23-year-old electrician from Middlesbrough created the fictitious Serbian teenage footballer Rajko Purovic in a forum posting and email to a journalist. The make-believe player was then linked with a move to Middlesbrough FC by the *Teesside Evening Gazette*, the *Daily Mirror*, the Press Association, Sky Sports News and Setanta Sports News.

Clearly, the routine journalistic process of checking with a second source is a key safeguard to avoid becoming the victim of such hoaxes. *The Guardian*'s Kevin Anderson also suggests (2009) technical tips to avoid being hoaxed, including:

- Pay attention to the URL: governmental sites tend to end in .gov; academic sites in .ac or .edu; and there are similar extensions for the military, NHS and police. Nonprofits end in .org but it is possible for an organisation that is not a charity to get a .org address.
- Who owns the site?: Anderson says: 'Finding out who owns a site is easy. Do a WHOIS lookup, and you'll find out not only who owns the site, but sometimes even their contact details. Most of the time this is corporate information that won't give you a person to ring, but as Alex says, he registered the site in his own name.'
- Hover over the links: 'Why? If you hover over the links, you would have seen they went to a different address.'
- Be wary of a Twitter account with only one update.

Other techniques include looking to see when the page was last updated (you can find tools online that will tell you this), looking at the raw HTML on a page (right-click and select View Source or similar), and using Google's advanced search to look for sites linking to the page (they may be pointing out the hoax). In images, look out for areas being repeated (e.g. background faces, smoke) and inconsistent lighting.

Also worth looking out for is 'astroturfing': faking grassroots support for a cause which is actually funded and supported by a large corporation. In one US campaign, for example, 'oil industry workers paraded as part of a supposedly spontaneous movement opposed to climate change regulations being considered by US legislators . . . Greenpeace learned that the "Energy Citizens" protest group was founded by the oil industry trade association and therefore indirectly funded by ExxonMobil, Shell and others. At the same time, a congressional inquiry found that letters to lawmakers attacking the proposed legislation – letters purporting to be from concerned members of the public – were also backed by energy groups.' (Johnson, 2009) Check the funding of organisations and the backgrounds of their founders to provide context to their position.

Summary

In this chapter we have looked beyond the generic term 'user-generated content' to analyse its different forms, the types of people that generate UGC, and why and how news operations have sought to tap into it. We have also looked at some of the issues to consider, from hoaxes and hijacks to issues of copyright and law.

Throughout the chapter two themes have recurred: adapting the news operation to serve the needs of the user-contributor technically and culturally; and allowing journalists to become an active participant in communities of production elsewhere. While UGC is often talked of in terms of the latest technical platform – mobile phone photos during the July 7 bombings or Twitter coverage of the Mumbai attacks – these are, ultimately, just tools. A genuinely effective UGC strategy looks at the people behind these tools, the communities that they are part of, and the reasons why they share content in the first place.

As an online journalist, you should not treat UGC as a virtual letters page or phone-in. The territory and the agenda are the user's, not yours. What is 'user-generated content' to a news organisation is, to those who participate, simply the set of online conversations taken part in as they go about their job or hobby. As people create and exchange photos and video, opinions and links, facts and corrections, you need to be there.

Imagine UGC as a series of virtual places where you might overhear a lead, meet an expert source, or spot an interesting photograph. These places are not empty or neutral – they have their own rules on acceptable ways to behave ('lurking' for a while to get a feel for those rules is often advised). As a journalist, you will have to demonstrate that you are not there simply to take without putting anything back, and the best way to do that is to contribute where you can. Once you become a useful member of these communities you'll find that not only will you know where to go when the big stories break, but that other members will be willing to help you too.

Activities

1. Draw up a POST strategy for user-generated content. Identify:
   - The *people* who are your audience (or intended audience), and what social media (e.g. Facebook, blogs, Twitter, forums, etc.) they use.
   - Your *objectives* for what you want to achieve through using UGC.
   - The *strategy* to achieve that. How will relationships with users change?
   - The *technology* that will be most appropriate to your audience, objectives and strategy.
2. Join a group on photo-sharing website Flickr (you can search for them at flickr.com/groups) and spend a week participating as positively as you can. Read David Higgerson's blog post on the topic for some ideas: http://davidhiggerson.wordpress.com/2009/11/11/running-a-group-on-flickr-tips-on-how-to-keep-everyone-happy
3. Create and maintain a group on a social network such as Facebook. Spend a week trying to recruit members and encourage participation. This post at Concise Content gives a good brief overview of the factors that help make a Facebook group successful: www.concisecontent.co.uk/2009/06/16/what-makes-a-successful-facebook-group/

Further reading

Bowman, S. and Willis, C. (2003) 'We Media: How Audiences are Shaping the Future of News and Information' USA: The Media Center at the American Press Institute.

Johnson, B. (2009) 'Astroturfing: A question of trust', *The Guardian*, September 7, 2009, www.guardian.co.uk/media/2009/sep/07/astroturfing-energy-citizens-us

Kelly, J. (2009) 'Red Kayaks and Hidden Gold: the rise, challenges and value of citizen journalism', UK: Reuters Institute.

Lasica, J.D. (2003) 'What is Participatory Journalism?' *Online Journalism Review*, August 7 2003, www.ojr.org/ojr/workplace/1060217106.php

Project for Excellence in Journalism: 'The Latest News Headlines – Your Vote Counts', September 12, 2007, www.journalism.org/node/7493

Rosen, J. (2006) 'The People Formerly Known as the Audience,' *PressThink*, June 27, 2006, http://archive.pressthink.org/2006/06/27/ppl_frmr.html

Rosen, J. (2008) 'A Most Useful Definition of Citizen Journalism', *PressThink*, July 14, 2008, http://archive.pressthink.org/2008/07/14/a_most_useful_d.html

Wardle, C. and Williams, A. (2009) 'ugc@thebbc: Understanding its impact upon contributors, non-contributors and BBC News', www.bbc.co.uk/blogs/knowledgeexchange/2009/05/ugcthebbc.html

Chapter 11

Law and online communication

By Edgar Forbes

This chapter will cover:

- Interactivity and UGC
- Freedom of expression
- Closer look: Hate-speech laws
- Privacy and data protection
- Closer Look: Mobile journalism and the Terrorism Act 2000
- Defamation and the Reynolds defence
- Contempt of court
- Copyright and content rights
- Closer look: Regulation

Introduction

> 'Tom pointed out that technically they weren't abusing the terms of Crown copyright and that, far from corrupting the data, they were in fact correcting it. But that was irrelevant – simply the fact that a citizen was using official information without having a licence from the government (e.g. asking permission) was the problem. 'We had no concept we were doing anything wrong,' Tom said. 'It's my data. I paid for it. It's about my government. If I'd corrupted it then I can see the government's concerns but we weren't doing that. We were making it more accessible and by making it so widely available we were improving the quality too as more people could scrutinise it.'
>
> Heather Brooke,
> *The Silent State* (2010) on the beginnings of the MySociety website

For the past decade or so the differences between 'the media' and 'the people' have been breaking down. If you publish on a blog, or on YouTube – even if you publish comments on Twitter and forums – you are, effectively, part of the media: publishing, and distributing, information. That not only opens up a world of opportunities in terms of audiences and stories, but also means you are subject to the same laws as more traditional publishers and distributors.

The UK broadcast regulator Ofcom refers to its remit over the media as 'regulator for the UK communications industries, with responsibilities across television, radio, telecommunications and wireless communications service'. This recognises the variety of 'media' over which it has regulatory authority. Whether viewed from a micro perspective of a local newsletter or from a macro perspective of an international news organisation or channel such as Reuters, CNN or Al Jazeera, the one unifying feature behind the term 'media' is a reference to communication – what's being delivered, how it's being delivered and who's delivering it.

So when we refer to the media we are talking about communication of one sort or another – including internet communication.

Rapid advances in technology and the proliferation of web-based content have led to convergence both in terms of the content being delivered over any given platform and the suppliers of such content. To this extent, traditional mass media is engaging with local (and international) audiences while localised media is widening its reach through the global availability of its online content such as video, podcasts and blogs.

So we now have mass communication being delivered via local means and local communication being delivered across mass mediums. This has completely changed the shape of media delivery as content and audiences blend across varying formats.

It could be argued that the economic and technological drivers behind current convergence in the industry is going to result in '*content burnout*' – the public will tire of recycled and reformatted content. Convergence is bringing about consolidation at a corporate level and consequently at the point and mode of delivery. The next step will be a consolidation of content. But insofar as the objection to media activity or a given report relates to the packaging, the law also has to assess when it is appropriate or proper for it to intervene. While the media may accept that it should subject itself to the jurisdiction and scrutiny of the legal process in relation to content, it may be less willing to do so in relation to how it chooses to package and deliver such content.

Interactivity and UGC

Interactivity has become a key component in programme formats and in attracting readers from print-based media into the online environment. While the media constantly seeks out wider audiences, the audiences now seek out the media and each other.

The growth area in recent years has been user-generated content (UGC). Journalists are trying to work out how best to use this new strand of content in an enduring and profitable way. And while YouTube set the scene for this type of content, its deal with Google was transacted on cautious terms (it being bought for shares rather than cash) and soon highlighted the risks such content poses in relation to copyright infringement. If one gets the business model right and finds a way of cost-effectively managing the rights issues then UGC still holds much potential for new entrants to the market.

For legal systems such as the English 'common law' model that traditionally rely on legislation being initiated and passed through the parliamentary system – and then complement and supplement this through a body of case law – changes in the make-up of the media present significant difficulties.

Such a system is more used to being responsive – to new legislation, cases brought by litigants, appeals in relation to cases – and it is faced with the task of 'responding' retroactively to the proactive activities of the media.

In doing so it is being asked to apply old laws to new situations. The 1959 Obscene Publications Act didn't have internet pornography in its contemplation. Similarly, legislation such as the 1981 Contempt of Court Act or 1996 Defamation Act isn't set up or equipped to deal with transjurisdictional offenders using the internet. The same is true of codified legal systems such as those in Germany, France, Spain or Italy.

In seeking to identify and rationalise the appropriate legal provisions and responses to the business and activities of the media we need to take a step back from the adversarial context of cases or complaint. If the media is being judged against the backdrop of its democratic remit as the 'mouthpiece of society' and the benchmark of 'responsible journalism' we need to explore what society wants from the media. In doing so we need to acknowledge both the democratic function of the media to inform as well as its commercial function of providing demand-led content.

So when it comes to media law we have a unique situation whereby the subject of regulation and legal control is at the same time part of the democratic and social process that exists to scrutinise those who would seek to impose and apply such controls.

This chapter aims to provide practitioners of online journalism in the emerging landscape of convergence with a useful overview of the key areas of law that affect them and guidance on how to navigate a safe path through them.

While the laws that currently exist are far from perfect, they do provide a framework that regulates the interaction between journalists, society and the state. Getting acquainted with the law will allow journalists to be more confident in their engagement with it. And as the law starts to change in response to new developments you may find yourself even shaping it.

Freedom of expression

Thoughts may be free but their expression comes with limitations

One of the principles upon which democratic societies are based is that people should be free to express their opinions, contribute to debate, scrutinise their politicians, adore and criticise their celebrities, be free to tweet on Twitter, post on Facebook, blog and generally interact as individuals within their society.

One of the principles upon which the internet was based, was to open up the ability to communicate, exchange ideas and knowledge, learn and bring the world closer together by uniting the world through a globally accessible medium.

Add these two principles to the rapid, accessible and affordable advances in technology and one has a very powerful tool that allows journalists immediate access to a global audience.

As the online journalist files their latest story via their laptop or phone they sit in a powerful position to publish globally and in real-time but, as we will explore throughout this chapter, such seeming power does not mean they can write or post what they like.

The internet may have swung the pendulum of power to express in the journalists' direction but those who seek to control power and the laws that allow them to do so have pulled the pendulum back in a manner that means journalists need to play by the rules.

So what are these rules?

The rules relating to freedom of expression are made up on the one hand of a mixture of national and international laws that provide for what an individual should be allowed to freely express in a democratic society. On the other hand are a series of laws and specific regulations relating to the press and media that define what can be expressed when and what the limitations to such expression are.

The key to good journalism is to balance the competing laws and regulations in a manner that allows the journalist to successfully tell their story and reach their audience. This requires an understanding of the laws that will be explored in more detail below.

Some of the earliest laws in the UK were actually ones that sanctioned freedom of expression and imposed criminal penalties for things such as libel, blasphemy or obscenity. Where the evolution of laws in the UK has differed from many other countries is that while there were laws that restricted or prevented free expression, there were no competing laws that specifically provided for it or protected the right of an individual to freely express themselves.

The UK does not have any legal or constitutional guarantee to safeguard the freedom of expression when it comes to the press. Contrast this with other countries such as the US where the First Amendment of the US Constitution sets out that: 'Congress shall make no law . . . abridging the freedom of speech, or of the press', or Germany where Article 5 of the Basic Law ('Grundgesetz') provides: 'Freedom of the press and freedom of reporting by means of broadcasts and films are guaranteed. There shall be no censorship . . .'

European law in the form of the European Convention on Human Rights (ECHR) did pave the way for some legal structure around the exercise of free expression but it, along with the UK Human Rights Act, have been seen as unwelcome rights bearers by successive political regimes.

ECHR – what you need to know

In relation to freedom of expression, the key article in ECHR is Article 10(1). This provides that:

> 'Everyone has the right to freedom of expression. This right shall include the freedom to hold opinions and to receive and impart ideas without interference by public authorities.'

While this may seem to offer some kind of guarantee to journalists this is swiftly constrained as Article 10(2) which states that:

> 'The exercise of these freedoms etc may be subject to such formalities, conditions, restrictions or penalties as are prescribed by law and necessary in a democratic society in the interests of national security, territorial integrity or public safety, for the prevention of rights of others, for the provision of information received in confidence . . .'

What this means is that while the right to free expression is granted, it is subject to whatever other laws and penalties are out there that may apply to the exercise of free expression.

As we have identified and will explore throughout this chapter, there are several laws that do affect the exercise of free expression in the UK.

The key question and one that has been the fundamental point of debate in several court cases over the years is this:
When is it 'necessary' in a democratic society to use or enforce such laws as are available to prevent or punish freedom of expression?

What ECHR provides is that to prevent free expression there have to be formalities, conditions, restrictions etc. that are prescribed by law AND it has to be necessary in a democratic society to enforce these in relation to what has been published (expressed).

What politicians and some judges in the UK have argued is that the fact there is a given law (e.g. libel) means that it is automatically 'necessary' to prevent or punish free expression. What others would argue is that it should depend on the circumstances and context of the publication as to whether the enforcement of the law is necessary.

The UK Human Rights Act 1998 (HRA)

Several decades after ECHR came into force, the UK finally managed to bring in a human rights law of its own which provided that it was 'unlawful for a public authority to act in a manner that was inconsistent with ECHR' – in other words, public authorities in the UK have to act consistently with and apply ECHR.

Public authorities include local councils, public bodies and the courts. So where a court is being asked to enforce a legal sanction against a journalist it will have to follow the principles of ECHR.

What is key to note here is that this means that ECHR only comes into play i.e. becomes 'engaged' when an issue – a complaint that a journalist has abused their power and written something objectionable, or that someone has in an unlawful manner prevented a journalist from accessing information or being able to report on a matter – gets put before a court to decide.

The UK Human Rights Act does have one specific section that does provide journalists with a hint of a 'free press' provision in the form of Section 12.

The effect of HRA section 12

The reason this section is important is that it provides journalists with a legal guarantee that safeguards against the indiscriminate use of legal sanction to prevent publication. When the section talks about 'relief' it means a legal sanction such as a court order or 'injunction' (an order that specifically prevents – 'injuncts' – something being done).

This most commonly arises where someone such as a celebrity or politician knows or thinks that a journalist (website or newspaper) is going to run a story about them, e.g. 'sex scandal shame' or 'expenses scandal', and they apply to the court to obtain an order to prevent the story being published – also commonly referred to as a 'gag' or 'gagging order'.

So how then does freedom of expression in relation to journalism operate in the UK?

One only has to look at the various websites or scan the front pages of the newspapers to conclude that in spite of there being no guarantee to free expression in the UK, there certainly does not seem to be any lack of it, especially where footballers, reality TV stars, royalty or politicians are concerned.

What has evolved in the UK is what one could argue is a typical journalistic response to the lack of a specific free press law, namely the 'see what you can get away with rule'. This is more properly referred to as the doctrine of prior restraint and means that journalists are, in theory, free to publish what they wish but if what they do publish breaks any law (e.g. by being blasphemous, obscene or a libel) then the journalist – or their media outlet – will be subject to legal sanction. This is where the saying 'publish and be damned' comes from.

The online journalist can take advantage of being able to publish without being damned by:

- Having an understanding of what they are allowed to publish.
- How they can be punished for publishing (and by whom).
- Or how they can be 'gagged' and prevented from publishing in the first place (and by whom).

What are the key constraints on freedom of expression under UK law?

Freedom of expression is a right that is recognised through ECHR and the UK HRA but only to the extent that it is subject to the constraints put on it by the other laws that exist to control, prevent or punish for the exercise of that right.

So what are these other laws and who might be seeking to use them to prevent journalists from freely expressing their views?

The constraints on a journalist's ability to exercise their free expression can broadly be placed into two categories:

1. Laws that regulate and control the activities of journalists in relation to specific matters (such as Contempt of Court, Freedom of Information or Data Protection).
2. Laws that can be used by others to prevent journalists from publishing or punish (e.g. by suing) them for having published certain information (such as Defamation law, privacy laws or the Official Secrets Act).

Points to consider

1. At the outset of this section we noted that freedom of expression was a key principle in democratic societies and that the evolution and purpose of the internet related to improving and facilitating free expression.
2. In relation to the exercise of free expression and the various constraints that journalists encounter in relation to being able to publish, it is important to remember that the various laws do not exist or operate in a vacuum.
3. Technological advances have made it much easier and cheaper to publish material and reach a global audience with such publication. To the extent an online journalist can readily and instantly access a global audience, they are also subject to not just UK but wider international and country specific laws – so online journalists need to exercise caution in relation to both where their material gets published and where it ends up.
4. The shape of the media and demand for content has and keeps evolving. The media is now no mere outlet to feed the thoughts of journalists into society as part of the democratic process. Rather, the media is a commercial commodity with profit margins, shareholder returns and other such commercial drivers. Online journalism is as much, if not more so, about providing as much content as possible to as many consumers as possible on commercially viable (revenue generating) terms.

Closer look Hate-speech laws

A number of laws forbid expression of 'hate speech' online in the UK. The Public Order Act 1986, the Racial and Religious Hatred Act 2006 and the Criminal Justice and Immigration Act 2008 cover, respectively, stirring up racial hatred (which can be based on nationality, colour, and ethnic origins); stirring up religious hatred; and inciting hatred on the basis of sexual orientation. If material published on your site comes under any of these categories you should inform the contributor of the legal basis under which you are removing the material.

5. To the extent that the media is commercial it is also more powerful and as such there will be people who wish to interfere with the way that freedom of expression is exercised. This can be internally, where a media owner wants journalists to focus on content that makes money rather than provides for socially valuable journalistic insights or investigations. This is however more frequently externally where powerful individuals and corporations or high profile celebrities or politicians seek to prevent the public finding out about all manner of things from drugs that don't work, to hospital waiting lists, to environmental pollution through to sex scandal, vote rigging and general corruption.

If today's online journalist wishes to secure tomorrow's scoop they will need to be aware of how the law interacts with their activities and how to use it as a shield to defend their freedom of expression against unfair and unjust attempts to gag them and prevent the public from reading their story.

Privacy

When is intrusion and exposure justified?

There may be a saying that goes 'what you see is what you get' but in the context of online journalism this has to be repositioned to read 'it's not what you can see but how you got it' that counts.

In other words, when it comes to obtaining and using material (be it information, photographs or video footage) that can be considered 'private' or 'personal', journalists have to be careful that they don't fall foul of an increasing willingness on the part of the UK courts to uphold a person's right to privacy against the media's use or intended use of private material.

In terms of the law in the UK, privacy and the protection of an individual's privacy against media intrusion, has evolved from what the courts used to view as a patchwork right that might apply depending on whether an existing (non privacy specific) law such as trespass, copyright or confidentiality had been breached, into a new right capable of its own enforcement.

What this means for journalists is that where privacy related matters attach to or form the basis for a story, they now need to be cautious of a set of changing rules of engagement as far as the application of law is concerned.

Privacy law

The first point to note is that in the UK, as opposed to other countries, there is no actual privacy law. As with freedom of expression and human rights law generally, the UK has been both slow and reluctant to feed these into the statute book such that there are specific laws (Acts of Parliament) that provide for a free press (as we have discussed above) or a legal right to privacy.

The UK approach to privacy has been to rely on existing laws (such as confidentiality, copyright or trespass) to protect things that are private.

The courts and politicians were, until relatively recently, happy to leave the law at that and rely on self regulation and this pick'n'mix of laws to do the job. The result was that there was inconsistency and uncertainty as to how privacy issues were protected and pursued through the courts.

This was both good and bad news for the media. On the positive side, they could follow the 'see what you can get away with' rules of engagement and – as many a web exposé will testify – did get away with an arguably more than their fair share of privacy intrusion. On the negative side, where a celebrity or footballer or politician had the money to wheel in their lawyers and take the media to court, the cost of uncertainty could be significant.

European law – privacy through the back door

To arrive at a sensible rationale for privacy protection one has to look to the European Convention on Human Rights (ECHR). Article 8 of ECHR provides that there is a right to privacy and that a public authority may not interfere with that right except to the extent that such interference is provided for in a law (e.g. Official Secrets or Anti Terrorism laws) and is necessary.

As with freedom of expression, the application of ECHR is brought into effect in UK law through the Human Rights Act (HRA – as discussed under Freedom of Expression above).

The problem here is the right given by the law – ECHR together with HRA – is not a proactive or 'positive' right in the sense that the law is required to actively protect privacy of an individual. Instead the way the law is framed means that the right takes the form of a 'negative' obligation on a 'public authority' not to interfere with an individual's privacy (except where legally necessary).

So how does this work in practice?

Self regulation provides guidelines on how the media should approach privacy and provides regulatory codes that the courts can use as a guide to assess to what extent the media have behaved within the agreed rules it has set for journalists in this context.

In the UK there are two principal self regulatory codes of conduct for the media. Print and online journalism are currently regulated by the Press Complaints Commission (PCC) while broadcast journalism is regulated by Ofcom (the independent regulator and competition authority for the UK communications industries).

The PCC Editors Code explained

1. In relation to privacy, editors (on behalf of their media outlets) have to make and be responsible for the final judgement call over whether to use material that may relate to or be invasive of someone's privacy. All online journalists generally are nevertheless subject to this code and should therefore comply with it.
2. Where there is a reasonable expectation of privacy, photographs taken in relation to such a setting should not be used without the person's consent.
3. Where the material the journalist wishes to use relates to the private life and matters of a person, then the journalist should not use such material except where:
   (i) the use can be justified by the context and/or circumstances.
   (ii) the person has already made similar or related disclosures in public.
4. The public interest element should always be assessed.
5. The pre-existing availability of the material in the public domain may (for privacy law purposes) also be relevant.

Privacy law – where are we at: what is the law now?

The position can be summarised as follows:

1. Individuals – such as celebrities, politicians etc – have a right to respect for privacy.
2. Journalists – collectively the wider media – have a right to freedom of expression.
3. The right of the individual to protect their privacy has to be balanced against the competing right of journalists to express themselves.

Privacy – example

A story appears on a national media outlet's website claiming a premiership footballer has taken part in a sex and drugs 'orgy' with prostitutes at a London hotel.

The footballer complains that the story online has violated his privacy and wants a court to prevent the website keeping the story online and sue them for damages for having published the story.

The journalist and media outlet who control the website say they are entitled to run the story and should be able to freely express their views about the footballer.

The journalist says that the footballer has recently 'sold' his story and pictures about his recent wedding to a national gossip magazine and has also made comments publicly about how bad drugs are and that footballers should be role models for young people.

The footballer calls his lawyers and the case goes in front of a judge who has to decide whether to allow the website to keep running the story.

Looking at the PCC Editors Code it would seem that there has been an intrusion into the private affairs of the footballer but that this could possibly be justified by the journalist. Why is it justifiable? – as allowed for in the code, the footballer has discussed his private life in public (he got paid for the photo-shoot in the glossy gossip magazine). Not only that, it appears he has also stated that drugs are bad and that footballers should be role models – this now appears to be a lie in relation to his activities. Looking at the 'public interest' aspect of the facts, it does seem that using that test, the public have a right to know about the footballer's activities.

The judge takes guidance from section 12 HRA. This states that if the judge is considering preventing the story from staying online (through an injunction) – which would be a clear constraint on freedom of expression – then they should not grant such injunction unless they are satisfied that the footballer would be likely to win a court case on the basis that the publication of the story should not have been allowed.

Section 12(4) of the HRA directs the judge to take account of the fact that the story is 'journalistic' (which it is as it has been published as a news story by a national media outlet) and whether it is in the public interest to publish it. It also directs reference to any relevant privacy code.

The judge concludes that given the facts it appears the footballer has lied about drugs, pretended to be a role model and against drugs, already put himself in the public eye and as such, the public has a right and interest to know about his 'sex and drugs shame'. The journalist was therefore entitled to publish it and the story can remain on the website.

4. To understand how journalists should be conducting themselves in relation to privacy one has to be guided by the PCC Editors Code.
5. Where a legal action is brought before the courts, the judge will weigh the competing rights through applying HRA Section 12 (as set out in the Freedom of Expression part of this chapter above).

Privacy law – the rules of engagement

The UK might not have a specific privacy law but that has not stopped celebrities, footballers, celebrity chefs or politicians complaining to the courts about how violated they have been at the hands of the media. What needs to be understood and taken account of are the competing rights and how circumstances can affect the extent to which such rights can be exercised.

Another aspect to consider is the range of pre-existing laws that can touch on privacy. Copyright law is a notable area where there may be a move in coming years for the UK to give more clarity around when something is an image right (in relation to a celebrity, etc.) and when something is a privacy right. Separating the use of celebrity images under licence as a copyright related image right from the use of celebrity pictures as something private would provide the media with more certainty. The application of the existing laws and PCC Editors Code already acknowledges that there is a sliding scale to the interpretation of privacy rights and their exercise – the Editors Code allows for account to be taken of whether a person has already made statements or appeared publicly in relation to their private life or private matters. Similarly, the HRA directs a judge to take public interest and privacy codes into account when deciding on privacy issues.

It is therefore fair to conclude that the more someone has 'put themselves out there' and enjoyed or benefitted from being a public figure or 'celebrity' in the public eye, then when it comes to complaining about privacy, the courts will look at what the complaining person has put out there. The more of a person's private life they have put into the public domain, the less guaranteed they are to subsequently be able to seek to protect that and prevent the media from discussing or revisiting what is already in the public sphere. This is something, used within the PCC and legal guidelines, journalists may benefit from.

Confidentiality

There is legal groundwork to be done if you are dealing with confidential information of any sort – e.g. information which has been communicated under a duty of confidence or which is covered by confidentiality agreements in a source's employment contract (trade secrets, government secrets and personal information may all be included here) – not only because you may be sued by a source or an organisation for betraying confidentiality, but also because they may seek an injunction to prevent publication of the confidential details.

There are public interest defences of your right to publish confidential information – specifically, if you are exposing crime, corruption, anti-social behaviour or injustice; exposing lies, hypocrisy, or misleading claims; protecting public health and safety; disclosing incompetence, negligence or dereliction of duty; or exposing exploitative or dangerous behaviour. If material has already been made widely available, or has been disclosed with consent (and you have proof of this) then this can also form the basis of a defence.

Harassment

The Protection From Harassment Act 1997 is occasionally used to prevent journalists from reporting on particular individuals. Specifically, any conduct which amounts to harassment of someone can be considered to a criminal act, for which the victim can seek an injunction (followed by arrest if broken) or damages. One example of a blogger's experience is illustrative of the way the act can be used with regard to online journalism, even if no case reaches court.

In January 2010 the Seismic Shock blog published a post linking an Anglican reverend with Holocaust denial and antisemitism. The reverend complained of harassment to his local police force – Surrey Police – who passed on the complaint to the police force covering the blogger's district: Yorkshire Police. Yorkshire Police visited the blogger and suggested he remove his blog. The blogger, feeling intimidated, complied. It was only when the reverend threatened another blogger (who had linked to the same evidence), boasting of his previous success (and falsely claiming that Seismic Shock had received a caution), that the Seismic Shock blogger talked publicly about what had happened and the story received national attention (Cellan-Jones, 2010).

Defences to a charge of harassment include if you were undertaking actions for the purpose of preventing or detecting crime, or that your conduct was 'reasonable' in the particular circumstances. The fewer the incidents, and the more spaced out the instances of those, the weaker the case. If you have complied with an internal code of conduct with regard to privacy and fairness this will also help you.

A further consideration with regard to harassment is if someone claims that they are being harassed on your website. While they can report the harasser to the police, they might also expect you to take action under the Equality Act 2010 if the harassment is sexual in nature or based on gender, sexuality, disability, age, pregnancy, race or religion. This legislation is useful to refer to if you wish to remove content that might be considered harassment, or bar a contributor for such behaviour. As always, clear terms and conditions outlining unacceptable behaviour that would result in such actions will strengthen your position.

Data protection

If you gather user information in any way – for example, requiring users to register to comment, upload material or to access your site, or 'crowdsourcing' details which include personal information – then you will need to be aware of the Data Protection Act.

The Data Protection Act 1998 stipulates how you should process any personal information you handle, and gives individuals powers to request access to information held about them. It requires that you use information 'fairly and lawfully' and only for the purposes for which it is gathered, and only for as long as it is needed; that you store it securely and do not transfer it outside the EU (unless you ensure adequate protection); that you keep it accurate and up to date where necessary; and that you provide avenues for users to access their personal data if they require it.

In practical terms this means that when you gather information you should be clear about what it is to be used for and how the user can gain access to information held about them. You should only provide access to user databases or spreadsheets containing personal details to members of staff who need that access to do what you said would be done with that information.

Importantly, the Act contains an exemption for information held only for 'journalistic, literary or artistic' purposes, which applies before first publication and if the publisher believes that publication would be in the public interest. If these conditions are met then the data must only be held securely and you are exempt from the other requirements. This is clearly important because otherwise the subject of a secret investigation could request any information that is held about them.

More information and advice about data protection can be found on the Information Commissioner's Office website at www.ico.gov.uk/for_organisations.aspx

Closer look Mobile journalism and the Terrorism Act 2000

Several photographers and video journalists taking footage in public places have found themselves confronted by police officers requesting that they stop taking photographs (and in some cases attempting to confiscate equipment) under Section 44 of the Terrorism Act 2000. In July 2010 this section was officially suspended, but if you are planning to take photographs or video in a public place you should be aware of your rights to do so.

The website I'm a Photographer, not a Terrorist! monitors these rights and provides useful material for understanding them. After Section 44 was suspended they noted that 'Unfortunately there are still a swathe of laws that police can and will still use to harass photographers, most notably Section 43, which is similar to Section 44 but requires an officer to suspect that you are a terrorist and Section 76 which makes it illegal to "elicit information about a police officer" which includes photographing them.'

The site includes a 'Bust Card' (http://PhotographerNotaTerrorist.org/bust-card) to stick in your wallet that says exactly what you should do if stopped by police in such circumstances.

Defamation

Investigative journalism – how to comply with the law

Defamation is probably the area of law that causes editors most sleepless nights and leaves media organisations counting serious costs when a court decides that they have misbehaved. This is especially true in an online setting where journalists are publishing to a potentially global audience. The added risk for online journalists is that what they upload in the UK may be read across the world and is therefore subject not just to UK law but to other laws, depending on where the story is read and who it relates to.

Defamation cases can therefore span the globe, as did a high-profile case a few years ago, where a Saudi businessman sued a US website and newspaper in the UK courts over what it had published about him. So journalists should beware that on the internet there are world wide laws that can come to bear and too rash a click of the mouse can often see them snared by an unwelcome legal trap.

Why is defamation such a contentious topic?

1. It relates to the legal protection of reputation and when celebrities, politicians or corporations and their bosses decide that their integrity and dealings have been called into question – invariably the very thing that have helped them gain celebrity status, political standing or corporate power – they will go to great lengths to protect themselves.

2. The very nature of journalistic endeavour is to inform, interrogate and expose (wrongdoing). It is part of a journalist's job to find out and write about things and people that their readers and viewers are interested in. In today's highly commercial and content-demanding media environment it is also a journalist's job to find stories that sell and this invariably takes them down the path of finding something new or scandalous that the person or persons in question would rather the public did not know about.

3. Get the story right and you can persuade a court that you have played within the rules and you have a great scoop which can go online. Get the story – or how you have gone about getting

or presenting it – wrong and you (and your editor and/or employer) could be looking at a six figure sum of damages plus costs being awarded against you.

4. It can be argued that it is a serious restraint on media freedom. It means that you cannot risk exposing wrong and expressing concern unless you are fairly sure that you have an excuse (in the form of legal defence) for doing so. As we will see, it is for the journalist to show they have not defamed, or were justified in doing so and not for the person exposed to justify their actions or necessarily show that they have suffered any financial loss. This coupled with the deterrent effect of high damages awards and legal costs means it is a brave or foolish journalist or editor who is willing to take a punt on a story without the backing of good defence and a big cheque book.

Types of defamation

There are three types of defamation, of which libel is by far the most common:

1. ***Libel*** – where something has been published in written and permanent form (i.e. 'fixed' form – this could be a web page albeit that the page may not be available indefinitely but it would suffice that is has been available to view and was capable of being viewed by people who could have reacted to its imputation in a defamatory manner).
2. ***Slander*** – where something is spoken or otherwise communicated in a transitory (non-permanent) manner e.g. during a council or shareholders meeting or at a public rally or demonstration. Where, however, something that may on the face of it be slanderous (i.e. not written down or printed but merely spoken) is captured in the form of a broadcast online, the law will treat that as a libel (as the recording and/or broadcasting of the statement will have 'fixed' it into a permanent form).
3. ***Malicious falsehood*** – this arises where something malicious and untrue has been written about someone and there has been financial loss.

The key difference between libel, slander and malicious falsehood is that in relation to libel and slander the person concerned does not have to show any financial loss and merely the potential for reputational harm whereas for malicious falsehood there is no need to show actual reputational damage but there is a need to show that what has been published is malicious, untrue and has led to financial loss.

Defining defamation

The relevant UK law, the Defamation Acts 1952 & 1996, do not provide an exact definition but in its overall sense, defamation can be summarised as:

Publication of a derogatory, offensive or objectionable imputation which is likely to tarnish or otherwise diminish the reputation of another without just cause or regard to their competing rights not to have such subject matter publicised.

How to interpret this

1. There has to have been *publication* in some form or another – in other words people must have been able to read, see, react to the expressed thoughts or writings of the journalist (or other person making the publication).
2. There has to have been an *imputation* – i.e. a suggestion – whether direct or indirect – that is strong enough to lead to an opinion or perception on the part of the recipient.

3. The imputation has to be *derogatory* or *objectionable* – i.e. it contains something that questions or exposes and/or which is untrue.
4. It is *likely* that this would *damage* the reputation of the person who is the subject matter.
5. The damage that would be *likely* to be caused to the other person has or would be caused *without a just cause* (i.e. legal defence) or regard to the person's *competing rights* (such as their right to a private and family life or freedom to practise religion or follow political beliefs – where such rights are protected by laws such as the European Convention on Human Rights).

The triggers for defamation can therefore be summarised as:

- Publication
- of defamatory subject matter
- that refers to the claimant – i.e. the person to whom the publication relates and who is making the legal claim for defamation.

Liability for defamation will arise where:

- The publication has been to a third party (e.g. writing something nasty in a letter will of itself not be defamatory if no one other than the recipient could read it).
- The defamatory imputation is either:
  - intended
  - can or could be anticipated
  - caused by lack of care.

What does this mean in practice?

- Check whether the story or item is true – check your sources and double-check any information you cannot readily corroborate.
- Can you prove that what you've produced is true?
- Can you show that you have exercised sufficient care and judgement over how you have researched, compiled and presented your story?
- Could you be covered by one of the defences – as we will discuss in relation to defences, you must ensure you have done your research and have substantive evidence to back you up.
- How likely is it that the subject concerned would sue? Dead people cannot sue, for example, and some public figures such as the Queen and Prime Minister will avoid situations where they might have to testify in court. Other public figures are notoriously litigious and protective of their reputation. Very large groups of people will find it difficult to make a strong case ('footballers', for example, would struggle to win a case in which you were accused of defaming all footballers), but companies and organisations can sue (so Manchester United could pursue a case if you defamed the club). Public bodies, however, cannot sue, following the judgment in Derbyshire County Council v Times Newspapers Ltd. But remember that an individual within a public body can (for example if you said that social services were badly managed that could be construed as defaming the manager of social services).
- Is it commercially justifiable/viable to run with the risk.

Closer look Note of caution for online journalists

Aside from the fact that it is quick and easy to upload your story you should also be aware that as opposed to a newspaper where there may just be one or two editions and so 'publications', in the online setting there is what is known as 'continuous republication'. What this means is that your story will remain available on your website and through any links to the site until it is taken down.

From a legal perspective it is therefore not just published once (at point and time of original upload) but is continually republished each time the web page is refreshed or newly viewed. The scope for more people to read and react to any defamatory imputation in your story is therefore greater and a court will assess the reach and continued availability and 'publication' of the story when it comes to the damages it awards against you in a defamation action.

The good news is that to the extent it's quick and easy to post potentially offending material online, it is equally quick and easy to remove it and so mitigate or limit the damage or potential for damage it could cause.

Lawyers will sometimes send threatening letters to people in other parts of the chain of publication – for example, the company hosting your website. The objective here is often to remove the content from distribution rather than winning a legal case. Many website hosts will take down content if they receive such a letter, regardless of whether they believe that there is a case to answer, because there will be little financial reason to do otherwise (this will depend on how much the hosting company earns from your custom, of course).

This tactic has been known to frequently backfire, however, in what is known as the 'Streisand Effect'. In these situations, although the approach succeeds in getting the original website taken down by the hosting company, dozens of 'mirror' sites spring up elsewhere not only containing the disputed content, but spreading publicity about the legal tactics employed to suppress it. If you are confident about your case you can also move your website to another host, of course.

Defences to defamation

To the extent that defamation law is and can be seen as a restraint on media freedom it does provide a set of 'get out' options in the form of the following defences:

1. Justification – i.e. what you've reported is true.
2. Fair comment – what has been said is fair in the circumstances and on the facts.
3. Privilege – this sets out circumstances and conditions where such matters are legally allowed to be said.
4. Innocent dissemination – i.e. you have not had any control over the publication.
5. Consent to publication – the person has already given you permission to publish.
6. Offer of amends – the person has already accepted a legal settlement.

Most of these will be covered in any general textbook on media law, which you should familiarise yourself with. With specific regard to newsgathering, production and distribution online, however, you should be familiar with the following developments and cases.

Fair comment – now 'honest comment' in the digital age

In December 2010 a landmark judgment enhanced the fair comment defence, renaming it 'honest comment' in an explicit reference to internet communication. In his comments on the judgment Lord Walker noted that the fair comment defence had developed 'in the context of published criticism of their works' by a small elite. Now, however, millions talk, 'and thousands comment in electronically transmitted words, about recent events of which they have learned from television or the internet.

> 'Many of the events and the comments on them are no doubt trivial and ephemeral, but from time to time (as the present appeal shows) libel law has to engage with them. The test for identifying the factual basis of honest comment must be flexible enough to allow for this type of case, in which a passing reference to the previous night's celebrity show would be regarded by most of the public, and may sometimes have to be regarded by the law, as a sufficient factual basis.'
>
> (Ponsford, 2010).

Reporting on the case The Guardian said that it was now not necessary 'that a comment must identify the matters on which it is based with sufficient particularity to enable the reader to judge for himself whether it was well founded. However, the court held "the comment has to identify, at least in general terms, the matters on which it is based" so that "the reader can understand what the comment is about and the commentator can, if challenged, explain by giving particulars of the subject matter of his comment why he expressed the views that he did". The court also made clear that a defendant was not permitted to rely in support of the defence of fair comment on matters that were not referred to, even in general terms, by the comment.' (Phillips, 2010)

Privilege

There are two types of privilege: absolute privilege, and qualified privilege. Qualified privilege refers broadly to 'fair and accurate' coverage of public proceedings and documents. Online coverage of such events needs to pay particular heed to the 'fair and accurate' part of privilege. If coverage of public proceedings is ongoing online, then this may need to be continuously updated to keep it 'contemporaneous' and 'accurate'

Absolute privilege refers to the ability to report on what takes place in the courts, inquests and in parliament. A good example of the use of absolute privilege in the internet age is the Guardian's 'Trafigura' investigation into the dumping of waste in Cote D'Ivoire. A key part of the investigation was the Minton Report into the disaster, which had been obtained by the newspaper and partners in other countries. Trafigura served a 'super injunction' preventing UK newspapers from mentioning the report – or even the fact that they had been served with an injunction. Although the Minton Report was then published on the document-leaking website WikiLeaks, no newspaper was allowed to mention this.

Paul Farrelly MP – a former journalist with The Observer – tabled a question notice in the House of Commons which mentioned the Minton Report, Trafigura, and its lawyers, Carter-Ruck. The plan was clearly that this question would then be covered by parliamentary privilege, and therefore exempt from libel law. However, Carter-Ruck managed to convince the legal authorities that their super-injunction extended even over the right to report parliamentary proceedings, and The Guardian was prevented from reporting the question.

The Guardian decided to make this restriction the focus of its strategy. The paper reported that it had been prevented by Carter-Ruck from reporting remarks made in Parliament and – crucially – editor Alan Rusbridger tweeted about it. As he wrote later:

'It took one tweet on Monday evening as I left the office to light the virtual touchpaper. At five past nine I tapped: 'Now Guardian prevented from reporting parliament for unreportable reasons. Did John Wilkes live in vain?' . . . By the time I got home, after stopping off for a meal with friends, the Twittersphere had gone into meltdown. Twitterers had sleuthed down Farrelly's question, published the relevant links and were now seriously on the case. By mid-day on Tuesday 'Trafigura' was one of the most searched terms in Europe, helped along by re-tweets by Stephen Fry and his 830,000-odd followers.

'. . . One or two legal experts uncovered the Parliamentary Papers Act 1840, wondering if that would help? Common #hashtags were quickly developed, making the material easily discoverable. By lunchtime – an hour before we were due in court – Trafigura threw in the towel. The textbook stuff – elaborate carrot, expensive stick – had been blown away by a newspaper together with the mass collaboration of total strangers on the web. Trafigura thought it was buying silence. A combination of old media – the Guardian – and new – Twitter – turned attempted obscurity into mass notoriety.'

(Rusbridger, 2009)

Innocent dissemination

The innocent dissemination defence comes from the 1996 Defamation Act and establishes that you are not liable for user-generated content created by others if you do not moderate the content. That said, you will find the innocent dissemination defence harder to maintain if you are seen to be encouraging infringing content in any way – for example, if you are initiating discussions asking people to identify celebrities who take drugs.

Generally speaking, the innocent dissemination defence is not particularly useful because, once you have been notified of the offending material, the defence no longer applies and you must investigate.

Unless you are instantly absolutely certain that you can defend the statement you should remove it, notify both the claimant and the creator of the content that it has been removed for investigation, and add a statement in its place to that effect, and then investigate the content accordingly. If you then decide that you can defend the content successfully, as detailed above, you should then reinstate it. If, however, you decide the content is defamatory and does not have a defence, then you should remove it permanently, explaining why to all parties and updating the statement on the site. Having a clear policy on how such content is treated will help – see the box opposite on creating terms and conditions for your site.

'Responsible journalism' – the Reynolds defence

The Reynolds defence was established in 1999 in the case of Reynolds vs Times Newspapers Ltd, and revised in a 2006 judgment. Broadly speaking, it allows journalists to successfully defend a libel case even where they cannot prove that the allegations are true – if they can prove that they have undertaken 'responsible journalism' in its production. More general media law books will provide further detail on how that might be demonstrated, but one area to be particularly wary of in the case of online publication is your online archives.

When The Times printed allegations of corruption against a police officer it managed to both win and lose the libel case that was pursued as a result. The newspaper successfully defended publication of those allegations in print because the paper demonstrated that it had practised responsible journalism in doing so. However, once an investigation into those allegations was completed – and the allegations against the police officer cleared – the newspaper had failed to correct the article in its archives. On that point, the newspaper lost its case.

Closer look Terms and conditions (T&Cs)

If you are running a news website of any form you can help limit any possible fallout from future legal issues by publishing or linking to a set of terms and conditions that users agree to adhere to. This is particularly important if you allow user-generated content on the site.

Any terms and conditions on a publishing site should cover the following: copyright and permissions (i.e. what permissions users give you to re-use any content, and that they agree not to upload copyright-infringing material); defamation (that they agree not to defame); ethics (these are up to you); how users can access information held about them or close their accounts; and how they can bring content that infringes the terms and conditions to your attention ('flagging').

Terms and conditions need not use legal language or be overly-long. The point is that they establish an explicit agreement between you and the users of your site about what is acceptable behaviour. If they then display behaviour that is not acceptable, you can point to the agreement that they signed up to. Likewise, users of the site can use it to hold you to account. And if anything on the site ends up in a court of law, you can demonstrate that you took reasonable steps to prevent that happening.

Contempt of court and court reporting

What you can and can't report when crimes have been committed and cases go to court

An area of legal control and constraint on free speech that is arguably more acceptable to and tolerated by journalists is that of contempt of court and court reporting restrictions. There is a general understanding and acknowledgement that in order for criminal investigations to be successful and courts to function without undue influence or impediment, some proceedings and aspects of those proceedings do require legal protection.

Recent years have, however, seen debate and contention focus on several aspects of contempt and court reporting laws.

First, there has been some judicial concession towards what has been a long-standing campaign to bring more openness into the family courts. While there is acknowledgement that the interests of children are best served by protecting them from unnecessary identification and reporting when it comes to legal proceedings, much of the criticism in relation to family proceedings has centred on the proceedings themselves and issues such as the credibility and integrity of expert witnesses and theories which courts have allowed to determine the fate and wellbeing of children and other vulnerable people. Allowing more scrutiny of proceedings while still preserving the anonymity rights of children is shining a long overdue light into the family courts.

Second, there have been some questionable instances of political interests being served through narrow and arguably inappropriate use of contempt laws to dissuade journalists from reporting on sensitive issues. When in the period between 2003 and 2006 journalists chose to question some of the decisions behind the political decision to wage war on Iraq and the treatment of prisoners there, there were several 'reminders' sent to news editors that they were subject to contempt laws.

Third, there is the uncertain and deeply unsatisfactory provision in Section 8 of the 1981 Contempt of Court Act that makes it an offence to 'obtain, disclose or solicit any particulars of statements made, opinions expressed, arguments or votes cast by members of a jury in the course of their deliberations in any legal proceedings'. While it is appropriate to shield the jury from influence while listening to a trial and arriving at their decision, it seems perverse that what is meant to be an open administration of justice criminally sanctions the discussion of cases and juries' decisions after the event. Fourth, there is the highly contentious issue of contempt of court law being able to be used to force journalists to reveal their sources. Section 10 of the 1981 Contempt of Court Act states that:

> 'No court may require a person to disclose, nor is any person guilty of contempt of court for refusing to disclose, the source of information contained in a publication for which he is responsible, unless it be established to the satisfaction of the court that disclosure is necessary in the interests of justice or national security or for the prevention of disorder or crime.'

The UK experience has been that when police or politicians play the national security or wider 'interests of justice' card, there has been considerable pressure on journalists to reveal sources. However, a recent ruling by the European Court of Human Rights serves as a useful reminder that at a European level (and as should be followed in the UK) suitable weight should be given to the freedom of expression provisions of Article 10 of ECHR and that prior to any judicial intervention in relation to journalists sources, there should be sufficient judicial investigation of the facts.

Contempt of court

In relation to online journalistic activity, contempt of court arises where the actions of the journalist have:

- Compromised the integrity of the court.
- Interfered with the administration of justice (either directly or indirectly).

This arises where a journalist publishes something that will:

- Undermine the legal process.
- Unduly interfere with or influence a juror (or witness).
- Breach a court order or other injunction that prohibits publication.

What this means for journalists and the media is:

- Paying close attention to court orders or directions of judges.
- Not reporting facts or comments that are forbidden in relation to proceedings.
- Not engaging in sensationalist journalism where court proceedings are likely or active

There are two types of contempt

1. Statutory contempt
2. Common law contempt

Statutory contempt

This is based around the 1981 Contempt of Court Act which creates a legal offence of *interfering with active court proceedings*. Section 2(2) of the Act makes it a 'strict liability' offence to interfere with active proceedings – in other words why or how a journalist might have interfered or thought they were or were not interfering is irrelevant, the fact that their actions may in some way have interfered is sufficient to engage and attract legal sanction under the law.

The law applies to any publication that *'creates a substantial risk that the course of justice in the proceedings in question will be seriously impeded or prejudiced'.*

Strict liability means that the law and legal sanction will apply:

- whether or not publisher intended to cause a substantial risk of – or serious – prejudice
- without any need to the part of the prosecution to prove ***intent***.

What this means is that where a journalist

- *publishes* something
- in relation to *active* court proceedings
- and that publication carries a *substantial risk* of *serious prejudice*

then strict liability contempt of court under the 1981 Contempt of Court Act (CCA) will apply.

Common law contempt

Contempt of court at common law is wider in its scope and does not require there to be any active proceedings. It extends to any action that could generally interfere with legal proceedings.

Common law contempt arises where there is:

Publication of material that is calculated to prejudice or otherwise interfere with proceedings that AT THE TIME OF PUBLICATION were PENDING or IMMINENT

What this means is that for common law contempt to apply it will need to be shown that the journalist or person publishing the information:

- Intended there to be prejudice.
- Proceedings were imminent.

Contempt – matters journalists should be aware of:

- Reports that assume guilt of defendant.
- Reports that assume outcome of preliminary hearings.
- Reports that contain information that may hamper police investigation (photographs and ID parades).
- Reports that contain detailed accounts of circumstances leading to criminal charges in question.
- Statements based on assertions of fact presented in advance of evidence.
- Material that would be inadmissible in a criminal case but could stick in the mind of a juror.
- Reports containing details of other proceedings in which defendant or witness has been involved.
- Reports containing information or comments about witnesses that may undermine their evidence.
- Reports which breach an order.
- Archive material which may contain prejudicial information (e.g. previous convictions, details about lifestyle). The Attorney General has said it is unlikely he would bring a prosecution on

these grounds unless the archive material was published again or attention was explicitly drawn to it.

- Material which jurors would not have access to in print (because newspapers are not distributed in their area) may be accessible to them online.

Court reporting

As applies in relation to the wider and general restriction that contempt laws exert over the media's freedom to report, the specific court reporting restrictions and laws provide a drilled-down regulation of what can be reported in relation to specific courts and those appearing in them.

The underlying and overriding principle of the protections the law seeks to offer and impose is to offer assurance that children, young persons and other members of society who could – depending on their mental status or predicament in relation to legal proceedings – be seen to be 'vulnerable' or at risk of influence or prejudice are protected by the legal process.

However, in contrast to this protectionist and 'closed door' approach that the law imposes lies the competing democratic principle that justice should be seen to be done and that the public and the media that serves that public should be allowed access to the justice system and courts to supervise and scrutinise the administration of justice and ensure that it is performing its role and serving its people.

At the outset of this section on contempt and court reporting we highlighted several areas where there has been debate around the balance between protecting the judicial process and those subject to it while at the same time making it open and accountable.

What follows is a summary of the rules that exist but the hope is that these will be refined and changed in the coming years to provide for a more up-to-date system of publicly accountable justice that better serves the interests of those it seeks to protect and entrusts juries and journalists to act responsibly in their engagement with the legal process.

Court reporting – key protections

The key concerns and accompanying restrictions in relation to court reporting arise in relation to the following categories of cases:

- Publication of reports relating to children and juveniles.
- Reports relating to young offenders.
- Sexual offences.
- Magistrates and Crown Courts.

Unauthorised recording of court proceedings

There is an outright ban on any recording being made of court proceedings except where expressly authorised by the court. This does not prevent journalists from reporting on proceedings but it does prevent them using any electronic device to record audio or video or otherwise capture pictures in relation to court proceedings.

Sexual offences

There has been debate over whether those accused of sexual assaults and rape should be identified prior to being charged with an offence. While the current coalition government has hinted that it may review some widening of the provisions to protect anonymity between the time of allegation and charge, this has not been widely welcomed and the current position is that it remains for the police and media to determine what level of identification is appropriate.

The Sexual Offences (Amendment) Acts 1976 and 1992 set out the range of offences and the protection afforded to the victims of such offences.

Copyright and content rights

Protecting your work, gaining permission to use other work and knowing what rights there are in content

The laws that apply to copyright and the use of content are and should be of particular importance to online journalists. With a fast paced medium where it is possible to exchange information and create and post content with relative ease, you as a content creator as well as content user need to be aware of the rules. This will enable you to protect and exploit your own work but will also help you ensure you do not copy or otherwise infringe the work of others.

It is all too easy and happens all too often that online journalists 'copy and paste' text, information, images or other media into their work and this information is subsequently used or published in a manner that is not permitted. In a global publishing environment you also have to be aware that any rights you obtain may only apply to certain territories: this is why many TV on demand websites only work in the UK or US. In a news context, a journalist can find themselves accused of copying and – aside from any legal action – have their reputation compromised as a result.

A good example of this is the *Cook's Source* case in the US. *Cook's Source*, a small local magazine, found an article and recipe online by a blogger called Monica Gaudio. Considering the article 'public domain', the editor of the magazine, Judith Griggs, published it in her magazine without asking for permission from Gaudio. This – and particularly Griggs' email response to Gaudio when she was approached about the issue – kicked off an internet backlash that led to advertisers withdrawing from the magazine and hundreds of users investigating possible copyright infringement elsewhere in the magazine. Even before any legal proceedings had begun, the reputations of Griggs and her magazine were irreparably damaged.

Bigger names have made similar mistakes. In 2009, the BBC News channel had to reach a settlement with Michael Bailey when they used his photo of the Birmingham skyline as a backdrop to a two-way discussion without permission. The image had been taken from image-sharing website Flickr, and the Creative Commons licence on the webpage clearly forbade it being used commercially and without attribution. In the same year Sky News – needing a picture to illustrate a shooting at Waterloo Station – used an image of the crime scene which had been posted to Twitter through the Twitpic service. The picture was credited to 'Joe on Twitter' but they did not obtain Joe's permission for its use, and he found out through a third party that his photograph had been used in this way. After getting the channel to change the credit on the photo to his full name, it took Joe a further two weeks – and negative publicity for Sky on Twitter and blogs – to get a positive response to his request for payment. He wrote at the time:

> 'I'm pleased that my picture has achieved good reach but I worry that the co-option of apparently free content from Twitter by big media is something that may become endemic and devalue the rights in photography. Rupert Murdoch has announced people will have to pay to access his sites from 2010 – meantime he doesn't seem to mind not paying for material and happily infringes on other people's work.'

All of these examples illustrate just what a battleground copyright issues have become online, with some news organisations demanding payment from online publishers who reproduce headlines or quotes from stories, even when it drives visitors to the original article webpage. When Associated Press suggested it might charge bloggers for using excerpts from its reports which would normally be considered 'fair use', one blog hit back by invoicing AP for $17.50 based on excerpts that the news agency had 'borrowed' from their posts. The media world is rife with national newspapers and broadcasters taking stories from local newspapers, local newspapers using content from hyperlocal blogs, and hyperlocal blogs quoting from reports elsewhere, and for every claim by the news media that websites and blogs are 'parasites' on their hard work, you will find equally strong accusations that the mainstream media will take content without permission whenever it can. So far most of these claims appear to be used as negotiating tactics or for political lobbying; very few have reached the courts to establish any case law.

What the above does illustrate is the equal risk that all your journalistic endeavours or hard-earned footage are misappropriated by another person or media outlet. While knowing the law in such circumstance will not always provide a remedy, it will help mitigate the risks that are involved when creating and dealing with content.

Intellectual property and copyright law – overview

Intellectual property or 'IP' is the means by which the law confers ***ownership*** on people's creativity or innovation. It provides a mechanism for letting people control and protect the use of non-tangible goods or creations which do not have a physical inanimate form. By means of example, when you buy a book, you own the book itself but you do not own the expression of its contents. While you may lend the book to a friend to read, you are not permitted to photocopy it and give it to them.

IP lets owners commercially exploit their work so they can sell it for profit or protect themselves against others who may wish to copy or profit from it against their wishes. The intent behind the law is to encourage innovation by letting people benefit from it in this way.

IP rights can arise automatically and owners do not necessarily have to register what they have created or invented. IP covers a broad spectrum of things 'intellectual' from products and designs to visual displays and performance rights. Just as your online copy and content is protected by IP, so too is that of your competitors and in the context of publishing online in a journalistic context this means you need to be aware of how the media and content providers and users process and use information at an operational and commercial level.

Copyright law

Copyright affects daily journalistic production activities and the use of content in commercial outputs. In the UK copyright is regulated through the **1988 Copyright Designs and Patents Act** along with several international treaties and protocols.

When considering copyright in relation to online journalism here are some of the questions which may arise:

- Why should copyright be relevant to online journalism and media production?
- How is this likely to affect the way your content gets used – or how you use others' content?
- Does there need to be a contract for there to be copyright?
- Does there have to be an express notice or disclaimer for copyright to arise?
- Can free content or that which is publicly available be used?
- What is the notion of 'public domain'?

- What is 'fair use'?
- How much of a source can be used?
- Does attribution negate infringement?

So what is copyright?

It is a legal right which protects an author's exclusive rights to control the reproduction, adaptation and distribution of their work.

Copyright protects 'any literary, dramatic, artistic or musical work, sound recording, film broadcast or typographical arrangement'.

Copyright does not apply to ideas, facts or concepts themselves but to the *form* in which they are *expressed*. In other words, someone has to do or have done something with an idea or fact for copyright protection to arise.

So, you cannot copyright the idea for an article, only the arrangement of information and phrases with which it is expressed. Likewise, you cannot copyright the facts of a story, only your report of them.

Copyright can be applied to parts as well as the whole of the *expression* so a phrase or section within a publication or website can be as protected as the entire work or site. Poetry is particularly relevant here, as small passages can still be covered.

When does it arise?

Copyright arises automatically as soon as the work or 'expression' is published, recorded or fixed in some material form. There is no need for formal registration as with patents for inventions or designs. In basic terms, if someone has put the effort into producing something then that something is likely to be protected (one would still have to prove its *form* in such a manner as the law would recognise).

However, the law does require effort to have been expended, so the work must not itself be a copy and should involve a degree of independent skill, labour and judgement. There is generally no requirement for that work to have artistic quality or literary merit, although this varies from country to country.

Databases whose creation involved a 'substantial investment' in obtaining, verifying or presenting their contents are also protected by law, thanks to the EU's Database Directive of 1996, implemented into UK law under the Copyright and Rights in Databases Regulations 1997. In addition, databases are treated as a class of literary work under the 1988 Copyright, Designs and Patents Act, as long as 'by reason of the selection or arrangement of the contents of the database the database constitutes the author's own intellectual creation'. A simple arrangement of information by date, size or position in the alphabet would not be considered such as 'intellectual creation'.

A good example of the difference between the two is illustrated by the football fixture list. In 2010 the High Court ruled that the fixture list was not covered by the EU Database Directive but was covered by database copyright, because, as Mr Justice Floyd explained: 'There were numerous stages in the process of allocation of matches to dates, and in the selection of the dates themselves where judgment and discretion in the relevant sense had to be exercised'. Unlike copyright, database rights only last 15 years after completion or publication, although if substantial changes are made the 15-year period starts again.

Database rights and database copyright are important to consider if you are compiling information yourself and wish to protect it. It is a good idea to record the resources and processes invested in that creation as this may be useful if you need to prove the 'substantial investment' required for database rights, or the intellectual work required for copyright. The cost of building of the database itself is also important to record.

When re-publishing information that has been compiled by someone else (such as the fixture list example above) – or when using programming scripts to 'scrape' and then republish data from other sources – check if a copyright notice is included alongside the data which indicates any conditions under which it can be used, and who to contact for permission to reproduce it. As previously explained, the absence of such a notice does not mean the data is copyright-free – it merely means you will have to do more work to find out who holds the copyright. If you are dealing with information from a public body, it is likely that you will encounter Crown Copyright.

Crown Copyright and the Open Government Licence

Material produced by public bodies such as government departments and local authorities is normally covered by Crown Copyright. This means that the source of the material must be identified and the copyright status acknowledged, and that the information must not be used in a misleading way. There may also be other conditions – Ordnance Survey data, for example, had a history of inflexible licensing, so check the relevant government website if you are using such material (Parliamentary Copyright may instead apply if the material relates to parliamentary proceedings).

Recently, however, there has been a trend towards more open licences, with Ordnance Survey data now covered by 'flexible licensing' depending on what you wish to use the data for. And in 2010 the UK government created an 'Open Government Licence' which was compatible with the Creative Commons 3.0 licence (this states that you can use material as long as you say who created it). This followed a similar move in 2009 by the White House in creating a new licence for images it shared on Flickr, while using Creative Commons 3.0 licences for images on its own website.

Can copyright protection be lost?

It is a common assumption that copyright protection is somehow lost if a work is freely distributed to the public – for example, over the internet – the argument being that the work has somehow fallen into the 'public domain'. **This is not true.** The concept of 'public domain' does not affect copyright protection. If you are writing a story about someone and you need a photograph, taking an image from their Facebook profile without permission is a breach of copyright.

How long does copyright last?

Copyright protection generally lasts for the life of the author of the copyright work plus 70 years in the UK and Europe. However, the period of protection varies from country to country and according to the type of copyright work in question.

What constitutes copyright infringement?

Copying of the whole or a *substantial part* of a copyright work without the consent of the owner is an infringement. In deciding whether a substantial part has been copied the following are taken into account:

- Size doesn't matter – the courts will look at the *quality* of the part that has been taken ahead of quantity. So if a small excerpt is taken from a short but highly specialist publication, this might be construed as infringement ahead of a larger excerpt taken from a bulky more general text.

- Changing the word order or paraphrasing will not necessarily avoid copyright infringement. You can't simply copy a sentence and get the thesaurus out to amend a few words.
- Similarities are more important than differences. Remember it's the *form of the expression* that is protected, so the overall feel when comparing one work against an allegedly copied one is important.
- *Innocence is not a defence.* Claiming not to know about the law, or that there might be something wrong in lifting chunks of text or information from another work, is not a defence.
- *Actual copying is required.* If one person happens to create or write about something in exactly the same way, but can show that this was mere coincidence as they *created* their work *independently* then that will provide a defence. Facts or ideas as such are not protected by copyright. Thus, if a text contained something factual like a celsius/fahrenheit conversion rate for temperature, then this could be used. But for less clear-cut cases it may well prove difficult to distinguish between an idea or fact and the expression of that idea or fact. Further, repeated taking of information from the same source may be copyright infringement and is likely also to give rise to infringement of database rights (see further below).

What defences are there?

There are certain defences to copyright infringement.

Consent – if the copyright owner has given consent to material being used then this will constitute an *absolute* defence. This can be either:

- *Express* – in the form of a written contract or agreement
- *Implied* – from circumstances, correspondence, usage, etc.

Express consent is better as there is less scope for there being misinterpretations or misunderstandings and also because an implied consent is likely to be tightly interpreted to have a narrow scope.

Fair Dealing – this is a public policy defence that allows limited use of copyright material without consent for specific purposes such as for private research, reporting current events or criticism. Journalists may rely on this defence when they are reporting current events, provided that they attribute the source. However, the fair dealing defence is extremely unlikely to help in the context of providing historical information services in a commercial setting (although this is likely to vary from country to country).

What are the consequences of copyright infringement?

There are both legal and commercial consequences, neither of which are desirable.

Legal:

- *Court injunction* – courts have the power to stop the material which infringes copyright from being distributed. This can have severe consequences, such as forcing the withdrawal of a product that contains infringing material from sale.
- *Damages* – courts can order the guilty party to pay money damages to the copyright holder. The amount of damages will either be calculated on the basis of the loss of revenue suffered by the copyright owner as a result of the infringement or on the basis of the profits made by the infringer.
- *Criminal* – yes, the go to jail card could be issued in severe cases, especially where there is evidence of extreme infringement or fraudulent activity in a malicious or premeditated way.

Commercial:

- Embarrassment – doesn't make your company look good.
- Harms credibility – who will trust your work now?
- Damages reputation – if you are faking it rather than making it.
- Can harm share price as any of above will effect the stock market.

Controlling copyright and content

The standard practice for controlling and obtaining permission to use content is through the use of contracts and licences. These will set out the the terms on which content can be used and define the scope of rights clearances obtained or granted under them.

Content and copyright in an online environment – summary of dos and don'ts

- *Always* work on the assumption that material is copyright.
- *Ensure that you adequately protect your own work through contracts, licences or other arrangements.*
- *When making use of content that has not been created by yourself then wherever possible* use content that is supplied to you or your media outlet under *contract* and ensure that the *scope of your use* is covered by that contract.
- *Wherever possible* ensure you have rights clearance in respect of the material you are using or proposing to use.

Remember: Online journalists should never assume they have the right to use content unless they have checked and confirmed the existence of that right first.

Closer look Regulation

How online media is regulated

In addition to the specific laws and legal provisions that have been examined, the activities of journalists in the online environment are subject to regulation by a number of bodies.

The Press Complaints Commission – the PCC

This is a self regulatory and independent body that monitors and deals with complaints about the content of newspapers and magazines and their respective websites.

www.pcc.org.uk/

Ofcom

This is the independent regulator and competition authority for the UK communications industries.

www.ofcom.org.uk/

▶

ASA – the Advertising Standards Authority

This is the UK's independent regulator of advertising across all media.

www.asa.org.uk/

ICO – the Information Commissioners Office

The UK's independent authority for upholding information rights in the public interest, promoting openness by public bodies and data privacy for individuals.

www.ico.gov.uk/

In addition you may choose to abide by the codes of conduct of any of the following bodies:

NUJ – National Union of Journalists

http://media.gn.apc.org/nujcode.html

BBC Editorial Guidelines

www.bbc.co.uk/guidelines/editorialguidelines/

Blogger's Code of Conduct

Tim O'Reilly proposed this in 2007 and dozens of people contributed suggestions via a wiki. The diversity of these resulted in a series of 'modules' which bloggers can pick from. The page also has links to codes from around the world:

http://blogging.wikia.com/wiki/Blogger%27s_Code_of_Conduct

Summary

When it comes to understanding the law, journalists and publishers operating online not only have to understand traditional areas covering what they can report, they must also weigh up the risks – and put measures in place to address these – of providing a platform for others to publish on. In addition to the well-trodden areas of defamation and contempt of court, in the digital age we must also understand database rights and data protection. And in our newfound ability to combine images, audio, text and video from all over the world – and to publish globally too – we need to be aware of the ease with which we can breach someone's copyright.

In the grey areas of law in the internet age, as businesses struggle to maintain old profit margins and establish new ones, countless battles are being fought to draw the lines that will determine practice for the decades to come. Is it acceptable for Google to scan thousands of out-of-copyright and out-of-print books to make them available to a new audience for free? Is the aggregation of dozens of links for clients considered 'fair use'? New law is continually established and old laws are reviewed as they become the target of abuse in a global marketplace of legal tourism, or as cultural change, accelerated by technology, makes them appear outdated.

I write this passage at the end of a week in which fair comment became honest comment, in which headlines were judged to be literary works and subject to copyright, and in which the website WikiLeaks found itself without a web address or a funding channel as the companies involved in its hosting and fundraising decided – without anything being decided in a court of law – that the site had breached their terms of service. In a networked society we are reliant on a chain of actors – from users who contribute content to the companies that host and distribute our own content – to uphold the law, but also to resist intimidation from lawyers if there is no legal basis for it.

Knowing the law, being prepared in the way that you go about your job, and being confident that you can mount a strong defence against any legal attack, can make a world of difference for a journalist. It is the difference between pulling your punches through fear of the unknown, and reporting with the confidence and strength of someone who knows how to defend themselves.

Activities

1. Draw up terms and conditions for your website. See the box in this chapter for guidelines, and look at examples on other sites to guide you. Try to keep it as succinct as possible.
2. Draw up a code of conduct for your blog. Look at examples from around the world and draw on the elements you feel suit your own ethics.
3. Look on a forum and see if you can identify any content that could be considered defamatory or in contempt of court. What would you do if this was your site? How would you defend yourself if you found yourself in court over it as a publisher?
4. You need an image to illustrate a blog post you are writing. How can you ensure that the image is not in breach of copyright?
5. The Ministry of Justice is inviting contributions as part of a review of libel law. Write a document outlining how you feel it needs to be changed for the online age, including evidence supporting your position. Try the same exercise for other parts of media law such as copyright, data protection, contempt of court and privacy.

Further reading

Further updates and commentary on the law and regulation can be found at Edgar Forbes' blog mediabeak.com

Other blogs worth following include:

Meejalaw.com
davidbanks.blogspot.com
blog.tech-and-law.com
martinjemoore.com

Channel 4 publishes an Independent Producer's Handbook online which includes a comprehensive chapter on media law.
www.independentproducerhandbook.co.uk

The Ministry of Justice holds consultations on changes to the law which you should follow and contribute to.

Jane Singer and Cecilia Friend's book Online Journalism Ethics (2007) is an excellent introduction to ethical dilemmas that so closely follow beside regulatory and legal ones.

Glossary

ABCe Audit Bureau of Circulations Electronic audits traffic figures for websites

API Method by which a software program interacts with other software programs

App ('application') Program designed for a specific task. The term was popularised by Apple when it expanded its iTunes service with the launch of the App Store in 2008 to distribute software to its mobile devices

Blog Online diary format for news and commentary

Blogosphere The web community inhabited by bloggers

Citizen journalism Journalism produced by untrained contributors

Convergence journalism Using a combination of media, platforms and technologies to produce content

CMS Content management system, which organises content and workflow of a website

Cookie Text file that is downloaded to a user's computer which remembers details such as preferences when that site is visited again

Creative Commons Copyright licences specifying terms under which content can be used and shared

Crowdsourcing News gathering by using contributions from outside sources such as readers and bloggers

CSS Cascading style sheets, the file which defines the style of a website

Download Transmitting a file from one computer system to another

Flash Program used for animation

HTML Hyper Text Mark-up Language. Programming code used for display of web pages. HTML5 is the upgraded version

Hyperlink The link that readers click on to go to another web page

Hyperlocal Collaborative community news websites

JavaScript Scripting language implemented in websites to improve features such as interactivity

Mashup Using a combination of content from different sources

Metadata Data providing information about other data

Microblogging Smaller form of blogging confined by amount of text that can be used, e.g. Twitter

Navigation Structure and design which helps readers find content on a website

Open source software Openly available software that can be distributed and developed

Podcast Audio files which can be downloaded

Pop-up An advert which pops up on screen

RSS Really Simple Syndication, allows web feeds to specific content

SEO search engine optimisation, improves search rankings of website content

Semantic web The new technologies which improve how computers understand information

Shovelware Denotes journalism that is cut and paste from print product with no thought given to the web medium

Social network Site which allows groups of people to connect and interact with one another

Streaming Multimedia that can seen or heard in real-time

Tag Metadata which describes content (can also described to describe elements of HTML)

Troll Online troublemaker who posts provocative comments or tries to divert user to other sites

UGC User-generated content

Unique users The number of individual users which read a website

Upload Publishing a file to the internet

URL Uniform resource locator, the unique address of a web document

Vlog Video blog

Webcast Audio or video broadcasts

Wiki A collaborative site where anyone can edit content, such as Wikipedia

Web 3.0 Next generation of technologies on the web

Bibliography

Adam, G. S. (1993) 'Towards a Definition of Journalism', The Poynter Institute for Media Studies, St Petersburg, Florida, www.poynter.org/media/product/20030123_141216_24094.pdf

Allan, S. (2006) *Online News: Journalism and the Internet*, UK and USA Open University.

Allan, S. and Thorsen, E. (2009) *Citizen Journalism: Global Perspectives*, USA: Peter Lang.

Ames, M. and Naaman, M. (2007) 'Why We Tag: Motivations for Annotation in Mobile and Online Media', CHI 2007, April 28–May 3, 2007.

Anderson, K. (2009) 'How to spot a web hoax' *Strange Attractor*, September 1 2009, http://strange.corante.com/2009/09/01/how-to-spot-a-web-hoax

Arthur, C. (2009a) 'MPs' expenses, by amount, on a map: does distance matter?' *The Guardian* Data Blog, 3 April 2009, www.guardian.co.uk/news/datablog/2009/apr/03/mps-expenses-houseofcommons

Arthur, C. (2009b) 'The mystery of the missing London parking tickets', *The Guardian* Data Blog, 29 April 2009, www.guardian.co.uk/news/datablog/2009/apr/29/transport-london-parking-tickets

Baird, S. (2010) '10 Tips for Designing Infographics', *Digital Newsgathering*, April 24, 2010, http://digitalnewsgathering.wordpress.com/2010/04/24/10-tips-for-designing-infographics

Barbaro, M. and Zeller, T. 'A Face Is Exposed for AOL Searcher No. 4417749, *New York Times*, 9 August 2006, http://query.nytimes.com/gst/fullpage.html?res=9E0CE3DD1F3FF93AA3575BC0A9609C8B63

Belam, M. (2008) *Measuring UK newspaper success with social media*, private report.

Berners-Lee, T. (1999) *Weaving the Web: The Past, Present and Future of the World Wide Web*, USA: Orion.

Betancourt, L. (2009) 'The Journalist's Guide to User Generated Video', *Mashable*, September 14, 2009, http://mashable.com/2009/09/14/ugc-video-guidelines/

Benkler, Y. (2006) *The Wealth of Networks: How Social Production Transforms Markets and Freedom*, USA: Yale University Press.

Bernoff, J. (2007) 'The POST Method: A systematic approach to social strategy', *Groundswell*, December 11, 2007, http://forrester.typepad.com/groundswell/2007/12/the-post-method.html

Blastland and Dilnot (2007) *The Tiger That Isn't*, UK: Profile Books.

Blood, R. (2006) 'Weblogs: A History and Perspective', *Rebecca's Pocket*, 07 September 2000; 25 October 2006, http://www.rebeccablood.net/essays/weblog_history.html

Bowman, S. and Willis, C. (2003) 'We Media: How Audiences are Shaping the Future of News and Information,' USA: The Media Center at the American Press Institute.

Bradshaw, P. (2008) 'When Journalists Blog: How It Changes What They Do', *Nieman Reports*, www.nieman.harvard.edu/reportsitem.aspx?id=100696

Bradshaw, P. (2010) 'Telegraph launches powerful election database', *Online Journalism Blog*, April 20, 2010, http://onlinejournalismblog.com/2010/04/20/telegraph-launches-powerful-election-database

Brooke, H. (2007) *Your Right to Know: A Citizen's Guide to the Freedom of Information Act*, UK: Pluto Press.

Brooke, H. (2010) *The Silent State: Secrets, Surveillance and the Myth of British Democracy*, William Heinemann.

Bughin, J. R. (2007) 'How companies can make the most out of user-generated content,' *The McKinsey Quarterly*, McKinsey and Company.

Burgess, J. and Green, J. (2009) *Online Video and Participatory Culture*, UK: Polity Press.

Casciani, D. (2005) 'Analysis: Britain's modern face', BBC News, 7 September 2005, http://news.bbc.co.uk/1/hi/uk/4220002.stm

Cellan-Jones, R. 'Seismic Shock: When blogging meets policing', *BBC News*, 26 January 2010, www.bbc.co.uk/blogs/thereporters/rorycellanjones/2010/01/seismic_shock_when_blogging_me.html

Cleveland, W. S. and McGill, R. (1984) 'Graphical Perception: Theory, Experimentation, and Application to the Development of Graphical Methods', *Journal of the American Statistical Association*, 79(387), 531–54.

Duvander, A. 'Mashups Are Dead, But the Web is Alive', *WebMonkey*, 25 November 2008, www.webmonkey.com/2008/11/mashups_are_dead__but_the_web_is_alive/

Deloitte (2009) 'The growing cost of free online content', www.deloitte.co.uk/TMTPredictions/media/Rising-cost-of-free-online-content.cfm

DiSEL (Digital Storytelling Effects Lab) (2005) 'HTML versus Flash: what works best – and when', Fall 2005, www.lauraruel.com/disel/DiSEL_report_one.pdf

Douglas, T. (2005) 'Shaping the media with mobiles', BBC News, 4 August 2005, http://news.bbc.co.uk/1/hi/uk/4745767.stm

Eaves, D. (2008) 'How Good Is The Mainstream Media At Linking Out?', The SEO Company: SEO Blog, July 16, 2008, www.seoco.co.uk/blog/how-good-is-the-mainstream-media-at-linking-out

Editors (2008) *The Huffington Post Complete Guide to Blogging*, USA: Simon and Schuster.

Eltringham, M. (2009) 'The Audience and News', in *The Future of Journalism*, Charles Miller (ed.), UK: BBC College of Journalism.

Fry, B. (2008) *Visualizing Data*, USA O'Reilly Media.

Fung, K. (2010) *Numbers Rule Your World*, USA: McGraw Hill.

Geary, J. (2009) 'Interview with an anonymous blog commenter', March 3, 2009, www.joannageary.com/2009/03/03/n-interview-with-an-anonymous-blog-commenter

Gillmor, D. (2004) *We the Media: Grassroots Journalism by the People, for the People*, USA: O'Reilly Media.

Glocer, T. (2006) 'Old media must embrace the amateur', Tom Glocer's Blog, October 24, 2006, http://tomglocer.com/blogs/sample_weblog/archive/2006/10/24/110.aspx

Greenslade, R. (2009) 'Who Will Fund Hyperlocal Start-ups?', Guardian.co.uk, April 14, 2009, www.guardian.co.uk/media/greenslade/2009/apr/14/digital-media-local-newspapers

Grey, S. (2006) *Ghost Plane: The Inside Story of the CIA's Secret Rendition Programme*, UK: Hurst & Company.

Guardian (2010a) *Blairometer: how Twitter rates Tony Blair at Chilcot*, www.guardian.co.uk/politics/blairometer/history

Guardian (2010b) *Brownometer: how Twitter rates Gordon Brown at Chilcot*, www.guardian.co.uk/politics/brownometer/history

Godin, S. (2009) *How to make graphs that work*, July 17, 2009, http://sethgodin.typepad.com/seths_blog/2009/07/how-to-make-graphs-that-work.html

Hall, J. (2001) *Online Journalism*, UK: Pluto Press.

Hamman, R. (2008) *BBC sport olympics map mashes up twitter, blog posts, coverage*, Cybersoc.com, 15 August 2008, www.cybersoc.com/2008/08/bbc-sport-olymp.html

Herrington, J.D. (2005) *Podcasting Hacks*, USA: O'Reilly Media.

Herrmann, S. (2008) 'Mumbai, Twitter and live updates', BBC – The Editors Blog, December 4, 2008, www.bbc.co.uk/blogs/theeditors/2008/12/theres_been_discussion_see_eg.html

Higgerson, D. (2009) 'Running a group on flickr: tips on how to keep everyone happy', November 11, 2009, http://davidhiggerson.wordpress.com/2009/11/11/running-a-group-on-flickr-tips-on-how-to-keep-everyone-happy

Hirst, T. (2008) *Data Scraping Wikipedia with Google Spreadsheets*, OUseful.info, the blog . . . October 14, 2008, http://blog.ouseful.info/2008/10/14/data-scraping-wikipedia-with-google-spreadsheets

Hudson, G. and Rowlands, S. (2007) *The Broadcast Journalism Handbook*, UK: Pearson.

Huff, D. (1954) *How to Lie With Statistics*, UK: Penguin.

Hunter, M.L. (2010) *Story-Based Inquiry: A manual for investigative journalists*, UNESCO, http://portal.unesco.org/ci/en/ev.php-URL_ID=29032&URL_DO=DO_TOPIC&URL_SECTION=201.html and http://markleehunter.free.fr/documents/SBI_english.pdf

Jarvis, J. 'Who wants to own content?' *BuzzMachine*, 23 August 2005, www.buzzmachine.com/2005/08/23/who-wants-to-own-content/

Jarvis, J. (2007) 'It's Not The Blog', *Buzzmachine*, December 9, 2007, www.buzzmachine.com/2007/12/09/its-not-the-blog

Jarvis, J. (2009) *What Would Google Do*? USA: Harper Collins.

Johnson, B. (2009) 'Astroturfing: A question of trust', *The Guardian*, 7 September 2009, www.guardian.co.uk/media/2009/sep/07/astroturfing-energy-citizens-us

Karp, S. (2008) 'Drudge Report: News Site That Sends Readers Away With Links Has Highest Engagement', *Publishing 2.0*, September 15, 2008, http://publishing2.com/2008/09/15/drudge-report-news-site-that-sends-readers-away-with-links-has-highest-engagement

Kelly, J. (2009) 'Red Kayaks and Hidden Gold: the rise, challenges and value of citizen journalism', UK: Reuters Institute.

Kiss, J. (2009) 'The Telegraph's wobbly experiment with Twitter and the budget', PDA: The Digital Content Blog, *The Guardian*, 20 April 2009, www.guardian.co.uk/media/pda/2009/apr/20/telegraphmediagroup-twitter

Kolodzy, J. (2006) *Convergence Journalism*, USA: Rowman and Littlefield.

Lasica, J.D. (2003) 'What is Participatory Journalism?' *Online Journalism Review*, August 7, 2003, www.ojr.org/ojr/workplace/1060217106.php.

Li, D. (2005) *Why Do You Blog: A Uses-and-Gratifications Inquiry Into Bloggers' Motivations*, Paper presented at the annual meeting of the International Communication Association, San Francisco, http://commonsenseblog.typepad.com/common_sense/files/Li_Dan_Aug_2005.pdf

Liu, Y. and Shrum, L.J. (2002) 'What is interactivity and is it always such a good thing? Implications of definition, person, and situation for the influence of interactivity on advertising effectiveness', *Journal of Advertising*, 31(4), 53–64.

Meek, C. 'Web 3.0: what it means for journalists', journalism.co.uk, October 23, 2008, www.journalism.co.uk/5/articles/532631.php

Meyer, P. (2009) *The Vanishing Newspaper: Saving Journalism in the Information Age*, USA: University of Missouri Press.

Microsoft Office Online, *Top Ten Ways to Clean Your Data*, http://office.microsoft.com/en-us/excel/HA102218401033.aspx

Miller, A. and Edwards, W. (2007) 'Give and Take: A Study of Consumer Photo-Sharing Culture and Practice', CHI 2007, April 28 – May 3, 2007.

Mills, J. (2004) *The Broadcast Voice*, UK: Focal Press.

Morgan, V. (2009) *Practising Videojournalism*, UK: Routledge.

Nielsen, J. (2004) *Designing Web Usability: The Practice of Simplicity*, USA: New Riders Publishing.

Nielsen, J. (2007) *Homepage Usability: 50 Websites Deconstructed*, USA: New Riders Publishing.

Niles, R. (2006) 'The programmer as journalist: a Q&A with Adrian Holovaty', *Online Journalism Review*, June 5, 2006, www.ojr.org/ojr/stories/060605niles

Nov, O. (2007) 'What motivates Wikipedians', *Communications of the ACM*, 50(11), 60–64.

Ofcom: The International Communications Market 2008, http://stakeholders.ofcom.org.uk/binaries/research/cmr/icmr08.pdf

Paulos, J.A. (2010) 'Metric Mania', *New York Times*, May 10, 2010, http://www.nytimes.com/2010/05/16/magazine/16FOB-WWLN-t.htm

Pegg, M. (2008) 'The Google Super Tuesday Map Mashup', *Google Maps Mania*, February 5, 2008, http://googlemapsmania.blogspot.com/2008/02/google-super-tuesday-map-mashup.html

Peña, N. de la (2010) 'Mapping technology provides journalists a new medium for story telling online', *Online Journalism Review*, May 18, 2010, www.ojr.org/ojr/people/nonnydlp/201005/1851

Perez, S. (2008) 'Where to Find Open Data on the Web', *ReadWriteWeb*, April 9, 2008, www.readwriteweb.com/archives/where_to_find_open_data_on_the.php

Phillips, G. 'Fair comment is dead. Long live honest comment', *The Guardian*, 1 December 2010, www.guardian.co.uk/law/2010/dec/01/libel-reform-medialaw

Ponsford, D. 'Libel landmark: Fair comment now "honest comment"', Press Gazette, 1 December 2010, www.pressgazette.co.uk/story.asp?storycode=46378

Project for Excellence in Journalism: 'The Latest News Headlines – Your Vote Counts', September 12, 2007, www.journalism.org/node/7493

Project for Excellence in Journalism: 'State of the News Media 2008', March 17, 2008, http://pewresearch.org/pubs/767/state-of-the-news-media-2008

Rosen, J. (2006) 'The People Formerly Known as the Audience', *PressThink*, June 27, 2006.

Rosen, J. (2008) 'A Most Useful Definition of Citizen Journalism', *PressThink*, July 14, 2008, http://archive.pressthink.org/2008/07/14/a_most_useful_d.html

Ruel, L. and Paul, N. (2007) 'Multimedia storytelling: when is it worth it?' *Online Journalism Review*, February 12, 2007, www.ojr.org/ojr/stories/070210ruel/

Ruel, L. and Outing, S. (2004) 'Recall of Information Presented in Text vs. Multimedia Format', September 2004, www.poynterextra.org/EYETRACK2004/multimediarecall.htm

Rusbridger, A. 'The Trafigura fiasco tears up the textbook', Comment Is Free, *The Guardian*, 14 October 2009, www.guardian.co.uk/commentisfree/libertycentral/2009/oct/14/trafigura-fiasco-tears-up-textbook

Shneiderman, B. (1996) 'The Eyes Have It: A Task by Data Type Taxonomy for Information Vizualisations', vol. 1, p. 336, 1996 IEEE Symposium on Visual Languages.

Shirky, C. (2002) 'Broadcast Institutions, Community Values', Shirky.com, September 9,

2002, http://shirky.com/writings/broadcast_and_community.html

Slobin, S. (2010) 'The 7½ Steps to Successful Infographics', MIX Online, March 25, 2010, http://visitmix.com/Articles/seven-and-a-half-steps-to-successful-infographics

Trippenbach, P. (2009) 'Video Games: a New Medium for Journalism', in *The Future of Journalism*, Charles Miller (ed.), UK: BBC College of Journalism.

Trippi, J. (2006) *The Revolution Will Not Be Televised: Democracy, the Internet, and the Overthrow of Everything*, USA: HarperPaperbacks.

Tufte, E. (2001) *The Visual Display of Quantitative Information*, p. 9, USA: Graphics Press.

Walsh, J. (2007) 'Build the perfect web community', *.net Magazine*, No. 165, pp. 39–43, August 2007, www.netmag.co.uk/zine/latest-issue/issue-165

Wardle, C. and Williams, A. (2009) *ugc@thebbc: Understanding its impact upon contributors, non-contributors and BBC News*

Weskamp, M. (2005) 'newsmap', *Marumushi*, April 3, 2005, http://marumushi.com/projects/newsmap

Whittaker, J. (2000) *Web Production for Writers and Journalists*, 2nd edn, UK: Routledge.

White, M. (2010) 'Open door', guardian.co.uk, April 19, 2010, www.guardian.co.uk/commentisfree/2010/apr/19/michael-white-open-door-election-reporting

Winnett, R. and Rayner, G. (2009) *No Expenses Spared*, UK: Bantam Press.

Wong, D. M. (2010) *The Wall Street Journal Guide to Information Graphics*, USA: W.W. Norton & Co.

Yang, Dennis, 'Infographic Does A Great Job Misrepresenting Opportunities Of The Digital Era', *Techdirt*, 14 April 2010, www.techdirt.com/articles/20100413/1647599007.shtml

Yau, N. (2009) '30 Resources to Find the Data You Need', *FlowingData*, October 1, 2009, http://flowingdata.com/2009/10/01/30-resources-to-find-the-data-you-need

Yau, N. (2010) 'The Boom of Big Infographics', *FlowingData*, May 6, 2010, http://flowingdata.com/2010/05/06/the-boom-of-big-infographics

Index